MAKING SENSE

MAKING SENSE

GEOFFREY SAMPSON

Oxford University Press

OXFORD NEW YORK TORONTO MELBOURNE

1980

Oxford University Press, Walton Street, Oxford OX2 6DP

OXFORD LONDON GLASGOW
NEW YORK TORONTO MELBOURNE WELLINGTON
KUALA LUMPUR SINGAPORE JAKARTA HONG KONG TOKYO
DELHI BOMBAY CALCUTTA MADRAS KARACHI
NAIROBI DAR ES SALAAM CAPE TOWN

British Library Cataloguing in Publication Data
Sampson, Geoffrey
  Making sense.
  1. Linguistics
  I. Title
  410   P121   79–41269

ISBN 0–19–215950–X

Photoset and printed in Great Britain by
Lowe & Brydone Printers Limited, Thetford, Norfolk

Preface

My *Liberty and Language* (Oxford University Press, 1979) alluded to a number of fundamental difficulties in contemporary linguistics which, in a book primarily concerned to make a political case, I was not able to analyse in detail. I thereby placed myself under a tacit obligation to treat these problems more explicitly in a separate work. Since writing *Liberty and Language*, furthermore, I have come to realize that even aspects of linguistic theory which I was then content to accept at face value involve what now seem to be fatal flaws. The present book, accordingly, attempts to discharge my debt to the discipline by attacking its various failings in a straightforward, properly documented, and responsible manner instead of backhandedly, and by compensating for this attack with an account of what I take to be the way towards a truer understanding of the relation between language and mind.

I thank F. B. D'Agostino, Noam Chomsky, F. W. Householder, J. R. Hurford, Geoffrey Pullum, and Yorick Wilks for criticism of various of the ideas in this book, Suzette Heald for advice on an anthropological question, and Angus Wilson for discussion of a point of usage; and I acknowledge with gratitude the permission of Cambridge University Press to reprint passages from my article 'Linguistic universals as evidence for empiricism' which appears in the *Journal of Linguistics*, vol. 14, 1978.

Since modern publishers commonly have offices in many towns, I have adopted the bibliographical convention of omitting the place of publication of books except when the locations listed do not include London.

Ingleton, Yorks.
14 October 1978

Contents

Language is not a finished product,
but an activity.

K. W. VON HUMBOLDT

I

This book is an attempt to analyse and rebut a certain nexus of beliefs about language and the human mind – beliefs which have a long philosophical ancestry, but which have recently been moved to the forefront of intellectual attention by the growth over the last two decades of the academic discipline of Theoretical Linguistics. Theoretical Linguistics both presupposes and claims to offer empirical support for a view of the human mind which I shall describe as the 'limited view of mind'. This phrase has an unfortunate question-begging air, but it means the belief that the mind is limited (in certain ways to be described); it is not intended to suggest a belief which is plausible only because its holders are blinkered. The 'limited view' of mind contrasts with a view which I believe to be both closer to the unphilosophical layman's view of human nature and in fact correct; I shall call this the 'creative view of mind'. On occasion it will be convenient to refer to people who hold or argue for the alternative accounts of mind as 'limited-minders' and 'creative-minders' respectively. Let me stress again that these terms imply no judgement about the quality of the minds of the thinkers concerned; they describe purely the opinions held by these individuals about the minds of human beings in general. In a society in which the creative view of mind is widely taken for granted, it may be a very creative intellectual achievement to propound the limited view of mind.

The creative view says, briefly, that it is in the nature of human minds to be always coming up with novel ideas – ideas which are in no sense implied by anything that has gone before, so that the workings of a man's mind are not predictable as machines or natural phenomena are. We may be unable to forecast the behaviour of a complicated machine or a complex natural phenomenon – the weather, say – in practice, but we feel that such things would be predictable in principle if only we knew all the controlling factors and could perform all the relevant calculations. We feel on the other hand – at least, many of us are inclined to feel – that a man's thoughts are not constrained by physical law in the same way that all material objects, including his body, are, so that no amount of calculation could enable us to foresee the future products of his mind. 'Whatever will they think of next?' we ask, without expecting to be answered.

The limited view of mind sees this attitude as a sort of myth born of ignorance. Human brains, the physical loci of our mental activities, are of course immensely complex structures, so there is nothing surprising in the fact that we cannot make predictions in practice. But, according to the limited-minder, in principle it would be possible, from an inspection of a man's mind as it is at a given time, to know what ideas he is potentially capable of formulating in future. What we ordinarily call 'originality' is not, as many of us are inclined to suppose, the creation *ex nihilo* of ideas whose potential existence could not be deduced from any aspect of the physical or intellectual world as it was before the ideas were invented; it is merely the birth into conscious awareness of elements of a fixed stock of ideas all of which were present in unconscious potential form in the thinker's mind from the start of his life, and beyond which he can never go.

To say that a man's thoughts are drawn from a fixed range is not, obviously, to say that it is possible to predict which elements of the range will enter the man's conscious mind in given circumstances. One can quite well hold that men have 'limited minds' while nevertheless believing that any detailed prediction of their intellectual biographies is impossible in principle. For our purposes this is a side issue. My quarrel is with the view that men are limited to specifiable ranges of ideas, so that for me the other question does not arise.

The classic exponent of the limited view of mind was Plato, who held that 'what we call learning is really just recollection' of things that we knew in former lives.[1] Plato argued that it is impossible for men to acquire by experience the concepts in terms of which they perceive the world, largely because our concepts are 'absolute' while the world is imperfect. Thus, we may think of a pair of sticks

[1] *Phaedo* 72e (translated by H. Tredennick in *The Last Days of Socrates*, Penguin, 3rd edn. 1969).

as 'equal' in length; but no two sticks we encounter are ever exactly equal, so our idea of absolute equality can be explained only as a *memory* of which we are reminded by the sight of the approximately equal sticks, just as the sight of a cat may remind me, through their similarity, of my own cat at home. If I did not already possess my idea of my own cat, the cat in the street could scarcely evoke that idea in me. The 'absolute ideas' with which Plato was concerned, such as equality, beauty, goodness, and the like, are never instantiated in the pure form in our grubby world, so our concepts of them must have been formed in previous existences.

A very similar view was held by René Descartes. Descartes was concerned less with the contrast between the imperfect world of experience and Plato's imagined world of 'ideal forms' (though contrasts of this kind did play a role in Descartes's thinking) than with the logical point that experience does not contain concepts. What impinge on a man's organs of sense are a kaleidoscopic and ever-changing array of visual, aural, and other stimuli, and these do not reach us labelled with the words we need in order to describe them. When I look towards my study window, my eyes are bombarded with an enormously complex mélange of green, brown, and grey light-waves, but no discrete elements enter my eyes corresponding to the words *tree, hill, sky* in terms of which I reduce the complex stimuli to simple statements. Still less do statements themselves, such as 'Two trees stand in front of a hill beneath an overcast sky', impinge on our organs of sense ready-formed. Yet we formulate such statements in response to such stimuli. For Descartes, the only possible solution was that the word-concepts and propositions are in us from birth, and only the truth-values of our inborn propositions remain to be settled by observation. 'I hold that all those [ideas] which involve no affirmation or negation are innate in us; for the organs of sense bring us nothing like the idea which awakens in us in response to them, and so that idea must have been in us beforehand.'[1] For Descartes as for Plato, 'learning' can scarcely be seen as the acquisition by a

[1] Letter to Mersenne, 22 July 1641; *Œuvres*, ed. by C. Adam and P. Tannery, 13 vols., Vrin (Paris), 1964-74, vol. iii, p̄. 418.

mind of ideas which it did not previously contain; he wrote that an infant, even in its mother's womb,

has in itself the ideas of God, itself, and all those truths which are said to be self-evident, no less than adults have these ideas while they are not attending to them; the child does not acquire them later, on growing up.[1]

Earlier that summer, Descartes had listed the ideas of 'God', 'mind', 'body', and 'triangle' as examples of 'true, immutable, and eternal essences' which as such were innate.[2]

This last passage implies that some ideas (less philosophically weighty than the concept of God or the self) are acquired by experience; Descartes fluctuated in the extent to which he claimed that *all* our ideas are innate. For that matter, Plato's argument appears to allow that our ideas of *imperfect* things might derive from experience (though that point may well be valid with respect only to the distorted version of Plato's philosophy which results from translation into our modern terms). But clearly both thinkers reject or ignore the creative view of mind. Plato and Descartes both argue that, if an idea does not derive from experience, then the mind must have been endowed with it from the first; the essence of the creative view is that this is a *non sequitur* because minds have the power of creating original ideas.

The modern discipline of Theoretical Linguistics was founded by Noam Chomsky of the Massachusetts Institute of Technology. Chomsky, and the many other theoretical linguists whose work has been inspired by the writings which Chomsky has published over the last twenty-odd years, see themselves explicitly as cultivating the approach to mind inaugurated by Plato and Descartes. 'From Plato to the present time', Chomsky writes, 'serious philosophers have been baffled and intrigued by the question . . . "How comes it that human beings, whose contacts with the world are brief and personal and limited, are nevertheless able to know as much as they do know?"'; and he answers the question, in a consciously Platonic and Cartesian manner, by saying 'we can know so much because in a sense we already knew it, though the data of sense were necessary to evoke and elicit this knowledge'.[3]

[1] Letter to *X*, August 1641; *Œuvres*, vol. iii, p. 424.
[2] Letter to Mersenne, 16 June 1641; *Œuvres*, vol. iii, p. 383.
[3] Chomsky, *Reflections on Language*, Temple Smith, 1976, pp. 5, 7.

For Chomsky, however, our innate stock of potential ideas are provided not by previous incarnations or by God but by biology: 'our systems of belief are those that the mind, as a biological structure, is designed to construct'.[1] That does not mean that every detail of a man's thinking is determined by his genes; Chomsky of course recognizes that a given child may grow up with any of a range of different conceptual categories and systems of belief, depending on his experience. But for that matter not every detail of a man's physiology is determined genetically either. Factors such as muscle tone, or hardness of the skin of hands and feet, are heavily affected by exercise, for instance, and are largely independent of an individual's genes. But in both cases, Chomsky argues, genes impose strict limits on the developmental flexibility of the growing organism. A human is no more free to formulate ideas that go beyond his inherited stock of possibilities than to grow a novel organ such as a pair of wings. For Chomsky and other linguists, Theoretical Linguistics is a science which is actually producing concrete evidence in favour of this version of the limited view of mind.

The fact that Chomsky's version of the limited view is stated in biological terms saves that view from a logical difficulty which assailed Plato's version even for those prepared to accept the doctrine of the transmigration of souls. If concept-formulation is merely the recollection of ideas acquired in previous incarnations, how were the ideas originally acquired? – if by 'learning' in the usual sense, according to which the idea learned was not previously present in the mind, then why is such learning not possible for contemporary men? Once we replace the somewhat mystical notion of the transmigration of souls with that of biological inheritance, the difficulty disappears. I did not 'learn' to grow a pair of eyes of the kind that human beings possess, and nor did any of my ancestors do anything that would usefully be called 'learning' to develop eyes; nevertheless, the processes of mutation and natural selection have changed an eyeless remote ancestor into modern Man via a long sequence of intermediate individuals each of which was developmentally inflexible with respect to his anatomy. If it makes sense at all to imagine that genes might determine concepts

[1] ibid., p. 7.

as well as anatomy (and I shall not claim that there is anything *logically* inadmissible in this suggestion) then the same process of biological evolution could explain how Man has acquired a rich structure of thought even though, allegedly, neither we nor our ancestors have created any ideas during our lifetimes – we have only shifted into our conscious awareness one or another of a range of potential ideas which, for each individual, was fixed from birth.

Chomsky, like Plato and Descartes, suggests that our innate ideas are in some sense 'good' or 'appropriate' – he often ascribes 'innate *knowledge*' to mankind, which implies that what is known is true. Chomsky does not suggest that we might have innate predispositions to analyse the world in terms of inappropriate concepts or to hold false beliefs, although logically this should be equally compatible with the notion of innately limited minds. For Descartes the goodness of innate ideas is guaranteed by the fact that they come from God, and for Plato perhaps by the notion that souls have spent part of their previous existence in an ideal world; in a biological limited-mind theory the concept of natural selection can play the role which God played for Descartes and the ideal world for Plato. (We shall see in due course that Chomsky has only small respect for Darwin's theory of biological evolution, but his criticisms would not affect what has just been said.)

Chomsky himself calls the point of view he advocates 'rationalist' as opposed to 'empiricist'. In earlier writings I have followed Chomsky in this, but that now seems to me a mistake; the issue I am taking up with Chomsky cuts across the debate between the rationalism of Descartes and the empiricism of, say, John Locke. There is a sense in which the Lockian, empiricist attitude that all ideas are derived by abstraction from experience is almost as much a 'limited-mind' view as is the Cartesianism against which Locke was concerned to argue. For Locke, our ideas were divided into simple ideas such as those of coldness and hardness, which '*are not fictions* of our Fancies, but the natural and regular productions of Things without us, really operating upon us', and complex ideas, such as those of beauty, gratitude, man, army, which are said to be compounds of simple ideas.[1] In other words, for Locke

---

[1] *Essay Concerning Human Understanding* (1690), ed. by P. H. Nidditch, Oxford University Press, 1975, §§ ii. ii. 1, iv. iv. 4, ii. xii. 1. Among the ideas derived by

the range of potential ideas is determined by external reality and the nature of our organs of sense. The simple ideas correspond to the ways in which the outside world can operate on our sense-organs, and the potential stock of complex ideas corresponds to the possible combinations of simple ideas. So, for Locke too, the mind is limited, but limited in a passive way to those elements impressed on it by Nature; for Descartes the mind is more active – it produces ideas from within itself – but in this activity it is limited to the stock of ideas with which it is unconsciously endowed from birth.

Chomsky is concerned to argue that the mind is active rather than passive in this sense, and, by an ironic quirk of intellectual history, he has often been led to use the word 'creative' to contrast the active conception of mind he favours with the much more Lockian view presupposed by descriptive linguists such as Leonard Bloomfield.[1] But (as I have argued at length elsewhere[2]) Chomsky's use of 'creative' in this connexion is Pickwickian, it flies in the face of the ordinary everyday usage of the word. Chomsky argues that minds do *not* engender new ideas which previously existed neither overtly nor implicitly – they only trot out one or another of an inventory of ideas with which we are all endowed from birth. Individual minds are, as it were, branches of a super-market chain rather than artists' studios.

The genuinely creative view of mind is represented in contemporary philosophy by Sir Karl Popper, lately of the London School of Economics. According to this view, men really do learn things they never knew in any sense before, but the acquisition of knowledge is a very active procedure. Understanding the world is a (never ending) process of interaction between guesses (or hypotheses, to give them a more dignified title) and evidence supplied by the senses which confirms or disconfirms the guesses. Lockian empiricism was correct in suggesting that no knowledge is innate; in many circumstances our guesses are likelier to be wrong than

applying mental operations to the 'simple ideas' Locke distinguishes 'relations' and 'abstractions' from 'compounds' of simple ideas, but these distinctions have no importance for present purposes.

[1] See e.g. p. 139 of Bloomfield's *Language*, Allen & Unwin, 1935.

[2] *The Form of Language*, Weidenfeld & Nicolson, 1975, pp. 53–9; *Liberty and Language*, Oxford University Press, 1979, pp. 101–11.

right, and the word-concepts in terms of which our guesses are formulated may well be inappropriate (no one nowadays thinks it worth while to try out *any* hypotheses about phlogiston or vampirism, for instance). But empiricism was incorrect in suggesting that experience determines our ideas; for Popper our guesses are the free inventions of our minds, and the concepts they employ are not in general mere compounds of simple sensory qualities such as coldness or hardness. (How could notions such as Locke's 'gratitude' or 'army' be reduced to qualities of sense, for instance? Prima facie it seems inconceivable that they could. If one insists dogmatically that there must be a translation of the term 'army' into some immensely complicated paraphrase mentioning only sense-qualities, then it seems hard to avoid the conclusion that people who do not know how to do the translation do not really know what 'army' means – which is surely nonsense.) The task of learning about the world has no end, because (to return to the supermarket metaphor) we are not limited to picking out the best tins from the grocery shelves but create our ideas *ex nihilo*; there will always be new ideas to be thought up, and some of them will prove to be valuable.

Since we have no guarantee of the appropriateness of our word-concepts or of the truth of our hypotheses, learning is a very slow, gradual business. Every new step we take is taken blind, so we cannot leap straight to complex theories about the world but must advance one pace at a time, always testing our new hypotheses against experience before shifting our weight onto them and exploring further. Thus, a contemporary man may conjecture that a wet summer leads to an abundance of greenfly, and he will probably think of the concepts 'wet', 'summer', 'greenfly', and so on as practically mere labels for obviously discrete elements of Nature; but his conjecture is possible only because, long ago, another thinker conjectured that the fluctuations in weather which he noticed during his lifetime followed a regular cycle, a guess which, once confirmed by further experience, enabled the concept 'summer' to enter the common stock of ideas; a further thinker conjectured that the various little flying things fell into discrete species each of which bred true, giving among others the concept 'greenfly'; someone else guessed that creatures might multiply not simply at the whim of the gods but in accordance with natural conditions; and so forth. The concepts we take for granted in formulating new hypotheses are themselves the descendants of earlier hypotheses (sometimes our own earlier hypotheses, often those of our predecessors) which were equally fallible when first produced, though in the event they survived the test of experience.

We are able to know much more than our remote ancestors, because we do not have to recapitulate individually the whole process by which previous generations have acquired knowledge; the institution of language, once we have mastered it, enables the previous generation to transmit the current results of that process to us, by-passing the long chain of guesses and refutations from which the results emerged. (Understanding a teacher may itself involve a process of conjectures and refutations, as any student of philosophy will surely agree; but it is much easier than understanding Nature, because the teacher co-operates actively in the process.) Thus we do 'inherit' the ideas of our ancestors, but not in the sense that they are built into us biologically (and are thus immutable for the individual). Cultural transmission provides each individual with the ideas of his predecessors as a foundation for his own thought, but these 'inherited' ideas will vary from one cultural tradition to another, and they do not bind the individual's mind; he may well find reason to reject some elements of his cultural inheritance, while accepting other elements as the basis on which to build further knowledge of his own.

Popper discusses the interactive process of knowledge-acquisition primarily in the context of the advancement of science.[1] But for Popper there is no philosophically significant distinction to be drawn between the process by which those particularly general elements of knowledge that we classify as 'science' grow and that by which ordinary men and women learn to understand their everyday world. 'Common sense' is just a name for the set of concepts and hypotheses which happen to have emerged and to have survived the risk of refutation over a long period in one's cultural tradition.

Since men's ideas are genuinely invented by them rather than

[1] e.g. in *The Logic of Scientific Discovery* (1934), English version published by Hutchinson, 1959.

given to them ready-made, it follows that the scientific method, one of the most powerful products of human thought, cannot be turned round and applied to thought itself. The essence of science is prediction; a scientific theory need not necessarily specify exactly what will occur in future in a given domain of enquiry, but it must at least specify a limited range of possibilities, so that it lays itself open to the risk of being proved wrong in the event. A wholly unrisky theory would tell us nothing because it would rule out no possibility. To construct a scientific theory about men's thought, then, would be to delimit a range of potential ideas outside which they were claimed not to venture; but that is exactly what the doctrine of intellectual creativity claims to be impossible. It is characteristic of human minds to create products which violate any norms that might be invented to describe their previous products. Popper actually suggests that there may be a logical paradox in the notion of applying the scientific method to human thought; to predict that an idea will be invented tomorrow (or even to predict that it belongs to the range from which tomorrow's new ideas will be drawn) would be to invent it today.[1]

It is worth noting at this point that Popper does *not* treat newborn minds as featureless 'blank slates', although he does deny that they contain any infallible knowledge. Most of Locke's 'simple ideas', for instance the ideas of 'cold' or 'yellow', corresponded to the various ways in which our sense-organs could be affected by stimulation; clearly it is a genetically-determined matter that we have sense-organs (eyes) which respond to electromagnetic radiation of 580-nanometre wavelength, so that in a certain sense we may be said to be born with the concept 'yellow', while we have no organ sensitive to 750-nanometre radiation, so that the concept 'infra-red' is a sophisticated product of scientific advance. Popper even suggests that we might be described as having some inborn propositional beliefs, for instance the belief that we will be fed at a nipple, and in his recent writings he has laid increasing emphasis on this aspect of our intellectual life.[2] Popper sees the conjecture-and-refutation process within the individual

---

[1] Preface to *The Poverty of Historicism*, Routledge & Kegan Paul, 1957.

[2] K. R. Popper, *Conjectures and Refutations*, Routledge & Kegan Paul, 1963, p. 47; K. R. Popper and J. C. Eccles, *The Self and its Brain*, Springer, 1977, p. 121.

human and within the human community as a very much speeded-up continuation, peculiar to our species, of the process of mutation-and-natural-selection within the biological world at large; and the intellectual evolutionary process begins not from scratch but from where the biological evolutionary process left off in our species. But the intellectual process is a *continuation*, not a standstill; we may genetically inherit some ideas, but we produce many more, and the new ideas are not predictable from or related in any simple way to the innate ideas.

Some people find the notion that minds engender ideas out of nothing unacceptable *a priori*. The assumptions underlying this judgement may be clarified by an analogy with an issue in the theory of cosmology. It has been established by empirical observation that the contents of the universe are moving away from one another in space, and the standard account of the situation (the 'big-bang theory') asserts that all matter was once concentrated in a single lump which has subsequently been spreading out and thus becoming ever less dense. There is an alternative, 'steady-state' theory which asserts that the universe has always had the same gross properties that it has today; it is not becoming less dense, because new atoms of matter are created at just the right rate to balance the eternal dispersal process. As I understand it the steady-state theory has proved empirically unsatisfactory, but that is beside the point here. What matters is that some have been reluctant to entertain the steady-state theory because they find intuitively incredible the notion that matter might be created *ex nihilo*, not just once for all in the remote past, but continuously in our own time. Others, of whom I am one, find it odd to strain at this particular item, when our investigations of cosmology force us to believe so many other remarkable things in any case.

I do not want to rest much on this analogy. There are large differences between the two cases; for one thing, it is quite possible for the cosmologist to avoid positing creation *ex nihilo* as either a continuous or a once-for-all event by arguing that the material of the universe has always existed, while the analogue of this view for the intellectual case (which would be panpsychism, the doctrine that there is no problem about the emergence of ideas in creatures of a certain biological level because all material objects have minds) seems extremely unattractive. The point I am making is merely that, if the creative view of mind appears unacceptable, this may be because of an unreasoned prejudice against creation *ex nihilo* rather than because of rational objections. In the material world (ignoring the steady-state theory) we find that nothing begets nothing; but we all recognize intuitively that human minds, whatever their relationship to brains, are a very special category indeed among the diverse furnishings of the world, and if the evidence points strongly in that direction there may be no good reason to deny that the ability to create *ex nihilo* may be one of the features differentiating minds from other things.

However, I do not in fact believe that the creative view of mind is less plausible than the limited view to the average member of our culture. I am convinced that the reverse is the case. Consider the admiration which is very widely felt for individuals who display an unusually large measure of intellectual or artistic 'originality', 'inventiveness', 'creativity'. Whatever the truth of the matter is, I am sure that those who feel this admiration *believe* that what they admire consists of something more than skill in picking out a suitable item from a fixed inventory of possibilities contained in all of us. It is hard to see how people could happily accept the institutions of patent and copyright, for instance, if they felt that the patented ideas or the copyrighted texts were already contained in their own minds (in inexplicit form, to be sure) before their fellow-citizen obtained his legal monopoly – if he *made* them, on the other hand, it seems quite just that he should reap the benefit.

I shall return to the question whether the creative view of mind may be unacceptable on *a priori* grounds in Chapter V below. For the moment, let me take for granted that the creative view is a possible alternative to the limited view. What implications would the creative view of mind have for the scientific study of language?

There appear to be two implications. (Doubtless there are others, but we shall consider two.)

In the first place, the creative view implies that a language can be described scientifically only to a limited extent. A scientific account of a phenomenon is an account which makes testable predictions – which says 'Thus and such, or so and so, may happen, but this, that, and the other cannot occur'; a creative phenomenon is one which constantly escapes the bounds suggested by its past history, so that any testable prediction about it will be falsified (unless it just happens to remain unrefuted by accident). Therefore scientific description of aspects of language which manifest human intellectual creativity is an impossibility.

This is by no means to say that any scientific linguistic description is impossible; there are aspects of our linguistic behaviour which seem to be quite mechanical and uncreative. Most obviously, our habits of pronunciation, although acquired rather than genetically fixed (different languages exploit the possibilities of our inherited vocal apparatus in quite different ways), are not consciously reflected on except by the few speakers who are trained in the technicalities of phonetics, and indeed there would seem to be little practical point for most people in 'intellectualizing' about such matters whether consciously or unconsciously (unless perhaps for purposes of social advancement). Scientific phonological description may be quite possible. On the other hand, the aspect of language which is most obviously dependent on the conscious intellectual activity of language-users is the semantic aspect. The meaning-structure of a language is closely tied up with (if indeed it can be distinguished from) the structure of beliefs of its speakers, which is very much a matter of conscious intellectualization. Therefore the creative view of mind suggests that scientific description of the semantics of a language should be impossible. One could describe the ways that the meanings of words have evolved up to the present, in the anecdotal, non-predictive style of the disciplines called 'humanities' or 'arts' – and this, of course, is just what the makers of good dictionaries such as the *Oxford English Dictionary* do; but it would be hopeless to try to entrap usage in more rigid scientific formalisms, because word-meanings will escape any cage they are put in. Between phonology and semantics lie the intermediate levels of morphology (word-formation) and syntax (the assembly of words into sentences); of these the former is commonly agreed to be about as mechanical as phonology, while the status of syntax is a question which I shall defer for the moment.

The other implication of the creative view of mind has to do with the diversity of languages. If the products of human minds are genuinely free creations rather than merely the realization of fixed possibilities laid down for our species through the machinery of biological inheritance, then insofar as languages are intellectual products they should be expected to show no more common characteristics than what are induced by cultural transmission. Where we find language-communities which are culturally isolated from one another, we shall not look to find any properties common to their languages, at least with respect to those aspects of language which are controlled by the speakers' thought rather than by their physiology or other considerations. (Thus, we may predict that no human language will use labiopalatal stop consonants, but that is because it is physiologically difficult or impossible for a human to induce plosion between lower lip and hard palate; and we may predict that all human languages will have some means of referring to phenomena such as sun and water, but that is because these things are as a matter of physical fact familiar to and important for all human beings irrespective of their particular ways of thought.) For the creative-minder, linguistics will be a matter of describing individual languages separately, and there will be no room for a general theory stating properties shared by all languages. Different languages will be simply . . . different.

The discipline of Descriptive Linguistics which flourished, mainly in America, late in the nineteenth century and for the first six decades or so of our century reflected these implications of the creative view of mind. The foremost nineteenth-century American linguist, William Dwight Whitney, argued against those who suggested that language might be the manifestation of specific innate mental endowments:

. . . as we approach man, the general capacities increase, but the specific instincts, the already formed and as it were educated capacities, decrease. It is among the insects that we find those wonderful arts which seem like the perfected results of training of a limited intellect; it is among birds that we find specific modes of nest-building and a highly art-like, almost artistic, song. Man is capable of acquiring everything, but he begins in the actual possession of next to nothing. Except suckling, he can scarcely be said to be born with an instinct. . . . There is no plausibility in the suggestion that he should have begun social life with a naturally implanted capital of the means of social communication. . . .[1]

The pioneer of substantive research on the structures of the 'exotic' languages of American Indians, Franz Boas, came to linguistics out of disillusionment with a geographical version of the limited view of mind; he began his ethnographic fieldwork with the assumption that human cultures were more or less predictable products of geographical circumstances, and when he found that this was not so he turned to the study of language as a component of culture which reflected the free human intellect relatively directly. Even Leonard Bloomfield, though like Locke he emphasized the role of experience rather than that of mental creativity in accounting for our intelligent behaviour, resembled Whitney in scouting the idea that language might be somehow 'built-in' in the mind; the child's acquisition of language is a matter of learning, it 'is doubtless the greatest intellectual feat any one of us is ever required to perform'.[2]

The Descriptive Linguists saw their subject as a 'science', but they attempted to treat scientifically only the 'lower' levels of language: phonology and morphology in great detail, syntax only to a limited extent, while attempts at formal description of the semantic structure of languages were unheard of. Furthermore, linguistics was very much a matter of producing separate descriptions of individual languages each in their own terms, and Descriptive Linguists frequently emphasized that one could look for no 'carry over' from a successful description of one language to the task of describing another language, unless the two happened to share a common ancestry. In a passage which I have quoted elsewhere but which is too apposite not to quote again, Martin Joos wrote of the 'American (Boas) tradition that languages could differ from each other without limit and in unpredictable ways'.[3] Insofar as 'General Linguistics' was more than a handy departmental title to cover work on diverse languages which (unlike

---

[1] W. D. Whitney, *The Life and Growth of Language*, Henry S. King, 1875, p. 289.
[2] Bloomfield, *Language*, p. 29.
[3] M. Joos, ed., *Readings in Linguistics*, American Council of Learned Societies (New York), 1957, p. 96.

Spanish or German) were too exotic to have university departments of their own devoted to them, it was seen by the Descriptivists as a tool-kit of useful *techniques* of description, rather than as
a *theory* of how all languages are structured.[1]

Since the rise to prominence of Noam Chomsky and his
approach to linguistics in the 1960s, this situation has wholly
changed. The new breed of 'theoretical linguists', while they are as
insistent as their descriptivist predecessors on the 'scientific'
nature of their work (indeed, they pay considerably more attention than the Descriptivists did to abstract questions of scientific
methodology, and the notion that linguistic descriptions should be
rigorously formal is taken even more seriously now than then),
apply their analytic methods as much to the syntactic and semantic levels of language as to the lower levels. Nowadays it is not
unusual to meet an established practitioner of linguistics who
works only on syntax and/or semantics and who is more or less
wholly unversed in the special techniques of phonological
analysis – a situation that would have seemed bizarre twenty
years ago. Furthermore, description of individual languages is
now seen as a mere means to the end of constructing a 'general
linguistic theory', a scientific statement of the common properties
of all human languages (this is why I call members of the new
school 'theoretical' linguists). These scholars claim to have identified a rich system of universal structural characteristics shared by
all known languages but not imposed on men's speech by their
physiological heritage, and not predictable on the basis of any
considerations external to Man. It is argued that these findings
reflect inborn, inherited mental organization of very much the
kind suggested by Plato, Descartes, or Kant.[2] To learn a language
would be 'an extraordinary intellectual achievement for a creature
not specifically designed to accomplish this task'[3] – so extraordinary that Chomsky cannot believe humans perform it. What
we learn is only the relatively superficial details that distinguish

[1] For a sketch of the Descriptivist school of linguistics, see ch. 3 of my *Schools of
Linguistics*, Hutchinson, in press.
[2] Chomsky's ideas are in some ways even more closely related to the philosophy of Immanuel Kant than to that of Descartes, whom Chomsky more
commonly cites as his predecessor. Cf. my *Form of Language*, pp. 31–3.
[3] Chomsky, *Reflections*, p. 4.

one language from another; the basic structural principles do not need to be learned, instead they 'grow in the mind, rather in the way that familiar physical systems of the body grow'[1] – under the control of a genetic program.

The influence that this view of language has enjoyed in recent years can scarcely be exaggerated. Not only has the Chomskyan approach to linguistic research, including its objections to Descriptive Linguistics (which the new men despise as mere fact-collection), been accepted with more or fewer reservations as authoritative by almost all members of the profession of linguistics, but that profession has itself expanded mightily; every second university now has a department of linguistics where, twenty years ago, such institutions scarcely existed. (It is true that some of this expansion is due to the general growth of higher education, which in Britain happened to coincide rather exactly with the rise to prominence of Chomskyan Theoretical Linguistics, and some to independent factors, but unquestionably an important share of the expansion was a response to the intrinsic attraction of Theoretical Linguistics as a discipline.) Moreover the new linguistics has exerted great influence on thought in other disciplines, particularly psychology and philosophy – something which was never true to anything like the same extent of Descriptive Linguistics. In the psychological case, for instance, Donald Broadbent finds it necessary to write a book *In Defence of Empirical Psychology* against what he identifies as a growing anti-empiricist drift in both academic psychology and the general intellectual scene, and Broadbent is clear that Chomsky's linguistics is the key to that drift.[2] And on the other hand Bryan Magee describes Chomsky's thought as so influential for contemporary philosophy that 'In the writings of philosophers today, I should say his name probably occurs as often as that of any living person'[3] – a judgement which certainly chimes with my own experience.

In this book I am concerned to argue three points.

First, the extent to which Theoretical Linguistics provides

---

[1] 'Noam Chomsky on the genetic gift of tongues' (interview with Bryan Magee), *The Listener*, vol. 99, no. 2554, 6 April 1978, p. 434.

[2] D. E. Broadbent, *In Defence of Empirical Psychology*, Methuen, 1973, pp. 188–9.

[3] Chomsky/Magee interview, p. 434.

evidence relevant to the limited- v. creative-mind issue is greatly exaggerated. Often the work of theoretical linguists simply *assumes* the correctness of the limited view of mind, and the plausibility of much of the linguistic analysis carried out by the new school vanishes as soon as one appreciates that the limited view of mind is only an assumption which need not necessarily be true. The fact that Chomsky leaves the creative view out of consideration as a potential account of our intellectual life is clear from remarks such as this: 'If we were plastic organisms without extensive pre-programming, the state that our mind achieves would . . . be a reflection of the environment, which means that it would be extraordinarily impoverished.'[1] In other words, for Chomsky as for Descartes, either the contents of an adult's mind are built-in in advance or they are contained in his experiences, and the third possibility – that they might be invented freely and unpredict-ably – is not entertained. It is chiefly (though by no means only) in the semantic area that the limited-mind view functions as an assumption rather than as a conclusion supported by evidence; I deal with semantics in Chapters II, III, and IV.

After a discussion of *a priori* problems in the doctrine of intel-lectual creativity in Chapter V, in Chapters VI to IX I turn to consider syntax. Here the claims of the theoretical linguists are, superficially at least, more convincing. I shall argue that some of the 'syntactic universals' to which linguists appeal as support for their limited view of mind are indeed true discoveries rather than mere artefacts of their assumptions, and that these universals cannot be explained away as logically necessary features of language, for they are not. Nevertheless, the theoretical-linguistic position is defeated even more soundly in the syntactic arena than in the semantic. Not merely do the syntactic universals fail to support the view that linguistic structure is inherited, as linguists claim; on the contrary, they turn out to constitute decisive evi-dence *against* the genetic inheritance of language, and in favour of the creative-mind supposition that individuals learn their mother-tongue from scratch as a feat of intellect. Linguists, in other words, have radically misunderstood the implications of their own find-ings – this is the second thesis of my book.

[1] Chomsky/Magee interview, p. 435.

The consequences of my arguments, if they succeed, will be destructive for the discipline of linguistics. I shall suggest that there is no room for a 'general theory of language', of the kind that so many contemporary linguists see themselves as contributing towards; that such features as are common to all natural languages are predictable on the basis of facts in other intellectual domains which are already well understood, so that a separate theory of linguistic universals is redundant. Furthermore I shall argue that the notion of extending scientific linguistic analysis to the level of semantics, even within an individual language, rests on a fallacy, so that linguistic description ought to retreat to the 'lower' levels which some linguists have begun to think of as the less glamorous side of the subject. (My objections to scientific semantics will also have implications for the discipline of 'Artificial Intelligence'.) My third general point, in other words, is that the Descriptivist approach to linguistics, which began to go out of fashion about twenty years ago, was broadly the right approach, and that the aspects of contemporary linguistics which clash with Descriptivist assumptions are undesirable developments. The last chapter, Chapter X, briefly considers what has led linguistics to take this wrong turning and draws the moral for the future.

I should stress that I regard the message of the book as an optimistic rather than a gloomy one. The kinds of linguistic research whose validity I am calling into question, though having their own appeal as intellectual exercises, are founded on a view of human nature which sees Man as something much less than the creative animal I take him to be. I hardly suppose that anyone *prefers* to think of himself as a machine with a fixed potential, however rich that potential may be, rather than as a creator whose responses to experience, while fallible, are limited by no internal or external constraints; and even those of us who belong to the profession of academic linguistics are surely human beings first and linguists only a distant second. To summarize the book in a sentence, I aim to show that the contents of our speech and writing – both the concepts denoted by our words and the logical forms into which our concepts are arranged – are not born with us but made by us. It is not only by a figure of speech that we are entitled to describe ourselves as *making sense*.

II

As I have already said, formal description of the semantic structures of natural languages was not practised by the Descriptivists. The first attempt at such a thing was J. J. Katz and J. A. Fodor's article 'The structure of a semantic theory', published in 1963.[1] This one article inaugurated what rapidly grew from a trickle to a flood of publications on 'Linguistic Semantics', as the new field has come to be called; it is now one of the most popular specializations within linguistics.

The various scholars contributing to the field naturally differ among themselves on many issues. One basic idea unites them, however. This is the notion that a scientific account of meaning in a natural language will involve a system of *translation* between that language and another language which has to be discovered by theoretical enquiry; the translation of a natural sentence into this other language is often referred to as the 'semantic interpretation' of the sentence. It is almost always assumed further that the vocabulary-elements of the hidden 'conceptual language', as one might call it, will be fewer and in some sense simpler than those of the ordinary language being described; words in the ordinary language will be semantic molecules compounded from atoms called 'semantic components', or 'features', or 'markers', in the conceptual language. Thus, the English word *boy* might translate into a set of three 'features' MALE, HUMAN, YOUNG. (It is conventional to name 'features' in small capitals to distinguish them from words of the natural language being described. Often the features are treated as variables taking two values – thus linguists write [+MALE] and [−MALE] rather than MALE and FEMALE – but this has little significance in the present context and will be ignored.) The meanings of features will not necessarily coincide exactly with those of any single words in the natural language. Thus it is usual to treat English *brother* and *sister* as compounds of

[1] *Language*, vol. 39, pp. 170–210; my page references are to the reprint in J. A. Fodor and J. J. Katz, eds., *The Structure of Language*, Prentice-Hall, 1964.

features MALE and FEMALE, respectively, added to a feature SIBLING representing the meaning common to *brother* and *sister*; but, apart from the fact that *sibling* does not occur in many Englishmen's vocabulary, *sibling* does not mean the same as SIBLING even for those who know the word: a twin is a SIBLING but not a sibling (*O.E.D. Supplement*, s.v.). There is no one-word English translation for SIBLING; *brother or sister* is the shortest one can manage. Other characteristics of the conceptual language, notably the syntactic rules governing the assembly of features into propositions, are more controversial.

In their original article Katz and Fodor did not commit themselves to the claim that there was one conceptual language shared by speakers of all natural languages[1] (and I shall argue that the view of semantic description as translation into a conceptual language is invalid whether or not such a claim is made). However, most subsequent writings on Linguistic Semantics have argued that the conceptual language ultimately to be discovered will be, or even must be, a linguistic universal, though they do not claim that they have completed the task of dissolving words of English or any other natural language into their ultimate conceptual constituents.

Thus, Paul Postal writes that 'the relation between the semantic primitives and their combinations . . . and the world is not learned but innate. What must be learned is only the relations between fixed sets of semantic primitives and sets of phonological and syntactic properties.'[2] Chomsky argues that general linguistic theory '*must* provide a general, language-independent means for representing the [phonetic] signals and semantic interpretations that are interrelated by the grammars of particular languages', and he welcomes Katz and Fodor's article as a step in this direction.[3] For Manfred Bierwisch, the notion that 'semantic features

[1] Katz and Fodor's 'semantic markers' were said to be drawn from a universal stock ('Structure of a semantic theory', pp. 516–17), but they also recognized a category of conceptual features called 'distinguishers' which seem to have been meant as specific to individual languages.

[2] Review article on A. Martinet, *Elements of General Linguistics, Foundations of Language*, vol. 2, 1966, p. 179.

[3] Chomsky, *Topics in the Theory of Generative Grammar* (*Janua Linguarum, series minor*, 56), Mouton (the Hague), 1966, pp. 12–13; my italics.

cannot be different from language to language, but are rather part of the general human capacity for language, forming a universal inventory used in particular ways by individual languages' ranks as a 'plausible hypothesis',[1] but the only consideration cited by Bierwisch as rendering it plausible is that it is difficult to think of men's concepts as derived directly from their experience of the world. For Katz, on the other hand, universality seems to have become a methodological requirement as it is for Chomsky: 'We . . . *require* a semantic theory to provide . . . a universal theory of concepts in which the notion "possible (cognitive) meaning in a language" is defined by a recursive enumeration of the set of possible senses.'[2]

With the postulate of universality, the notion of a 'conceptual language' is clearly a limited-mind theory of the Platonic/Cartesian kind: the word-concepts potentially available to a human are exhaustively defined by specifying the list of atomic semantic features and the principles governing their combination into semantic 'molecules'. Notice that the features are by no means restricted to Lockian 'simple ideas', i.e. immediate sensory qualities such as 'cold', 'yellow'; properties like YOUNG or MALE are only distantly related to the qualities which our physical organs of sense are designed to detect, so linguists are solving the problem posed by the fact that we have ideas not directly derived from experience by holding that such ideas are built-in from birth.

The question arises, then, how linguists justify their belief in a conceptual language underlying the ordinary languages that we hear people speak.

One interesting answer to this question is provided by J. A. Fodor in his book *The Language of Thought*,[3] which is possibly the most explicit defence by any linguist of the notion of a 'conceptual language'. According to Fodor, 'The only psychological models of cognitive processes that seem even remotely plausible represent such processes as computational', and 'Computation

---

[1] 'Semantics', in J. Lyons, ed., *New Horizons in Linguistics*, Penguin, 1970, pp. 181–2; and cf. p. 3 of Bierwisch's 'Some semantic universals of German adjectivals', *Foundations of Language*, vol. 3, 1967, pp. 1–36.

[2] J. J. Katz, *Semantic Theory*, Harper & Row, 1972, p. 32; my italics.

[3] Crowell (New York), 1975.

presupposes a medium of computation: a representational system'.[1] For behaviour to be goal-directed implies that the behaving organism must in some sense be able to predict the likely outcomes of the various actions physically open to it, and to compare these outcomes with its goals; this prediction and comparison presupposes some sort of internal symbolic representation system for describing and drawing conclusions about outside-world states of affairs, and such a system might as well be called a 'language' even if it is not equipped, as English and French are, with a medium of expression permitting the work of prediction and comparison to be shared with other organisms.

So far this is reasonable enough, but I still see no reason to posit a 'conceptual language' *in addition to* languages such as English and French; surely it is simpler to say that my internal symbolic representation system is just the English language, that a Frenchman's internal representation system is the French language, and so forth? However, Fodor has anticipated this reply, which according to him just cannot be taken seriously.

The obvious (and, I should have thought, sufficient) refutation of the claim that natural languages are the medium of thought is that there are nonverbal organisms that think. . . . considered action, concept learning, and perceptual integration . . . are familiar achievements of infrahuman organisms and preverbal children. . . . So either we abandon such preverbal and infrahuman psychology as we have so far pieced together, or we admit that some thinking, at least, isn't done in English.[2]

I find this quite *ins*ufficient as a justification for the notion of 'semantically interpreting' natural languages into a distinct conceptual language. Like Fodor, I see little profit to be gained from debating what it means to attribute thought to organisms which cannot speak. I readily agree that infants and animals do exhibit, e.g., goal-directed behaviour, that this shows that they must have available some internal system for representing states of affairs and drawing conclusions about them, and that if such a system were equipped with a medium of expression we would certainly call it a 'language'. On the other hand, what one can observe of the

[1] op. cit., p. 27.
[2] ibid., p. 56.

behaviour of infants and animals suggests that their internal 'languages' must be extremely limited and crude by comparison with English or French; the plans which appear to govern their goal-directed behaviour are very short-term, simple, and concrete by contrast with those in accordance with which adult humans run their lives. It therefore seems odd to suggest that adult humans who demonstrably have mastered a highly subtle symbolic system such as the one we call 'English' actually do their thinking, not in that language, but in another language in some way more akin to the crude symbolic systems whose existence we can infer from the behaviour of infants or animals.

Fodor recognizes, of course, that adult humans' thinking is a more sophisticated thing than the 'thinking' of languageless infants, but he suggests that this is purely because English, say, provides convenient one-word abbreviations for concepts whose conceptual-language equivalents would be far too complex and cumbersome to be usable in practice.[1] In other words, Fodor seems to be going back, here, on his earlier suggestion that languages such as English are not 'languages of thought' at all; but he is going back only to the extent of suggesting that such languages make some thoughts thinkable in practice that in the conceptual language (which he takes to be genetically inherited and therefore available to infants as well as to adults) are thinkable only in principle, rather as Arabic notation for numbers makes it easy to do multiplication problems which in principle can be done in Roman-numeral notation but which are extremely cumbersome in that notation. Fodor still does not concede that a natural language such as English creates the possibility of thoughts which are unavailable even in principle to infants or animals. Yet my own behaviour, for instance, is governed on many occasions by axioms such as 'If the fuel gauge is low I should check the mileage to the next service area'. I see no reason to believe that a proposition such as this has *any* translation, no matter how cumbersome, into the internal representation system used by children of a few months. It is true that experimental psychologists are able to demonstrate that the intellectual world of newborn children is somewhat richer than the layman might have guessed; for

[1] ibid., p. 85.

instance it seems that the category 'human face' is inborn rather than learned by experience. But to say that the system is somewhat richer than is apparent to a casual observer is *very* different from saying that the system is so rich that in principle it permits the construction of all concepts available to any adult.

Fodor has been oddly ambivalent in his attitude to these issues. In the same year, 1975, in which he published *The Language of Thought*, arguing that the notion of a universal conceptual language is virtually a logical necessity, he co-authored an article[1] which argues that there is no reason even to posit a 'conceptual language' underlying any individual natural language, let alone a universal conceptual language common to all natural languages. However, Fodor's attempt to resolve this paradox[2] clearly places him back in the limited-mind camp. All he means by objecting to the notion of semantic interpretation, Fodor ends up saying, is that once we have learned to abbreviate a constellation of universal semantic atoms, say YOUNG MALE HUMAN, as a single word such as *boy*, the atoms cease to play any role in the psychological processing that occurs when we use or encounter the word *boy*. Fodor suggests that this gets him out of the apparent absurdity of suggesting 'that children are born with concepts like "airplane" ready formed'. But Fodor's resolution of his contradictory arguments in no way goes against – in fact it reasserts – the limited-mind principle that our possible concepts are definable in advance in terms of a set of primitive concepts and rules for compounding concepts; whether compounds, once formed, are processed by our psychological machinery as compounds with internal structure or as unanalysed units is (in the context of the present enquiry) a comparatively trivial issue of neural engineering. The problem about sophisticated concepts such as 'aeroplane' is not merely that newborn children do not appear to possess them but also that they cannot be paraphrased in terms of those concepts which can plausibly be ascribed to the newborn.

Furthermore, Fodor's theory yields highly implausible empirical predictions. Thus the concept 'dog' must abbreviate some set

---

[1] J. D. Fodor, J. A. Fodor, and M. F. Garrett, 'The psychological unreality of semantic representations', *Linguistic Inquiry*, vol. 6, 1975, pp. 515–31.
[2] On pp. 152–6 of *The Language of Thought*.

of semantic atoms including ANIMAL (a dog is a certain kind of animal), so the word *animal* ought to be learned by a child earlier than the word *dog*. Usually the reverse is the case, and Fodor is forced to reconcile this with his theory by suggesting that when a child first uses *dog* he may use it to mean 'animal' rather than 'dog'. To judge by my own experience (as father rather than as linguist) this is just not true, and Fodor gives no serious evidence in favour of the suggestion.[1] As soon as one gives up the insistence that all concepts are compounded from a stock of primitive concepts, there ceases to be any reason to expect it to be true.

I have begun with Fodor's justification of the 'conceptual language' notion because of its ingenuity rather than because it is representative – it is not. It seems likely that many linguists think of semantic interpretation into a conceptual language on the analogy of translation out of a foreign language. The only occasions when questions about the meaning of a sentence or other linguistic form arise in practical life are when the form is in a language other than one's native tongue, or involves unfamiliar vocabulary, and on these occasions what one wants is a translation into the language one knows. It might seem to follow that for a linguist to say what an ordinary sentence of his own language

[1] There has been surprisingly little empirical research in recent years on young children's acquisition of vocabulary, as opposed to syntax (for a survey of what has been done, see Melissa Bowerman, 'Semantic factors in the acquisition of rules for word use and sentence construction', in D. M. and A. E. Morehead, eds., *Normal and Deficient Child Language*, University Park Press, 1976; and cf. references to earlier work in footnote 1 to page 40 below). Eve Clark has argued for a theory about the development of word-meaning which supports Fodor's position with respect to concrete nouns such as *dog* ('What's in a word?', in T. E. Moore, ed., *Cognitive Development and the Development of Language*, Academic Press, 1973). But Mrs. Clark concedes that her account represents a somewhat speculative interpretation of data she has found scattered through various late-nineteenth- and twentieth-century publications. It is not at all clear why she believes that these data confirm the strong hypothesis that children systematically misinterpret concrete nouns as standing for concepts superordinate to the 'correct meanings' in the adult's conceptual taxonomy (as predicted by her and Fodor's semantic theory), rather than the common-sense view that children unsystematically mistake the sense of adults' words. Cf. the conclusion drawn by Philip Dale (*Language Development*, 2nd edn., Holt, Rinehart & Winston, 1976, p. 175). Andrew Lock offers a relatively congenial account of this and other aspects of language-acquisition in *The Guided Reinvention of Language*, Academic Press, 1979.

means must be to translate it into a language which is somehow even more perspicuous. But that is silly. A man's own language is by definition the most perspicuous language for him; translating its forms into another language, whether natural or artificial, cannot make them more comprehensible to him whatever other virtues such a procedure may have.

The original Katz and Fodor article suggested that the point of 'semantic interpretation' was that it accounted in a systematic way for such properties of and relationships between sentences as ambiguity, anomaly, and paraphrase. (A sentence is 'anomalous' if it is grammatical but senseless; a standard example is *Sincerity is triangular*. The example Katz and Fodor use is much subtler than this and might well be regarded as not anomalous at all; I defer discussion of it at this point.) In an article published shortly afterwards,[1] Jerrold Katz added to the earlier list the properties of analyticity (a sentence is said to be 'analytic' if it is true by virtue of its meaning, e.g. *Bachelors are unmarried*), contradiction (contradictory sentences are false by virtue of their meaning, e.g. *Bachelors are married*), and syntheticity (synthetic sentences are neither analytic nor contradictory, e.g. *That man is a bachelor*).[2]

The property of ambiguity, although treated by Katz and Fodor as the most central of all the phenomena they discuss, can scarcely justify the complex apparatus of translation into 'conceptual language'. It is *possible* to indicate that sentences containing the word *bill* are ambiguous by requiring all sentences to be translated into conceptual language and providing alternative translations for *bill*; but if that were one's only goal, it would be much simpler just to say that there are two words *bill*$_1$ and *bill*$_2$ and to leave other words unchanged.

However, the conceptual-language notion is prima facie more attractive with respect to the other semantic properties

---

[1] 'Analyticity and contradiction in natural languages', in Fodor and Katz, *The Structure of Language*.

[2] It is not quite clear whether Katz saw these latter properties as part of the data which a semantic description sets out to capture, or rather as theoretical constructs which emerge from a semantic description based exclusively on data of ambiguity, anomaly, and paraphrase. The former of these positions seems more reasonable, since the various semantic properties are very much on a par with one another with respect to their pre-theoretic availability to the analyst.

mentioned. Katz and Fodor's system for translating English into conceptual language represents the relation of paraphrase between sentences by providing the same translation for each; it represents anomaly by failing to provide any translation (the rules for translating into conceptual language are organized in such a way that they break down just when the input to them is an 'anomalous' sentence); it represents analyticity by providing a translation having a certain simple formal property (which will not in general be found in the original natural-language sentence); and so on. These matters could scarcely be treated more simply, e.g. by extending the system of numerical subscripts to natural-language words, so perhaps specification of a system of translation into an artificial conceptual language is a good way of describing the semantics of a natural language in an economical, elegant way.

There are several points to be made here.

In the first place, paraphrase, semantic anomaly, analyticity, and the rest are only various special cases of the general relationship of *inference*. Inference is the relationship that holds between a set of sentences and an individual sentence if, given the truth of the former, the truth or falsity of the latter is guaranteed merely by virtue of the meanings of the respective sentences. Thus, if I accept that *John is foolish* and that *Only wise men know the value of freedom*, I am bound to reject *John knows the value of freedom* and to accept *John does not know the value of freedom*. Two sentences are paraphrases if each can be inferred from the other. A sentence is analytic if its truth can be inferred given no premisses at all, and contradictory if its falsity can be inferred in the same situation. 'Semantic anomaly' is not usefully distinguished from contradiction. (Katz and Fodor call *Bachelors are married* contradictory and sentences like *Sincerity is triangular* anomalous because the negation of the former is an analytic truth which might usefully be uttered e.g. to someone who did not know what bachelors were, whereas it is hard to imagine any use for *Sincerity is not triangular*, though it is also an analytic truth; but this is not an important distinction.)

It is quite correct that a semantic description of a language would need as one of its central tasks to represent the relationships of inference obtaining between the declarative sentences of the language, but there is no obvious value in picking out the special categories of inference relations discussed by Katz and Fodor and attempting to construct a system that deals just with those cases. It would seem more sensible to set out from the general case, whereby a group of *n* sentences implies the truth or falsity of another sentence, in the expectation that a system which handles the general case will equally handle the special cases of analyticity and contradiction (where *n* = 0) and paraphrase (which is definable as mutual inferability). What a system handling inference in general will most obviously need will be rules for moving from one sentence or group of sentences to another, akin to the rules of inference used by formal logicians, which allow them to derive conclusions from sets of premisses (in the artificial languages they work with) by applying rules step by step to build up chains of propositions known as 'derivations'. To understand the words *buy* and *sell*, for instance, is in part to know that, granted *Mick bought a car from Roger*, it follows that *Roger sold a car to Mick*; in order systematically to represent this and the many other similar inferences in English we must state a rule something like 'Infer *A sell B to C* from *C buy B from A* and vice versa', with *A*, *B*, and *C* understood to range over the various noun-phrases of English.

Now it might be that a convenient system for specifying the inference-relations in a natural language would work by translating forms of the language into an artificial scheme of representation and by defining inference rules for the artificial formulae rather than directly for the natural sentences. Possibly the greater economy of inference rules defined for a regular, artificial language might outweigh the need to specify rules for translating between the artificial and the natural language. Indeed the example just mentioned made such an assumption, when it reduced the inflected form *bought* of the natural sentence to the root form *buy* in the rule. Differences of tense and the like, indicated by verbal inflexion in English, would need to be represented somehow in the artificial 'semantic interpretations' of English sentences, since such distinctions are meaningful (i.e. they affect inference relations); but English conjugation is very complicated and 'quirky', and it might well be that the formal inference rules could be simplified if the information contained in inflected forms of verbs were regimented into some unnatural but more logical structure. The syntactic 'transformational rules' posited by linguists (see Chapter VI below) often seem to be designed to relate natural sentences to 'deep structures' for which relatively simple rules of inference are available (though this is not their stated purpose, and such inference rules are never made explicit).

The notion of 'semantically interpreting' natural sentences into a 'conceptual language' might, then, be justified as a device for defining inference relations economically. But this consideration could be used only to motivate the postulation of independent conceptual languages for each natural language; it in no way leads us to expect that different natural languages will share the same conceptual language. (It might turn out as a matter of empirical fact that patterns of inference in various natural languages are such that the most economical way to regiment the sentences of any one language will resemble the way which is most economical for other languages, despite outward differences between the natural languages themselves, but we have no reason to assume this before doing the research.) So, if this is the rationale of the 'conceptual language' idea, it hardly supports the limited view of mind.

However, it seems in any case unlikely that this consideration will lead us to treat natural *words* as semantically complex. The kind of regimentation for the sake of inference-rule simplification just discussed could clearly serve a purpose in connexion with the *grammar* of natural sentences, but I cannot think of a case where inference rules would be simplified by translating words into clusters of semantic atoms. Thus we *could* if we wished handle the inference from, say, *John is a bachelor* to *John is unmarried* by translating *bachelor* as UNMARRIED MALE and *unmarried* as UNMARRIED, and stating an inference rule something like 'From A is X Y infer A is X' (e.g. UNMARRIED MALE implies UNMARRIED); but surely it would be simpler just to dispense with the translation into 'features' and write rules something like 'From *bachelor* infer *unmarried*', 'From *bachelor* infer *male*'? In the case of *brother* and *sister*, rather than inventing a feature SIBLING corresponding to no concept of which most Englishmen are consciously aware, why not write 'From A is B's *brother* infer *A's parents are B's parents and A is male*', and similarly for *sister*? It is not logically absurd to suppose that Englishmen unconsciously entertain a concept SIBLING in their minds, but it seems perverse to believe this when the facts can be stated perfectly straightforwardly without resorting to such devices. (And it would be hopelessly naïve to suggest that English children normally use *brother* to mean SIBLING before they learn that it means 'brother'.)

To take another standard example, to kill someone is to cause them to die, but that is no sufficient reason to say that the 'semantic interpretation' of *John killed Bill* is 'JOHN CAUSE (BILL DIE), or more extravagantly still, 'JOHN CAUSE (BILL BE (NOT ALIVE))'; the inferences that English-speakers can draw between sentences containing these words could equally well be stated in rules such as 'From *A kill B* infer *B die*', 'From *dead* infer *not alive*', and so forth, which involve only actual words of the English language. If the translations into 'universal semantic features' say something subtly different from the rules dealing with ordinary words, then the translations misrepresent the facts; if they say precisely the same, then the system of universal semantic features is redundant.

It is worth briefly pointing out, furthermore, that the device of translation into conceptual language does not even handle all the semantic facts of the categories (such as paraphrase) for which it was invented. Paraphrases that arise from the substitution of synonymous groups of 'monadic predicates' (properties of individuals) for one another can be treated readily in terms of conceptual language; one can capture the relationship between, say, *Genevieve is a female schimmel* and *Genevieve is a roan mare* by translating *female* as FEMALE, *schimmel* as ROAN HORSE, *roan* as ROAN and *mare* as FEMALE HORSE (though one could equally well write inference rules such as 'From *schimmel* infer *roan horse* and vice versa', 'From *mare* infer *female horse* and vice versa', which would leave the sentences as distinct sentences but would allow us to derive one from the other and thus tell us that they are paraphrases). But *Roger sold a car to Mick* and *Mick bought a car from Roger* are also paraphrases of one another, and we have seen that it is easy to write inference rules to reflect this; what translation of *buy* and *sell* into 'features', on the other hand, would give the sentences the same conceptual translation, which is what is required by the theory of 'semantic interpretation' in cases of paraphrase? Obviously it will not do to

give the words *buy* and *sell* themselves the same conceptual translation, because they have very different meanings. The problem
arises from the fact that *buy* and *sell*, like many verbs, are not
properties of single individuals but relations between sets of
individuals, and the device of 'features' is of little help in indica-
ting relations. One could give other examples of how the notion of
semantic interpretation is unsatisfactory even with respect to the
category of data for which it was invented; inference rules are
inherently more flexible, and since it seems redundant to use both
devices in a semantic description the obvious choice is to use only
inference rules.[1]

Conceivably there might be some set of inference relations in a
natural language the statement of which really could be significantly simplified if the words involved were replaced by constel-
lations of semantic atoms. But it is not clear to me what an
example of this situation would be like, and as far as I am aware no
linguist has ever attempted to make such a case; usually 'linguistic
semanticists' more or less wholly ignore the notion of inference.
Linguists simply assume that ordinary words must be compounds
of conceptual atoms, because they assume the limited view of
mind. People have always taken it for granted that speaking
involves mastering a set of conceptual units and putting them
together in different combinations on different occasions; linguists
say in effect 'Yes, that is the general idea, but the units are quite
different from what you know as words and the rules for assembling them are quite different from grammar as you know it'. An
assumption which leads to such an apparently bizarre conclusion
surely requires to be supported by better arguments than have
been provided for the limited-mind approach to semantics.

I know of only one category of concrete evidence that has been
claimed to offer direct support for the notion of 'lexical decompo-

---

[1] The above criticism of Linguistic Semantics was made by Yehoshua Bar-
Hillel in 'Universal semantics and philosophy of language', in Jaan Puhvel, ed.,
Substance and Structure of Language, University of California Press, 1969. Some
linguists have recently begun to incorporate inference rules (under the name
'meaning postulates') into their semantic descriptions, without appearing to
appreciate that they make the notion of translation into semantic features
redundant; see e.g. Ruth Kempson, *Semantic Theory*, Cambridge University Press,
1977, § 11.2.

sition', i.e. the idea that words are compounds of semantic atoms. This has to do with the syntactic phenomenon of anaphora; good examples of the type of argument in question have been constructed by W.C. Watt.[1] Anaphora is the name for a situation in which one element of a sentence derives its meaning by referring back to an earlier element; an obvious example is reflexive pronouns – *herself* in *Mary cut herself* is understood as co-referential with *Mary*, and *Mary cut himself* is not a well-formed utterance unless the hearer is prepared to suppose that *Mary* is being used, unusually, to name a male. Another anaphor is the phrase *do so*; thus, in the sentence *John swam the river and Mary did so too, did so* means 'swam the river'. However, Watt found experimentally that a fair proportion of English-speakers accept sentences such as *Dognog wanted to nail the boards together, but Gripsnake made him do so with adhesive tape*, which makes sense only if *do so* is taken to mean, not specifically 'nail the boards together', but more generally 'fasten the boards together'. Watt's own reaction to the sentence (and mine) is that it is ill-formed or silly; *do so* necessarily refers back to the actual words used previously, and one cannot 'nail boards together with adhesive tape'. But, Watt suggests, *nail the boards together* might well translate into conceptual language as something like (FASTEN THE BOARDS TOGETHER) WITH NAILS, so the reactions of the roughly half of Watt's sample of subjects who were happy with the quoted sentence could be explained by saying that they use English in such a way that anaphors are allowed to find their antecedents in the semantic interpretation of the sentence (in this case, the element in brackets) rather than necessarily in the superficial wording of the sentence. Clearly this explanation would work only given that the verb *nail* is indeed decomposed as suggested at the level of semantic interpretation.

However, the reactions of Watt's subjects could obviously be

[1] 'Late lexicalizations', in K. J. J. Hintikka, J. M. E. Moravcsik, and P. Suppes, eds., *Approaches to Natural Language*, Reidel (Dordrecht), 1973. There are also articles in the literature, such as Paul Postal's 'On the surface verb "remind"' (*Linguistic Inquiry*, vol. 1, 1970, pp. 37–120), which purport to demonstrate the reality of lexical decomposition from syntactic data other than anaphora, but these works suffer from failure to draw the crucial distinction between syntactically ill-formed word-sequences and grammatical sentences which are non-sensical or pointless (an issue which I discuss at length in e.g. my *Form of Language*, pp. 80–84).

explained also in many other ways. At the simplest level, the subjects in question might have been happy to accept the sentence because they were not very fastidious about usage. More interestingly, the sentence may have been unobjectionable because, for the subjects who accepted it, *do so* is an anaphor of a rather different kind from *herself* (a kind of which other examples occur in all versions of English). Contrast an ordinary personal pronoun such as *she* with the reflexive *herself*, for instance. *She* may be used to refer to someone mentioned earlier in a sentence, as in *Mary felt hungry when she got up*, but this is not necessary; in general *she* will be taken by the hearer to refer to the female nearest his mental focus of attention, and although the hearer's attention may have been drawn to the female in question by the fact of her just having been named a few words ago, she may have come to the hearer's attention in some way quite unconnected with language. If you and I are gazing wordlessly at a passing girl, you will not misunderstand if I say to you *She's a stunner*. Reflexives, on the other hand, must refer back to actual elements of the preceding clause; if, in the situation just sketched, I say instead *What do you think of herself?*, you will surely be startled (unless of course I stress *herself*, in which case you will take me to be speaking Irish for a joke). Reflexive pronouns such as *herself*, we may say, are 'true anaphors', while non-reflexive pronouns such as *she* are only 'quasi-anaphors'.

Now, for Watt and for me, *do so* is a true anaphor; but we have only to make the scarcely extravagant assumption that some English-speakers use *do so* as a quasi-anaphor and we can understand that the sentence about Dognog and Gripsnake will be acceptable, with *do so* understood as the general kind of activity suggested by the specific instance of nailing the boards together – namely, fastening them. If the word *so* in that sentence were replaced by the quasi-anaphor *it*, the sentence would be acceptable to me too in that sense.[1] In quasi-anaphora, even when the anaphor is understood by reference to an antecedent linguistic form rather than to the passing scene in general, any association of sense between the antecedent and the intended meaning of the

---

[1] Cf. § ix of my 'Thoughts on the recent marriage of philosophy and linguistics', *Foundations of Language*, vol. 12, 1975, pp. 537–60.

anaphor will suffice for the anaphor to be understood, and it is not necessary for the intended reference to be actually included in the verbal material. We understand the *it* of *They left the disgraced General alone with a loaded pistol but he could not bring himself to do it,* although no linguist would suggest that features corresponding to 'shoot himself' occur in the 'semantic interpretation' of any of the material preceding *it*.

Watt has taken issue with me on this, and has suggested other examples for which, he claims, the possibility of avoiding lexical decomposition by resorting to the notion of quasi-anaphora is not open.[1] I have used Watt's examples in an experimental survey of my own, the results of which are reported elsewhere;[2] they appear decisively to refute Watt's account of his examples in terms of lexical decomposition, while being entirely compatible with my account in terms of quasi-anaphora.

Lexical decomposition, then, seems a gratuitous assumption, and one which would scarcely support the notion of a *universal* conceptual language even if it could be justified (unless one were to argue that the very discovery of a hidden range of concepts underlying but distinct from the concepts encoded directly in the vocabulary of a natural language would suggest that the former must be universal – I am not sure why one should take this view unless one were predisposed to believe in a universal conceptual alphabet, but the question is too hypothetical to spend much time on).

Apart from alleged evidence in favour of lexical decomposition, the other type of evidence that has been used by advocates of the limited-mind view of semantics is comparative linguistic and psychological data from diverse cultures. The best-known example is the work of Brent Berlin and Paul Kay on the colour terminologies of a wide range of languages of many unrelated language-families.[3] It has long been known that languages differ in their ranges of 'basic colour terms' – that one cannot expect another language to contain words which cover just the areas of the spectrum covered by, say, English *red, orange, yellow, green,* and

---

[1] 'Good intensions', *Journal of Linguistics*, vol. 14, 1978, pp. 83–8.
[2] 'The irreducibility of words', *Journal of Linguistics*, vol. 15, 1979, pp. 39–47.
[3] B. Berlin and P. Kay, *Basic Color Terms*, University of California Press, 1969.

so on, and indeed that languages vary greatly even in number of basic colour terms, with some languages dividing up the whole range of distinguishable tints beween as few as two or three words while others have systems as rich as or richer than that of English. Descriptive linguists often cited these facts as a relatively clear example of the semantic independence of natural languages from one another. Berlin and Kay argue, however, that there is a considerable degree of system underlying this apparent diversity; the number of basic colour terms of a language increases with cultural level, but the order in which various terms emerge is fixed, so that if one knows how many colour terms a language has one can predict what they will be.

There is much to object to in Berlin and Kay's research methods, and in other writings I have pointed out some of the weaknesses in their theory and referred to the objections of others.[1] These criticisms certainly do not destroy the validity of the claim that colour-naming conforms to a universal system. What emerges, rather, is that the physiology of the human eye implies greater sensitivity to some tints than others, and languages evolve names for colours to which our eyes are highly sensitive (and which therefore look bright to us) sooner than for the duller tints.[2] It has even turned out that some of the variation between languages which Berlin and Kay themselves attributed to purely cultural differences are in fact consequences of physiology. Berlin and Kay note (as William Ewart Gladstone did a century before them) that languages of advanced cultures have more 'basic colour terms' than those of primitive communities; one example of this is that languages of primitive civilizations often lack words for short-wavelength hues such as blue. Many of these languages are spoken by dark-skinned races, and W. H. R. Rivers suggested as early as 1901 that the facts might be explained by saying that pigmentation of the retina tends to absorb light at short wave-lengths, so that blues are perceptually less salient for black men than for whites.[3] Berlin and Kay treat Rivers's idea as the product

[1] *Schools of Linguistics*, ch. 4.
[2] G. A. Collier, Review of Berlin and Kay, *Language*, vol. 49, 1973, pp. 245–8.
[3] W. H. R. Rivers, 'Primitive colour vision', *Popular Science Monthly*, vol. 59, 1901, pp. 44–58.

of naïvety about the relationship between language and perception, and as 'almost certainly wrong',[1] but detailed research by Marc Bornstein has subsequently shown that Rivers was quite correct.[2] (It is not suggested, however, that all variation between languages with respect to number of colour terms can be explained physiologically.) Bornstein has also shown in an ingenious experiment that four-month-old infants categorize various shades perceptually, as adults do, into reds, yellows, greens, and blues, long before they can label such categories verbally, and he refers to studies by other scholars showing that species other than Man likewise perceive hue categorically.[3]

Work comparable to Berlin and Kay's on colour has been carried out by Eleanor Rosch on shape.[4] Rosch ran an elegant experiment in New Guinea with members of the Dani tribe who had not been exposed to external cultural influences. The Dani, who live in what has been called an 'uncarpentered world', lack vocabulary for geometrical forms such as square, triangle, and circle; and Rosch began by establishing that her subjects did not spontaneously use such categories when given drawings of various figures that we would regard as perfect or more or less imperfect examples of these three shapes and asked to sort them into groups, or to say which of two figures a third figure resembled more closely. Rosch then set out to teach her subjects various concepts of shape, corresponding to different subsets of the figures; some subsets consisted of a perfect square, circle, or equilateral triangle together with various distortions of it, while in other subsets a 'distorted' figure (as we would see it) was central and the other members of the set departed in different directions from that figure. The results of the experiment make it clear that, despite the subjects' lack of previous awareness of the concepts, square, circle,

[1] Berlin and Kay, op. cit., p. 148.

[2] M. H. Bornstein, 'Color vision and color naming', *Psychological Bulletin*, vol. 80, 1973, pp. 257–85; 'The influence of visual perception on culture', *American Anthropologist*, vol. 77, 1975, pp. 774–98.

[3] M. H. Bornstein, W. Kessen, and S. Weiskopf, 'The categories of hue in infancy', *Science*, vol. 191, 1976, pp. 201–2; cf. Eleanor Rosch, 'On the internal structure of perceptual and semantic categories', in T. E. Moore, ed., op. cit., pp. 114–23.

[4] Eleanor Rosch, op. cit., pp. 123–30.

and triangle were 'good' shapes for them as they are for us. Furthermore, while square was a 'better' shape for the Dani than (non-square) rectangle, equilateral triangle was no 'better' than other perfect triangles. Thus it is apparently no accident that English has a single word for 'equilateral rectangle', and a word which is considerably commoner than the words *rectangle* or *oblong* (namely, the word *square*), but has no single word – only a learned phrase – for 'equilateral triangle'; in this respect English merely reflects the relative perceptual salience of these shapes.

Some may regard findings such as these as supporting the limited view of mind; Berlin and Kay (though not Rosch) offer their own work in this spirit,[1] and many linguists have seen it as having such implications. I cannot agree. To my mind what is significant about work such as Berlin and Kay's and Rosch's is that the areas in which it has been possible to demonstrate what might be called innate concepts are areas in which the concepts are immediate qualities of sense-data, Lockian 'simple ideas', the innate status of which is not a matter of controversy. Quite obviously biology gives us organs of sense which are sensitive to certain qualities in the stimuli impinging on our bodies and not to others; nobody suggests that humans 'learn' as a cultural or individual matter to perceive yellow light but not infra-red light, plainly that choice is made for us by our genetic endowment. Since our physical organs of sense are highly subtle devices, there is nothing surprising in the fact that the pattern of discriminations they make is not immediately apparent and that, for instance, they react in a categorial fashion to a range of stimuli (such as light of different wavelengths) which is physically continuous.

The creative-minder will certainly expect that all languages will tend to have words for stimulus-qualities to which our organs of perception are particularly sensitive. What he insists, however, is that each language will have many words which are not simply names for qualities of sense-data or paraphrasable in terms of such qualities, and that *these* words will not be fixed for all languages but will vary from culture to culture. Descartes claimed not only that 'triangle' was an innate concept but also that 'God' and 'mind'

[1] Berlin and Kay, op. cit., pp. 109–10.

were innate concepts. I am quite willing to grant Descartes 'triangle', and I know no evidence forcing me also to grant him 'God' or 'mind', which I should be very unwilling to do.

I suggested earlier that a semantic description of a natural language would consist, at least in part, of a set of rules specifying the relations of inference that hold between the various sentences of the language; but a language is not an entirely self-contained system, and clearly the inference rules would have to be supplemented by rules correlating certain linguistic forms with the physical stimuli that evoke those forms in the mind of the perceiver. Thus, as well as rules of the form, say, 'From *banana* infer *yellow*', there will be rules such as '*yellow* = 580-nanometre light'. The creative-minder need have no objection to the notion that the latter set of rules are genetically fixed (although in fact I believe they are likely to be fixed only initially, so that e.g. when I learn that yellow wine is called 'white' I may cease to see it as yellow); he need insist only that there are many words which do not occur in rules of the latter class, and that the former rules are not exhaustive enough to turn the words occurring in them into mere abbreviations of sets of words occurring in the second kind of rule.

Since the creative-minder does not think of the other concepts as built up from the so-called 'simple ideas' which correspond to the categories of perception, as Locke suggested, he will not expect the latter ideas necessarily to take any precedence e.g. with respect to date of emergence in a child's speech, and they do not. I have examined a list of about eighty words prepared by my wife and myself as a record, as complete as we could manage, of the vocabulary of our first child at the age of 22 months (done purely as a matter of parental interest rather than with a view to finding evidence for the theoretical issue under discussion). Not one of the words could plausibly be regarded as a Lockian 'simple idea', even given that in some cases the concepts attached to the words by our daughter may have been somewhat different from what we mean by them. (Typical items are *sock, banana, bye-bye*.) Six months later our child still does not appear to have acquired any colour names, for instance, although these are fairly common in the speech addressed to her. This evidence is admittedly anecdotal, but it is quite typical.[1] I have certainly never heard of children who began with words such as *yellow*, *soft*, *straight*, *triangle*, and the like and proceeded to acquire words for common physical objects such as *sock* or *banana* later.

(One might ask how a child can know a banana when he sees one, if *banana* is not some sort of abbreviation for a complex set of sense-qualities? The answer is that he cannot, and nor can anyone else; we *guess* that what we see is a banana, and sometimes our guess is refuted by subsequent experience.)

Noam Chomsky has claimed that there are observable universal constraints on word-concepts other than those correlating directly with perceptual properties. He offers, as examples, the suggestions that 'terms designating objects . . . must designate objects meeting a condition of spatiotemporal contiguity', and that 'artifacts are defined in terms of . . . human goals, needs, and functions instead of solely in terms of physical qualities'.[2] Chomsky stresses that these statements are empirical claims rather than tautologies; thus 'there are no logical grounds for the apparent nonexistence in natural languages of words such as "LIMB", similar to "limb" except that it designates the single object consisting of a dog's four legs'.[3]

There are two points to be made here. The first is that the mere fact that a universal property of language is not *logically* necessary does nothing to suggest that it is innately determined, provided there is an alternative explanation available for its ubiquity. Since vocabularies of natural languages must surely have evolved to fit the needs of practical life, any feature of a vocabulary that makes it

---

[1] Even William Preyer, whose pioneering studies of child development aimed explicitly to provide evidence for a theory of biologically inherited intellectual structure very like Chomsky's theory, could not argue that the earliest concepts verbalized by infants were 'simple' or 'central' with respect to the conceptual scheme of adults; for instance one of Preyer's child's first words was the German for 'wardrobe'. See pp. 111–25 of W. T. Preyer, *The Development of the Intellect*, Pt. 2 of *The Mind of the Child* (*International Education Series*, vols. 7 & 9), D. Appleton (New York), 1888–9 (German original published in 1882). For more systematic records see e.g. Wilhelm Ament, *Die Entwicklung von Sprechen und Denken beim Kinde*, Ernst Wunderlich (Leipzig), 1899, or W. F. Leopold, *Speech Development of a Bilingual Child*, vol i, Northwestern University (Evanston, Ill.), 1939.

[2] *Aspects of the Theory of Syntax*, M.I.T. Press, 1965, p. 29.

[3] ibid., p. 201, n. 15.

relatively convenient is likely to be universal whether or not it is innately determined. To repeat an analogy I have used elsewhere: if crop-rotation leads to better harvests, then we shall be foolish to infer, from the fact that farmers everywhere rotate their crops, that they are born with an instinct for doing so. It seems very likely that words for artefacts sharing a common function will tend to be more useful (to creatures with *any* kind of mind) than words for ranges of artefacts which are physically similar but serve unrelated purposes, and that the entities with which any creature interacts as units, and for which he will accordingly coin names if he has the power of reason, will tend to be spatiotemporally continuous. However, the second point is that if (as it seems) Chomsky's two claims are intended as absolute constraints they are both false. The second claim quoted is refuted by the noun *hardware*, which designates a range of artefacts whose common features have to do with their physical qualities rather than with the human 'goals, needs, and functions' that they serve (which are extremely diverse); while the first claim is refuted by the French singular noun *rouage*, which designates the object consisting of the road-wheels of a vehicle and is thus a very close match to Chomsky's allegedly impossible 'LIMB', or by the word *constellation*, which is applied to sets of stars that are in many cases about as uncontiguous as any known objects.[1]

Chomsky has told me in correspondence that he does not regard *rouage* as a genuine counterexample to the first of his claims quoted above because it does not designate 'a scattered object in . . . the sense of the calculus of individuals. Thus, the left half of the front wheel and the middle of the back wheel do not constitute a part of the "rouage"'. I do not understand the force of this reply. In the first place, I should have thought that in suitable circumstances (i.e., if there were any reason to do so) Chomsky's pair of wheel-segments would be counted as a part of the *rouage* – I can imagine talking about them as 'the rusty part of the *rouage*', if just those

---

[1] In the same passage Chomsky also makes a claim about a universal constraint on colour terminology – that 'color words . . . must subdivide the color spectrum into continuous segments' – which again is both unsurprising and, as has been pointed out by Noriko McNeill ('Colour and colour terminology', *Journal of Linguistics*, vol. 8, 1972, pp. 30–31), not absolutely true.

segments were rusty, although admittedly I am not a native speaker of French. More important, Chomsky's claim mentioned nothing about the 'calculus of individuals'; he predicted that no language would have a word like 'LIMB', not that there were limits on what would count as part of a 'LIMB' in languages containing such a word.[1]

One reason why theoretical linguists are inclined to favour the notion of a universal conceptual language may have to do with an accident of their education which gives them an excessively 'Anglocentric' view of language ('Anglo-' in the linguistic rather than the national sense, that is). Part of the Cartesian approach to language is the view that, since various languages each encode the same universal concepts, 'there should be no fundamental difficulty in translating from one language to another', as Chomsky puts it.[2] Theoretical linguists often throw out hints which suggest that they take this to be axiomatic; thus, Fodor argues in favour of his version of the conceptual-language theory that 'if it is true, it goes some way toward explaining why natural languages are so easy to learn and why sentences are so easy to understand'.[3] Now it may well be appropriate to regard modern scholarly English,

---

[1] Apart from the specific claims by Chomsky discussed above, there is a more general point quoted by many linguists as a semantic universal, namely that individual words always replace constituents, rather than arbitrary sub-sequences, of the conceptual-language translations of sentences. Thus English has a verb *grow* found in sentences such as *John wants to grow*, corresponding to a conceptual translation such as JOHN WANT (BECOME BIG) in which the elements BECOME BIG go together as the object of WANT; on the other hand (it is claimed) no language could have a verb replacing the elements WANT BECOME, since these do not form a logical unit. (That is, in no language could one say something like *John flims big* to mean 'John wants to grow', with *flim* meaning 'want to become'.) Susan Schmerling calls this claim the 'major element of content' of the theory of lexical decomposition (in her review of D. Parisi and F. Antinucci, *Essentials of Grammar*, *Language*, vol. 54, 1978, p. 406). But only given the theory of lexical decomposition does the possibility that words might *not* be constituents arise; and even for those who accept that theory it seems that this generalization is true by stipulation rather than as an empirical finding (cf. p. 72 of J. D. McCawley, 'Lexical insertion in a transformational grammar without deep structure', *Papers from the Fourth Regional Meeting, Chicago Linguistic Society*, 1968).

[2] *Cartesian Linguistics*, Harper & Row, 1966, p. 96, n. 63.

[3] *Language of Thought*, p. 156. (One reader has suggested to me that Fodor may here be referring specifically to *first*-language acquisition; however, psychologists do not normally describe this as 'learning'.)

German, and French – languages which most linguists know – as merely alternative outer garments for a common stock of ideas; but then scholars of modern Europe and America form a fairly homogeneous *cultural* community, and the ideological differences that do divide them often cut across national and linguistic borders. While the Descriptivist school flourished it was standard practice for apprentice linguists in America to be set to study American Indian or other languages of cultures quite unrelated to their own; and of course until quite recently it could be taken for granted that a scholar on either continent would have spent many years during childhood learning Latin and Greek. Neither of these things is true today. The study of classical languages at school no doubt over-emphasized mechanical memorization of formal details at the expense of understanding the conceptual content of the literature, but it did have the great virtue of exposing large numbers of educated people to the thinking of members of cultures separate from ours, and thus giving them the opportunity, at least, to sample the diversity of thought-patterns open to our species.[1] After my own experiences of struggling with impenetrable concepts and texts of classical Chinese, I find it very difficult to sympathize with a theory that explains 'why natural languages are so easy to learn and why sentences are so easy to understand'.

Reading between the lines of some linguists' works, one almost gains the impression that 'natural language' and 'English' are, for them, synonyms (which, if it were true, would of course turn the doctrine of the universality of the conceptual system underlying English into a mere truism). One linguist tells an amusing anecdote, claimed to be genuine, of a mechanical-translation expert who succeeded in winning a grant from an American foundation with a research proposal in which the goal was stated, by an

---

[1] In this connexion it is particularly interesting to examine some remarks on language by Arthur Schopenhauer in *Parerga und Paralipomena* (1851; vol. ii, §§298–9 in the English version published by Oxford University Press, 1974). Like Chomsky (cf. Chapter VI below) Schopenhauer believed in a universal grammar determined by instinct in the same sense as the structure of a bird's nest or of bees' honeycombs; but Schopenhauer, on the basis of a deeper knowledge of classical and modern languages than is common nowadays, was clear that the meanings of individual words do not in general coincide from language to language and that novel vocabulary is constantly being coined.

oversight that was never noticed, as the development of a computer program for translating 'from French into natural language'. Indeed, the reader will have noticed Fodor's slip, in the passage quoted on p. 23, of arguing that research on the psychology of pre-verbal children and non-human species forces the sceptic to admit that 'some thinking, at least, isn't done in English'. As for classical Chinese, which no one could hope to mistake for English in unfamiliar pronunciation, Henry Rosemont has argued explicitly that it does not count as a natural language.[1] (I find his argument engaging but unconvincing.)

Apart from the Anglocentrism instilled by recent educational trends (and leaving aside the not inconsiderable point that faith in the 'language of thought' notion provides theoretical linguists with congenial research tasks), I believe that the other reason why the idea of a universal conceptual language is more attractive to contemporary linguists than the facts would seem prima facie to warrant is that linguists are confused about whether the idea is an empirical hypothesis for which linguistic research may be claimed to provide evidence, or a necessary truth – a methodological stipulation without which the notion of 'semantic description' is thought to be incoherent. We have already seen examples of this ambivalence; and indeed it can be illustrated within the writings of individual linguists. Paul Postal writes that 'It is a *reasonable hypothesis*, if one enormously difficult to verify, that underlying each language is a set of universal semantic primitives and conditions for their combination'; but the reality of these is taken for granted a few sentences later when he writes that 'It is a difficult, if *real enough*, problem for linguistics to study the set of semantic primitives. . . . Such research *must* in any event *obviously* precede any serious study of the relation between the combinatorial linguistic semantic structure and the nonlinguistic world.'[2] Likewise, in 1966 Jerrold Katz felt that the notion that 'each natural language is built up out of the same phonological, syntactic, and semantic elements' was a falsifiable theory which

---

[1] 'On representing abstractions in archaic Chinese', *Philosophy East and West*, vol. 24, 1974, pp. 71–88 – see particularly p. 85; cf. pp. 51–2 of T. Wasow, 'The innateness hypothesis and grammatical relations', *Synthese*, vol. 26, 1973.

[2] Review article on Martinet, *Foundations of Language*, vol. 2, 1966, pp. 179–80; my italics.

'receives its empirical support from empirically successful descriptions of particular languages that conform to its prescriptions';[1] six years later, as we have seen, he held that 'We . . . *require* a semantic theory to provide . . . a universal theory of concepts' in the form of an 'enumeration of the set of possible senses'.

The truth of the matter seems to be that when theoretical linguists talk about their discipline in general terms they often insinuate that it has discovered copious evidence in favour of the limited-mind view of semantics, but when they actually attempt to justify the notion of an innate conceptual language they do so almost exclusively by arguing that our concepts cannot be explained as mere reflections of our experience. In other words, they support their own version of the limited view of mind by arguing that *an alternative version of the limited view* is inadequate. Thus linguists do not refute the creative view of mind, they simply ignore it. The limited view functions, at least in discussions of semantics, as an unquestioned presupposition rather than as a discovery.

[1] *The Philosophy of Language*, Harper & Row, 1966, pp. 10–11.

III

I have argued that an adequate semantic description of a natural language would involve statements about relationships between words of that natural language, rather than about units of a hidden 'conceptual language', and that there is little reason to suggest that the respective conceptual stocks of various languages must be identical or related in any particular way – that is a gratuitous assumption, and an implausible one. I go on to argue now that it is equally unwarranted to suppose that there can be such a thing as an 'adequate semantic description' of a natural language at all. The creative view of mind suggests that any attempt to produce a rigorous, scientific account of the semantics of a human language must be as futile as chasing a rainbow. What linguists have observed of people's semantic behaviour does nothing to make this conclusion seem doubtful.

Thus, consider a typical question of the kind which would have to be given some definite answer in a semantic description of English: the question whether possession of a handle is a criterial feature for the application of the word *cup* to an object. *Cup* is one of a group of words, including *mug, tumbler, beaker, vase*, and others, whose meanings are similar but not identical; prima facie it seems plausible but not certain that possession of a handle might be a factor relevant for the use of the word *cup* as opposed to some of the other words. A linguistic semanticist would typically phrase the question as: 'Should the lexical entry for *cup* include a feature [+HANDLED]?'. Given the argument of Chapter II, it would be more sensible to reword this as: 'Should a semantic description of English contain a rule "From *X is a cup* infer *X has a handle*"?', or as: 'Is the sentence *Cups have handles* axiomatic?'. However, as questions about the English language, I suggest that none of these is meaningful. At best they could be construed as questions about the state of mind of an individual English-speaker at a particular point in his biography; but it is not at all clear to me that the questions will necessarily have answers (let alone discoverable answers) even when understood in this way, and certainly an answer to such a question could not count as a scientific prediction – this is just the kind of issue on which a thinker is liable to change his mind at any time, which means that no future behaviour by an individual could be incompatible with a positive or negative answer to the question with respect to that individual at a given moment.

How, after all, does an individual acquire a word – *cup*, or any other? It is fairly unusual to learn the meaning of a new word by being given an explicit definition; and even when this does happen, unless the word is a technical term the definition is unlikely to exert a decisive influence on how one subsequently understands and uses the word. (If theoretical linguists admit that they are very far from being able to specify the correct 'semantic interpretations' of the elements of our vocabulary, it is hardly likely that the average parent will manage a masterpiece of semantic analysis on the spur of the moment when asked by his child for the meaning of a word; yet the child will grow up using the word as competently as anyone else, unless it is unusual enough for the child to have no opportunity to correct his understanding of it.) Indeed, even in the case of technical words such as *atom*, though society arranges things in such a way that they receive standard definitions to which a considerable measure of authority is ascribed (this is what we mean by calling them 'technical'), nevertheless there is a limit to the influence of that authority. Were there not, it would have been impossible for scientists ever to have discovered that atoms are composed of particles, since at one time (as the etymology suggests) the stipulative definition of *atom* implied that atoms have no parts. Had the meaning of the word *atom* been determined by the stipulative definition, the discovery that things previously called 'atoms' were composite would have led people to cease applying the word *atom* to them; what happened instead was that the word remained attached to the same things, and the new knowledge about those things changed the meaning of the word.

In general we do not learn new words of our mother-tongue through definitions; we learn them by hearing them applied to particular examples.[1] We encounter a noun applied in practice to certain physical objects, say, and we guess as best we can how to extend the noun to other objects. A child hears its parents call certain things which resemble one another in some ways but differ in other ways *cups*; he may notice that one property shared by all of them is the possession of a handle, and if so he may conjecture that cups have handles as a matter of course. But any particular object has an endless variety of properties; there can be no guarantee that the resemblances which the child notices coincide with the features which led the parent to apply the word *cup* to the various objects in question. (The child may of course be aided in his conjectures about the criterial features for applying a given word by working out more general rules about the *kinds* of feature relevant for applying whole classes of words, for instance he may notice that colour is very rarely relevant for applying nouns, while function is frequently crucial so that, if a *cup* is used for drinking, the chances are that a similar object used to put flowers in will not be called a *cup*. But these more general rules are themselves creative and fallible conjectures.)

Some linguists seem to accept that this is how we learn words but to suggest that it is a fact only about the process of language-acquisition rather than about the nature of the language acquired. They suggest that the child has to guess his way towards the correct set of criterial features which control the adult's usage. But we are all in the same boat; we all spend our time guessing what sets of criterial features would explain the application of given words to given things in the speech we hear around us (and in the writing we read), while trying to conform our own usage to our conjectural reconstructions of each other's criteria in order to be understood. It is not clear what it could mean in such a situation to talk of a standard of correctness which a given speaker either has or has not achieved with respect to his use of a given word. That notion suggests that learning to use words correctly is like discovering the right combination to open a combination-lock, which is a problem with an objective solution independent of

---

[1] Fodor, in his *Language of Thought*, briefly notices this point (pp. 153-4), without drawing the negative conclusions I go on to draw below for the possibility of semantic description.

people's opinions. It would be more appropriate to compare the acquisition of a word-meaning to the problem of dressing fashionably in a very clothes-conscious society; here it would seem absurd to suggest that there was an objectively 'right' costume to wear, rather what is right is what people think right.

It is worth pursuing this analogy a little way. In the dress case, one solution which may be perfect if it is practicable is to dress exactly like someone recognized to be fashionable; I believe there have been societies in which fashion has led to rigid uniformity in this way. The counterpart of this principle in the case of language would be that one cannot go wrong in applying a word to the very same individual thing to which it has been applied by people who already know the word. But in the case of language one cannot restrict oneself to doing this. One constantly needs to refer to things (whether physical objects, actions, properties, or any other category of referent) about which, as individual instances, one has not heard anyone else talk. We have to *extend* terms that we have encountered used of other individual entities to the individual entity that confronts us now – an entity which, perhaps, no one has ever mentioned before. No two individual things share all their properties. The thing we want to refer to now will in various respects resemble various other individual things to which we have heard people give names, but it will not be identical to any of them; so we have to make a guess (an 'educated' guess, of course, not just a random stab in the dark) that entity Alpha, which we have heard referred to by words X, Y, and Z, was called Y by virtue of possessing the very properties which Alpha shares with the entity we want to talk about now – so that it is legitimate for us to call this thing a Y too.

The counterpart of this situation in the case of dress would be a situation in which it is normally impossible to copy someone else's costume exactly because garments are not made up to customers' specifications, rather there exist a large and diverse range of individual garments and accessories lying around for anyone to take and wear, each of which is unique in its details. In such a situation one would have to guess what properties of a dandy's costume lead to its being admired; given any limited set of properties one could assemble a costume of one's own sharing those properties, but duplication of the admired costume in all respects would not be possible. (The situation in our own fashionable society is actually not unlike this, not because exact duplication is impossible but because it is not admired – a point to which there is no analogy in the case of language.) One would ask oneself (consciously or unconsciously) questions such as 'Is it the cut of Dandy Lion's clothes that matter, or the colour, or the texture? If the colour plays a role, is it the general hue which counts, or the degree of contrast between the various elements, or what? Is the vaguely Oriental appearance of his costume relevant, so that I could get high marks by wearing something quite different but also Oriental in flavour? Perhaps it is only on tall men that three-piece suits are admired?' – and so on.

The counterpart of a linguistic semanticist would approach the dress situation with the assumption that the range of possible questions of this sort that a would-be dandy could ask himself form a finite, specifiable set, and that underlying the dress behaviour of the fashionable crowd are definite answers to these questions. Newcomers to the community know the questions when they arrive, work out the answers by observation, and then dress fashionably, and that is all there is to it (except that occasionally the fashion changes in some definite respect – i.e. a word undergoes a well-defined 'change of meaning' by dropping one feature or acquiring another). But in the dress case, surely, nobody would entertain this account of the situation for a moment? It seems quite obvious that there is no determinate set of possible questions to be asked about what makes fashionable costume fashionable, and that there are no authoritative answers to the questions one thinks of asking. Dandy Lion may be better at dressing fashionably than a newcomer to society, but he has no rules that guarantee fashionability. Everybody has to make up new ensembles day by day (i.e. mature speakers, as well as learners, have to extend words to items not exactly like things they have already heard words used for); Dandy Lion keeps as sharp an eye on the rest of the smart set as they do on him, since they are all equally at risk of being seen to have missed the trend. In such a world, standards of fashionability would gradually drift in various directions over time, but not in identifiable, discrete steps; and at any given time one could give only vague, sketchy indications of what currently counted as fashionable – the concept of a rigorous, predictive scientific theory of contemporary fashion would be quite inapplicable.

(Many readers will very reasonably feel that a society as narcissistic as the one I describe would be too contemptible to be worth thinking about, and they may take me to be suggesting that there is something frivolous about our semantic behaviour. But this would be to press the analogy far beyond the limits of its applicability. The dandies I describe seek to imitate each other's dress behaviour because they want to be admired, but real humans seek to imitate each other's semantic behaviour because they want to be *understood*, and there is nothing frivolous or untoward in that motive.)

If the reader agrees that there is no 'right answer' to a question about what is fashionable in the case of dress, but yet feels that the notion of scientific semantic description is an appropriate goal for the linguist, he must explain what relevant difference between the two domains has been suppressed in the above discussion. I believe the analogy is a fair one.[1] I know no evidence in favour of the idea that words of ordinary language have meanings that are more well-defined than the fashion analogy suggests; all the evidence I know of supports that analogy.

Consider for instance the work of Jeremy Anglin, a psychologist heavily influenced by Linguistic Semantics who tried to find experimental evidence for a 'lexical decomposition' approach to word meaning.[2] Anglin tells us that he began work on his doctoral

---

[1] There are certainly respects in which the analogy breaks down. Thus we commonly find ourselves choosing a word to name a given thing rather than seeking a thing to which a given word applies, which is the analogue of choosing a costume in order to be recognized as fashionable; and there is no analogue in the dress case of the fact that we have a vocabulary of many different words for each of which the conditions of use must be guessed, although this could be built in to the analogy e.g. by saying that what counts as fashionable is very different in different domains (the 'right' clothes for a cocktail party are unrelated to the 'right' clothes for going to the races, the 'right' kind of interior decoration is different again, etc.) and that people must simultaneously make independent guesses for each domain. These limitations of the analogy, in any case, do not affect its force as against the assumptions of Linguistic Semantics.

[2] J. M. Anglin, *The Growth of Word Meaning* (*Research Monograph* 63), M.I.T. Press, 1970.

thesis with, among other assumptions, the 'preconception' that the meanings of words were (at least to a close approximation) determinate sets of semantic features, and he used various experimental techniques to try to check that the feature-composition of certain English words in the speech of children and adults had the particular structure he expected. When the design of Anglin's experiments made it possible for them to do so, however, his subjects (both children and adults) persisted in behaving linguistically in ways which refuted successively weaker hypotheses about the observable consequences of *any* feature analysis, though their behaviour was recognizably sensible. Anglin concludes by asking 'How helpful has it been to view semantics in terms of features·. . ?', and answers 'The notion of a feature . . . has taken a beating. In retrospect it required considerable innocence to attempt to specify' the semantic features relevant to Anglin's word-set.

> Adult subjects appear to be able to generate a myriad of equivalence relations [i.e. common features] which for them make two words similar. A *boy* and a *horse* may both be *animals*, *beings*, *objects*, and *entities*, but they also both *eat*, *walk*, and *run*, they both have *legs*, *heads*, and *hair*, they both are *warm-blooded*, *active*, and *social*.[1]

Anglin here discusses the problem of identifying shared semantic features common to a pair of words; it is all the less likely that one could specify a determinate set of semantic properties for any individual word, when subjects can imagine a 'myriad' properties possessed by the entities to which they know the word to apply.

Fashion – to return briefly to my analogy – can be described, but only in the anecdotal discourse style of the arts rather than by the rigorous techniques of science. One can make impressionistic statements about current fashion, and write histories of the vicissitudes of fashion up to the present, but any attempt to be more exact about the present state of play or to make predictions about future developments would represent a misunderstanding of the nature of the subject. Similarly in the case of language one can give approximate, non-definitive accounts of the current meanings of words (which is what most dictionaries do) and

[1] ibid., p. 94.

describe the developments of word-meanings during the past (which is the additional goal of a dictionary such as the *Oxford English Dictionary*), and for either of these tasks ordinary English is as adequate a medium as any. When linguistic semanticists offer to formalize the meanings of words in quasi-mathematical notation, they are claiming (at least implicitly, but usually explicitly) to be able to define word-meanings more rigorously than is possible in the ordinary English of dictionary entries and to make testable predictions about utterances of words other than the particular utterances they have observed; to suppose that these goals are achievable even in principle is to misunderstand the nature of language.

Notice that the point I am making is not answered by the suggestion that the 'semantic interpretations' of words should be probabilistic rather than absolute. I chose the word *cup* as my example because it has been used in an interesting series of experiments by William Labov, who set out to attack the Linguistic Semantics dogma that words have essences – criterial features necessary and sufficient for the word to be applicable.[1] Labov elicited from subjects names for a variety of containers differing in respect of a number of variables, some of which were discrete (e.g. having or not having a handle) and others continuous (e.g. how wide they were for their height). The orthodox linguistic semanticist should predict that some of the features will be crucial and the others wholly irrelevant to the question whether a given container is called a *cup* rather than anything else, and that, if a continuous variable such as width-to-height ratio is relevant at all, what will count will be whether or not some more or less sharp threshold value is exceeded. Labov found instead that the different variables contribute various *increments of probability* that an object will be called a *cup*, and increasing values on a continuous variable contribute smoothly-increasing probability-increments with no threshold value.

One might conclude from such findings that all that is wrong with the picture of a semantic description as a set of inference rules

[1] W. Labov, 'The boundaries of words and their meanings', in C.-J. N. Bailey and R. W. Shuy, eds., *New Ways of Analyzing Variation in English*, Georgetown University Press (Washington, D.C.), 1973.

linking the words of the language is that the rules need to be equipped with statistics. Rather than a rule 'From *X is a cup* infer *X has a handle*', say (which makes a handle part of the essence of *cup*, so that something without a handle just cannot be a cup no matter how cup-like it may be in other respects), we should write, perhaps, 'From *X is a cup* infer with *n*% reliability that *X has a handle*', filling in some suitable value of *n*. The mathematics might need to be a little more sophisticated than this in order to explain how values of different variables interact to produce a decision about naming, and how the contributions of continuous variables are factored in, but this would be a purely mathematical problem (about which Labov makes some detailed suggestions) – it would leave unaffected the principle that natural-language semantics can be rigorously defined.[1]

From the point of view advocated here, however, a Labovian semantic description – although it can perhaps be welcomed as a step towards a better understanding of semantics – embodies the same fallacy as that underlying a non-statistical semantic description of the kind envisaged by most linguistic semanticists. Notice that the variables differentiating Labov's containers were supplied by the experimenter; Labov decided that possession of a handle, width-to-height ratio, use for liquid rather than solid food, and half a dozen other characteristics might be relevant to the meaning of *cup*, and he constructed his test objects accordingly. In other words, his experiments did not test whether the range of properties of an object relevant for calling it a *cup* are determinate; the experiments tested only the manner in which a certain few properties that *are* relevant influence the application of the word.

What I am arguing is that the set of properties that speakers may use to justify the application of a word is not determinate, because objects do not come to our attention labelled with a fixed set of properties and our minds do not impose a fixed set of categories on our experience. It was not for nothing that Anglin, in the passage quoted above, wrote of his subjects 'generating' (rather than 'noticing') a 'myriad' common properties for pairs of

[1] George Lakoff makes proposals similar to Labov's in 'Hedges: a study in meaning criteria and the logic of fuzzy concepts', *Papers from the Eighth Regional Meeting, Chicago Linguistic Society*, 1972, pp. 183–228.

words; we *create* ways of seeing things as similar. The invention of
the word *picturesque*, for instance, institutionalized a way of seeing-
as-similar two sights as physically dissimilar as, say, a romantic
garden and a Mediterranean fish-market. It seems absurd to
suggest that *picturesque* might abbreviate some compound of
Lockian simple ideas – for instance one of the features of a garden
that may lead us to call it 'picturesque' is that it is 'romantic'
rather than 'classical', and *romantic* seems no closer to the immediate properties of sense-data than *picturesque* itself is. And it would
surely be a gratuitous assumption to hold that *picturesque* corresponds to a category innately implicit in the human mind, because
the concept is a quite recent product of our culture, lacking near
equivalents in languages of other cultures or, as far as I know, in
the English of Chaucer or Shakespeare. We are surely bound to
admit that the concept 'picturesque' is an original creation by an
individual which has succeeded in becoming institutionalized in
our society. It is always possible, of course, to keep saying of each
apparently novel concept thrown up by an individual or a culture
that it must have existed implicitly all along; but if this becomes
merely a mechanical assertion of dogma, devoid of any testable
implications about future conceptual innovation, what value has
it?

I do not suggest that in seeking to master the use of the word *cup*
an English speaker will typically invent properties as novel as the
property 'picturesque' was when it was invented. Commonly,
perhaps, one distinguishes in the objects one hears called *cups*
properties which can be spelled out in terms of words one has
already mastered – 'having a handle', for instance. Given one's
previous vocabulary, the set of properties which can be defined in
its terms *is* in principle specifiable, though inconceivably diverse.
But examples such as *picturesque* establish the point that we do, at
least sometimes, invent properties that cannot be spelled out in
terms of previous vocabulary, and indeed such invention is probably relevant for *cup*: no doubt for many speakers, as for Labov's
subjects, width-to-height ratio is relevant (too wide a container is
a *bowl* rather than a *cup*, too tall is a *mug* or a *vase*), but how many
people have an adjective for the particular width-to-height ratio of
a 'good' cup? Furthermore, although many of the properties we

pick out as possibly relevant for the use of a word are definable in terms of our previous vocabulary, very few of them will be reducible in this way to ideas that it is plausible to regard as innate. One obvious property of many cups is that they have a handle, but the concept 'handle' is no more a mere compound of sense-qualities than 'cup' is. There is no escaping the creativity of semantic behaviour.

Cup is not in fact the best of examples for the case I am arguing, for reasons which have to do with the fact that cups are artefacts. Manufacture, and modern mass-production even more, lead to the existence of ranges of objects which appear to lend support to the 'essentialist' view of semantics because they are designed by speakers of the language. Thus, suppose it is commonly held that from *X is a cup* one can reliably infer *X has a handle* but not *X has a saucer*; if a few pottery manufacturers believe this, it may soon happen that everything sold in a package marked 'CUP' does indeed have a handle, though some come with saucers and others without. Mass-production creates a series of object-lessons in the theory of absolute semantic essences, and it may be no accident that that theory appeals to late-twentieth-century linguists who in most cases inhabit highly urban environments in which they are surrounded by human manufactures. It is possible that words for manufactured objects may be relatively stable in meaning for this reason. Let me give a more favourable example from the less mass-produced area of human emotions and relationships, namely the recent development in meaning of the word *gay*. This is of course a word which has modified its meaning so greatly in a short period as to have become notorious; that makes it an unusually clear example for expository purposes, but I suggest that the process exemplified by *gay* is typical qualitatively though not quantitatively of the life of much of our vocabulary.

Not many years ago *gay* (applied to a person or a social environment) meant, to me, something like 'happy or enjoyable in a witty and carefree way'. (I deliberately give a personal impression of the meaning rather than quoting an authoritative dictionary, because part of the point I am making is that shifts in meaning occur through the workings of individual, non-authoritative minds.) By now I have become used to the fact that for many people it means something like 'homosexual, but with connotations of allegiance to a style of life deemed to be as honourable as others rather than in a clinical sense'; since people are anxious not to commit unintended sexual double-entendres, the previous sense of *gay* is rapidly becoming extinct.

It is easy to see how such a transition was possible, given that the hearer of a word can only guess what properties of a referent evoked that word from a speaker. If people are carefree, it is often because they are irreverent, disrespectful of authority. While homosexual acts between males were illegal, groups of homosexuals who decided not to be ashamed of their inclinations were necessarily disrespectful towards the authority of the law (and although the law has changed, public opinion is another and more conservative kind of authority). Homosexual society is also supposed to be unusually 'bitchy', and witty talk is often malicious although the two ideas are quite distinct. One can well see how a speaker might have referred to a 'gay crowd' thinking of them as carefree and amusing, and a hearer have taken him to refer to the characteristics of irreverence and verbal malice which the group in question also displayed; when the hearer in turn became a speaker he would then refer to other groups as 'gay' who were irreverent without necessarily being carefree, and so the semantic drift would proceed.[1]

Indeed, it is not necessary to restrict ourselves to the hypothetical; I can quote a real example of the kind of usage that could have encouraged the semantic drift *gay* has undergone. On p. 57 of Angus Wilson's *Hemlock and After*,[2] Elizabeth Sands confronts her father Bernard with her discovery of his homosexuality; she has met Sherman Winter, one of his homosexual associates, who, affecting not to know her relationship with Bernard,

'. . . treated me, well, like any other queen's woman, dear.' She at last got out one of the terms ['which she had so determined not to evade'], but it really made her seem more gauche than her straight embarrassment. 'He remarked on your absence from the gay scene. . . .'

[1] It may be that someone can produce evidence that *gay* changed its meaning by a route quite different from that reconstructed here; this would not destroy my general point, though it might rob the example of its persuasive force.

[2] Secker & Warburg, 1952.

Anyone who had not already got a fixed view about the precise meaning of *gay* might well take this passage to suggest at least that it had connotations of social and/or sexual unorthodoxy, and if his previous experience of the word did not rule such an interpretation out he might even take *gay* here to mean 'homosexual', as it does nowadays. This might then be reinforced by the passage on p. 193 of the same novel where Wilson refers to the *gaiety* of Eric Craddock, an adolescent who is being drawn into the world of homosexuality.

In fact the interpretation of *gay* as 'homosexual' is certainly wrong here; Wilson assures me in correspondence that when writing *Hemlock and After* he had never heard *gay* used for 'homosexual', and he explains his usage by saying that 'people like Sherman (but not necessarily homosexuals) aspired to being thought always on the crest of a wave'. Indeed, on p. 194 of *Hemlock and After* there is a use of *gay* which is incompatible with the modern equation '*gay* = "homosexual"', since it refers to the relationship between Eric and his mother; but this relationship is sufficiently emotionally charged to make a slight hint of sexual unorthodoxy in our understanding of *gay* not altogether inappropriate even here. The reader of *Hemlock and After* could easily be led to add an implication of vague sexual unorthodoxy to his understanding of *gay* whether or not such an implication existed for the novelist. Furthermore, it seems unlikely to have been pure coincidence that Wilson repeatedly used a word which has subsequently acquired an explicitly sexual sense in contexts of sexual unorthodoxy; though Wilson thought of the word as referring to a quality of emotion or behaviour not peculiar to homosexuals, it is permissible to suppose that the semantic drift which has by now run its full course had already begun for Wilson, so that the emotions or behaviour which the word implied for him were ones more commonly displayed or more commonly aspired to by homosexuals than by the population at large.

Such a view is unavailable to the linguistic semanticist, however. For him, a change of meaning is a sharp transition corresponding to the acquisition or dropping of a particular semantic 'feature', so that Wilson's use of *gay* must be dismissed as mere coincidence and his novel cannot be seen as relevant to the recent development in meaning of the word.

Yet the ambiguities of interpretation I have discussed in connection with *gay* are the very stuff of real-life discourse. Even the single short passage already quoted from *Hemlock and After* offers another good example, in its use of *straight*. *Straight* often means 'ordinary, basic, without special admixture', and it is also used nowadays to mean 'heterosexual' – whether as a development from the usage just given, i.e. 'ordinary in sexual inclinations', or from *straight* as 'morally upright', given widespread assumptions about the immorality of homosexuality. When Wilson writes about Elizabeth Sands's 'straight embarrassment' this can perfectly well be read either as 'basic embarrassment deriving from the overall situation, as opposed to the special awkwardness of talking about "queens" in those circumstances', or as 'embarrassment of a heterosexual confronted with homosexuality'. In this case there is no objection to taking the word in either sense, or even to supposing that Wilson intended it in both senses at once, in the way described by William Empson[1] as characteristic of poetic language; but, however the word was intended, the fact that one interpretation could plausibly be imposed on the word by a reader when the writer had intended the other illustrates again the notion that usage does not rigorously determine meaning.

There remains a question why one particular development of meaning becomes widespread, given that on my account a particular word will presumably be developing in unrelated ways in different individuals' conversations. The question is not unanswerable; in the case of *gay*, perhaps the contemporary sense caught on because it answered a need on the part of homosexuals newly emancipated from legal discrimination for a non-pejorative means of self-description. Whether that is right or not, surely it is incredible that a semantic drift of the sort exemplified by *gay* could have occurred in discrete steps, at each of which the current implications of the word were clear-cut? A human social group is a very obvious case of an entity in which an imaginative onlooker can see an endless diversity of characteristics. Now that the new sense of *gay* has led to incorporation of the word into the title of formal institutions such as the Gay Liberation Movement, it may be that

[1] *Seven Types of Ambiguity*, Chatto & Windus, 1930.

the sense has become relatively rigid – such an institution is likely
to equip itself with articles of association defining the meaning of
gay, which turns the word into a technical term like *atom*. But
during the transitional period the implications of a given use of
the word must surely have been very fluid, indeterminate,
unpinnable-down?

So far I have argued that the meanings of words must be
indeterminate because individuals have to learn which aspects of
their world correlate with use of a word, and the possible hypotheses are endless while the data are limited. There is a further
factor: the 'world' to which individuals have to try to relate the
words they encounter is itself changing in unpredictable ways,
both subjectively (i.e. the individual is learning more about it) and
objectively (natural conditions change, and human life is altered
as a result of innovatory thinking by other individuals, e.g. tech-
nologists or politicians).

This means that the semantic fluidity or indeterminacy of
language is a very good thing. There are occasional changes in our
world which are so clear-cut and public that we can react to them
by clear-cut, public changes in our language, specifically by the
creation of new words. A quite novel form of transport is invented,
and a new word *hovercraft* is coined to go with it. But the great
majority of the changes in an individual's understanding of the
world will be subtler and more gradual than this, and furthermore
they will not in general run in parallel with the learning of other
individuals. Much of what we learn about the world is learned
from our own experience rather than from school lessons, and
different individuals often reach different conclusions. Such
developments in people's structures of belief cannot possibly be
reflected by public changes in the language such as innovation in
vocabulary; even if we neglected the problem of disparities
between different individuals' learning, the gradual and unceas-
ing character of many of the developments in our world would
require a state of permanent revolution in our lexicon, and people
simply could not learn all the new words. So, given that the words
themselves must remain broadly constant with only a limited
number of additions and subtractions to reflect the grosser, more
sudden and public modifications in the pattern of our lives, then if

our vocabulary were not semantically fluid either the language would rapidly become unusable in face of the many subtler and more private developments in our beliefs, or (more realistically) those developments would be prevented from occurring. Indeterminacy of word-meaning is a necessary condition for the growth of individual thought; and it is the fact that individual humans can think creatively, rather than being tied from birth to fixed instinctual patterns that remain rigid in face of an unpredictable world, that places Man in a position so much superior to brute beasts.[1]

Modifications to word-meanings induced by modifications in purely individual knowledge or belief are difficult to illustrate, simply because any particular process of evolution of an individual's thought is not likely to be paralleled in the average reader's biography. But it is easy to illustrate the dependence of word-meanings on beliefs in connexion with more public belief-changes. Consider, for instance, the case of the word *father*.

Typically, the linguistic semanticist will analyse *father* as a semantic molecule composed of the atoms MALE and PARENT.[2] PARENT, as a primitive, is left undefined, but the analysis is plausible only if we take PARENT to be synonymous with the English word *parent*, i.e. one of the partners in the act of conception. The difficulty is that there exists a large class of English-speakers who use the word *father* frequently and, on the great majority of occasions, in a quite standard fashion who certainly do not mean this by the word: namely young children. The fact that children use *father* in another sense is demonstrated by occasional mismatches between their usage and that of adults; thus the linguist Barbara Partee reports that

[1] I do not intend to presuppose here that Man is the only animal species with a creative intellect; it is not necessary for me to take a position on this issue either way. Experiments with other apes have shown them to exhibit many apparently intelligent patterns of behaviour, and Jane Hill goes so far as to argue that apes are likely to be fully as intelligent as men, and that their failure to evolve complex languages and high culture can be explained by factors unrelated to intelligence which prevent them using language in the wild ('On the evolutionary foundations of language', *American Anthropologist*, vol. 74, 1972, p. 311).

[2] See Bierwisch, 'Semantics', in J. Lyons, ed., *New Horizons in Linguistics*, Penguin, 1970, p. 172, and cf. Charles Fillmore's discussion of work by Anna Wierzbicka on pp. 140–41 of his article 'The future of semantics' in Robert Austerlitz, ed., *The Scope of American Linguistics*, Peter de Ridder Press (Lisse), 1975.

One year when I was living alone in a house in an area populated mainly by families, the small children in the neighborhood would repeatedly ask me whether I had a father and if so, where he was, and we had a number of perplexing conversations on the subject before someone pointed out to me that what they really wanted to know was whether I had a *husband*.[1]

For the children, a *father* was the adult male who acts as head of a family unit, and conception did not enter the picture for the obvious reason that they were too young to know about the role of males in reproduction. When in due course children are taught about this, they recapitulate what was once an intellectual discovery made by some long-past generation; Malinowski has shown us that there are cultures in our own time that have not yet made the discovery.[2]

Now one might explain the facts by saying that children first analyse *father* as something like MALE HEAD-OF-HOUSEHOLD, and that when they learn about sexual reproduction they drop the latter feature and slot in PARENT in its place.[3] But this is surely implausible. When children growing up in a society of stable marriages learn the sexual facts of life, they do not suddenly take themselves to have misunderstood the word *father* until that time; rather, they register a new *fact* about what fathers do, and the word *father* is not thereby changed in meaning. Only later, as they become gradually aware of the variety of child-rearing patterns in the larger world, are they forced to make a decision as to whether initiation of conception or role as head of a child's family is decisive for the use of *father*, and they find that when the criteria clash members of their society invariably prefer the former (if we ignore compound expressions such as *stepfather*, *foster-father*). While the child's experience remains compatible with either the head-of-

---

[1] Austerlitz, *The Scope of American Linguistics*, p. 198.

[2] Bronisław Malinowski, *The Sexual Life of Savages in North-Western Melanesia*, Routledge, 1929, ch. 7, §§3–4.

[3] Note that it is axiomatic for Linguistic Semantics that 'semantic primitives', being innate, do not themselves evolve in meaning; the word *parent* presumably develops its meaning in parallel with the word *father*, but the semantic feature PARENT must always mean something to do with conception – young children simply are not yet consciously aware of the idea PARENT which nevertheless exists implicitly in their minds.

household or the initiator-of-conception sense of *father* (i.e. while the two criteria always or almost always pick out the same individuals in the child's world) it is surely meaningless to ask which of the two *is* the sense of *father* for the child; the matter is genuinely indeterminate. If the individual child discovers independently of talk about 'fathers' that there are many cases of male conception-initiators deserting their families, there is no saying whether the child will decide to think of such men as *fathers* or not – the decision is not pre-empted by any aspect of his prior mental representation of the word *father*, and children invariably opt in due course for the same usage only because there already exists a convention, the many adult parties to which 'outvote' any contrary decision by an individual child.

But, the linguistic semanticist may reply, however he manages it the child does after all end up with the analysis MALE PARENT for *father*. So long as we claim only to describe *adult* English – and granted that it may be preferable to substitute inference rules, such as 'From *A is B's father* infer *A is male* and *A was a partner in the conception of B*', for reduction of words to molecules of semantic 'atoms' written in small capitals – we are perfectly justified in setting out to produce a rigorous semantic analysis of the language.

This is not true, because people do not stop learning when they reach adulthood. Again the point can be illustrated from the word *father*.

Until recently, a person's sex was a fixed given. There is now a surgical operation which converts men into women; since James Morris became Jan Morris and published *Conundrum* in 1974 the phenomenon has decisively entered the arena of public awareness, and by now instances are becoming scarcely more a matter of surprise than, say, divorces were at the turn of the century. Persons who undergo the operation of course do not emerge identical in all respects to persons who were born female, but they change sufficiently for them to be counted as 'women' and referred to as 'she' (even by those who know that they used to be men) – indeed this, as I understand it, is the point of the operation.

Now consider the case of someone who fathers children and then undergoes the operation. Does she remain the children's *father*, or become their second *mother*, or is neither word now applicable?

In fact I have the impression that the first of these three usages is becoming standard. If so, then it is no longer true that a father is 'by definition' a male parent; some fathers are female. We would need to correct a semantic description of the word to something along the lines of 'parent who *was* male at the time of conception' or 'parent who supplied the seed'. But the chief point is that it would surely be misleading to describe what has happened, as a linguistic semanticist presumably must, by saying that before the invention of the sex-change operation linguists had difficulty in discovering whether *father* meant 'male parent' or 'seed-supplying parent', and that cases such as Jan Morris's have demonstrated that their original guess was wrong when it was made. Rather, before the invention of the operation the question whether *father* meant 'male parent' or 'seed-supplying parent' *did not arise* – not merely did linguists not think to ask the question, but it would have been a meaningless one if they *had* thought of it. Once the operation arrived on the scene, the language had to move in one direction or another, but nothing in its previous state pre-empted the decision. Nobody could know beforehand which way the cat would jump.

In view of cases such as this, I suggest, the notion of trying to establish a rigorous scientific analysis of word-meanings is as misguided as would be the proposal that scientists ought to work out a theory enabling us to predict, now, whether there will be a General Election in the year 2000. There is no answer, now, to that question; when the year 2000 comes, the question of an election will be determined by free decisions that have yet to be made and which will be taken in the light of considerations that we cannot now know about. In the linguistic case, before sex-change operations became a reality an individual Englishman could have asked himself how he would talk about hypothetical cases of the kind discussed, and he would have been free to *decide* to call ex-male parents 'fathers' or 'mothers', but whichever decision he made he could not have been accused of imperfect mastery of his mother-tongue, and whichever decision he made he would have remained free to change his mind. Thus to ask for an analysis of the meaning of a word of 'the English language' is to ask what decisions would be made by English-speaking individuals about an indefinitely large series of hypothetical questions which many of the individuals may never have consciously considered; the reply must always be that, unless we are told what concrete situation (such as the invention of the sex-change operation) might force Englishmen in general to reach a decision about a particular question, we cannot even guess which answer to it would be likely to become conventional in the English linguistic community (and even if we are given the situation we can do no more than guess). As Wilhelm von Humboldt put it, language 'is not a finished product, but an activity'.[1]

The linguistic semanticist's next move may be to suggest that I am cheating by representing an exceptional phenomenon as normal. Granted that the sex-change operation has shaken up some of the semantic relationships in our language, he may say, nevertheless such innovations are very rare; in between times the semantic relationships are static and can be rigorously described, and it is not objectionable to say that novelties as unusual as this do indeed force a well-defined change in the language so that adults have to re-learn certain aspects of English.

Clearly there is a sense in which the sex-change operation is an exceptional phenomenon; the belief it overthrew, that sex is fixed, was particularly well entrenched (and emotionally significant). But, in the first place, the sex-change operation did not (or did not only) change the semantic structure of English when it was invented; it drew attention to an indeterminacy in that structure that had existed for centuries if not millennia previously, and thus cast doubt on the notion that a language ever has a determinate semantic structure. Furthermore, a belief does not have to be as longstanding and firmly established as the belief that sex is fixed to play a part in inference. If I decide that Manchester is a poor town for shopping I shall be disposed to infer, from sentences such as *John has a lot of shopping to do*, that *John had better not go to Manchester*. The difference is that no one would be inclined to argue that a

---

[1] '*Die Sprache* ... *ist kein Werk* (Ergon), *sondern eine Thätigkeit* (Energeia).' K. W. von Humboldt, *Ueber die Verschiedenheit des menschlichen Sprachbaues*, Dümmler (Berlin), 1836, p. 57.

semantic description of English should include a rule 'From *Manchester* infer *bad for shopping*' (or that the word *Manchester* should include a feature [− GOOD-FOR-SHOPPING]). My opinion about Manchester is clearly 'knowledge about the world' rather than 'knowledge of English'. What the sex-change example shows is that even the kind of principles which one *might* think of as part of the English language are sometimes overthrown by events independent of the language; there is no real distinction between knowledge of the world and knowledge of the semantics of the language. We are tempted to assign a principle to the latter rather than to the former category when it is one of relatively long standing, so of course it is true that the kind of beliefs implicit in a typical essay at semantic description by a linguist change less often than the sort of beliefs which the linguist ignores. It is tautologous to say that beliefs which remain constant for long periods do not often change.

(These considerations may excuse what some readers will feel to be my excessive resort in this chapter to examples concerning sexual matters. Sex is very prominent in theoretical linguistic discourse – as is violence: the two transitive verbs that occur most commonly in linguists' example-sentences are probably the verbs *hit* and *kill*.[1] These preoccupations may have something to do with the quiet lives that most of us linguistic scholars lead, and in certain cases they represent merely a juvenile desire to shock; but I believe there is also a more serious reason for them. Sex and violence are very 'basic' matters, and it is emotionally important to us that questions about them have clear-cut answers; we want essentialism to be applicable in these domains, as Linguistic Semantics suggests it is everywhere.)

I might add, however, that I do not see cases such as the sex-change operation as being so *very* exceptional as one might imagine from the writings of linguistic semanticists. These scholars often seem to presuppose a dreary, static world in which

[1] A remarkable symptom of this tendency was the recent withdrawal from sale of a book about syntactic theory on the eve of publication, when the respectable university press that had accepted it developed cold feet about the possibility that some of the Johns, Bills, and Marys who were made to misbehave in diverse ways in the example-sentences might decide to sue!

nothing ever crops up which is the least bit unusual from the point
of view of a sheltered academic living in their particular time and
place. Such a world is not recognizable to me as the one that I or
anyone else inhabits; real life is full of surprises. (To quote only
one, by no means extreme, case of this attitude: Katz and Fodor's
paradigm example, in their 1963 article, of a semantically
'anomalous' sentence is *He painted the walls with silent paint*. It would
leave me quite unstunned to learn that, say, when sprayguns are
used for applying paint, certain types of paint make a noise on
leaving the nozzle; and in that case I should *expect* sentences like
Katz and Fodor's to occur in the speech of paint-sprayers.) The
linguistic semanticists' attitude contrasts with a more widely held
principle of academic life which suggests that thinkers should be
open to new possibilities and should not expect the world to
conform to their prior assumptions. Only given the premiss that
reality is almost always unsurprising, however, does the programme of Linguistic Semantic analysis become at all plausible.
As the philosopher Imre Lakatos puts it: 'Science teaches us not to
respect any conceptual-linguistic framework lest it should turn
into a conceptual prison – language analysts have a vested
interest in at least slowing down this process [of conceptual
change].'[1]

Little in the above critique of Linguistic Semantics is original.
Almost everything I am saying about semantics was stated, with a
wealth of examples, in an excellent book by Karl Otto Erdmann
published in 1900.[2] Erdmann's book went through a number of
editions, the most recent being issued in 1966, but I have never
encountered a reference to it in the writings of the linguistic
semanticists. In our own generation, while the creative view of
mind has not been explicitly advocated by many philosophers
other than Popper, the corollary of that view for language has
become virtually a cliché of post-war philosophy. Not only
Popper's objections to 'essentialism' but equally Ludwig
Wittgenstein's doctrine of 'family resemblances' as the basis for

[1] *Proofs and Refutations*, Cambridge University Press, 1976, p. 93, n. 1.
[2] *Die Bedeutung des Wortes*, Eduard Avenarius (Leipzig), 1900. For references to
earlier, eighteenth- and nineteenth-century statements of the ideas in question
see ch. 1, §3 of L. J. Cohen, *The Diversity of Meaning*, Methuen, 1962.

the application of words, or W. van O. Quine's objections to the analytic/synthetic distinction, all amount to claims that people's semantic behaviour cannot be predicted by rules because it is determined by creative thought. Almost all English-speaking philosophers of recent decades who discuss language have done so within the general framework of assumptions of one or all of these figures.[1] (For that matter, some of the obvious difficulties in the Katz/Fodor notion of lexical decomposition were pointed out from within the discipline of linguistics by Dwight Bolinger in an article[2] published in 1965 which goes largely unmentioned in subsequent Linguistic Semantics writings.) The fact that a number of influential scholars are agreed on a particular issue does not imply that they are necessarily correct. However, it does suggest strongly that any group setting out to advocate incompatible views ought to take some trouble to explain why they believe the former scholars are mistaken. Linguistic semanticists do very little of this.

It is true that Jerrold Katz has devoted considerable attention to Quine's objections to the analytic/synthetic distinction. If inference in a language is governed by specifiable rules, there ought to be a clear contrast between sentences whose truth is guaranteed by the semantic rules irrespective of the truth of other sentences (i.e. analytic sentences) and sentences whose truth-values are left open by the semantics of the language (synthetic sentences). Quine argues, as I have done, that sentences we think 'analytic' are merely sentences of whose truth we feel unusually confident, so that there is at most a difference of degree between the two categories of sentence.[3] Since a semantic description of the

---

[1] One leading modern philosopher whose treatment of language might seem somewhat more compatible with the linguists' approach is J. L. Austin, who would have counted as a 'language analyst' in the terms of the Lakatos quotation in the previous paragraph. However, Austin's view of language seems self-defeating, for reasons elegantly set out by Keith Graham in ch. 2 of *J. L. Austin: A Critique of Ordinary Language Philosophy*, Harvester Press (Hassocks, Sussex), 1977. In the last few years essentialism of a sort has been making something of a come-back in connexion with the theory of 'possible-world semantics', but (like some others) I am unable to see this theory as anything more than a giant exercise in question-begging.

[2] 'The atomization of meaning', *Language*, vol. 41, 1965, pp. 555–73.

[3] W. van O. Quine, 'Two dogmas of empiricism', 1951, reprinted in Quine's

Katz/Fodor type predicts a sharp difference between the categories, Katz sets out to refute Quine. But his 'refutation' boils down in essence to describing an experiment (in which speakers sort sentences into categories) that could settle the issue, explaining how the results of the experiment establish the validity of the distinction, *but not actually performing the experiment* – the results Katz quotes are what he expects to find rather than what he has found.[1] This is all the more remarkable when one considers that Quine's original writings quoted similar experiments that actually had been performed and had yielded results unfavourable to the analytic/synthetic distinction.[2] A number of more recent experiments have been no more successful from Katz's point of view. Katz refers to none of the actual experiments.

This is a very rum way to carry on an academic debate. If we overlook this, however, we might allow that Katz could defend himself against the negative findings of published experiments by referring to the distinction between linguistic 'competence' and linguistic 'performance' – individuals' observable linguistic behaviour does not always conform perfectly to the linguistic rules stored in their minds (and which linguists set out to describe) because the behaviour is subject to interference from extraneous factors.[3] In this case, the idea would be that the semantics of our language is governed by clear-cut inference rules but that when drawing inferences in practice we sometimes make mistakes in following the rules. This would be a fairly desperate defence of Katz's position, since if we make so many mistakes that the rules cannot be inferred from what we say or do it is not clear what substance there could be in the claim that such rules exist inside us. In case that difficulty is felt not to be fatal, however, let me quote the results of a further recent experiment on the analytic/

From a Logical Point of View, Harvard University Press (Cambridge, Mass.), 1953.

[1] See e.g. Katz, *Semantic Theory*, Harper & Row, 1972, pp. 249–51; cf. my *Form of Language*, pp. 154, 209–10.

[2] Quine, *Word and Object*, M.I.T. Press (Cambridge, Mass.), 1960, p. 67, n. 6.

[3] Katz and T. G. Bever in fact adopt this defence explicitly in their article 'The Fall and Rise of Empiricism', in T. G. Bever, J. J. Katz, and D. T. Langendoen, eds., *An Integrated Theory of Linguistic Ability*, Harvester Press (Hassocks, Sussex), 1977.

synthetic distinction which is particularly interesting in this connexion.

Linguists who appeal in their research methodology to the notion that performance diverges from competence (a notion introduced by Chomsky in connexion with syntactic research) hold that it is possible to overcome the difficulty by using the intuitions of people trained to discount the disturbing factors summed up as 'performance'; thus a trained grammarian will be able to say whether a given word-sequence really is grammatical or not in his language, although a lay speaker of the language might take the sentence to be 'ungrammatical' merely because it reports a bizarre situation or uses vocabulary associated with stigmatized social groups, say.[1] In the case of the analytic/synthetic distinction, if one seeks a group who have been formally trained to draw the distinction explicitly the answer will presumably be the class of professional philosophers. Accordingly, Nigel Morley-Bunker compared the behaviour with respect to the analytic/synthetic distinction of two groups of subjects, one composed of university teachers of philosophy and the other arbitrarily chosen (it included undergraduates and teachers of another subject).[2]

The subjects were not, of course, asked in so many words to classify sentences as analytic or synthetic, since that would raise great problems about understanding of the technical terms. Instead, Morley-Bunker adopted the experimental technique advocated by Katz, presenting subjects with two piles of cards containing sentences which to members of our contemporary society seem rather clearly analytic and synthetic respectively, and allowing subjects to discover the principle of classification themselves by sorting further 'clear cases' onto the piles and having their allocations corrected by the experimenter when they clashed with the allocations implied by the analytic/synthetic principle. After subjects had in this way demonstrated mastery of the distinction with respect to 'clear cases', they were given eighteen sentences of more questionable status to sort. The exper-

[1] There are of course important objections to this appeal to 'trained intuition', but I ignore them here in order to give my opponents the benefit of the doubt.

[2] N. Morley-Bunker, 'Speakers' intuitions of analyticity', unpublished B.A. thesis, Lancaster University.

iment involved no assumptions about whether these sentences were 'in fact' analytic or synthetic; the question was whether individuals of either or both groups would be consistent with one another in assigning them to one or other of the two categories.

On the whole, as would be expected by a non-believer in the analytic/synthetic distinction, neither group was internally consistent. Two sentences were assigned to a single category by a highly significant ($p < 0.005$) majority of each group of subjects, and for each group there were three more sentences on which a consistent classification was imposed by a significant majority ($p < 0.05$) of members of that group; on ten sentences neither group deviated significantly from an even split between those judging it analytic and those judging it synthetic. (To give examples: *Summer follows spring* was judged analytic by highly significant majorities in each group of subjects, while *We see with our eyes* was given near-even split votes by each group.) Over all, the philosophers were somewhat more consistent with each other than the non-philosophers. But that global finding conceals results for individual sentences that sometimes manifested the opposite tendency. Thus *Thunderstorms are electrical disturbances in the atmosphere* was judged analytic by a highly significant majority of the non-philosophers, while a (non-significant) majority of the philosophers deemed it synthetic. In this case, it seems, philosophical training induces the realization that well-established results of contemporary science are not necessary truths; in other cases, conversely, clichés of current philosophical education impose their own mental blinkers on those who undergo it – *Nothing can be completely red and green all over* was judged analytic by a significant majority of philosophers but only by a non-significant majority of non-philosophers.

All in all, Morley-Bunker's results argue strongly against the notion that our inability to decide consistently whether or not some statement is a necessary truth derives from lack of skill in articulating our underlying knowledge of the rules of our language. Rather, the inability comes from the fact that the question as posed is unreal; we *choose* to treat a given statement as open to question or as unchallengeable in the light of the overall structure of beliefs which we have individually evolved in order to make sense of our individual experience. Even the cases which seem 'clearly' analytic or synthetic are cases which individuals judge alike because the relevant experiences are shared by the whole community, but even for such cases one can invent hypothetical future experiences which, if they should be realized, would cause us to revise our judgements.[1]

As already suggested in connexion with *cup*, the notion that word-semantics is rule-governed is most plausible in fields where human decisions control the realities to which words correspond; then, if people decide to adopt a certain semantic rule, they can manipulate reality so as to avoid the need to drop the rule. It is interesting to recall that the notion of analysing words as clusters of meaning-features was originally invented, by anthropological linguists, as a tool to describe one particular area of vocabulary, namely that of kinship terms.[2] Kinship classification is very clearly an area in which reality is determined largely by the wish to make situations clear-cut; our society, for instance, goes to con-siderable lengths (in terms of ceremonial, legal provisions, etc.) to ensure that there shall be no ambiguity about whether or not someone is a *wife*. It is also, of course, an area in which Nature has happened to operate in a relatively cut-and-dried way; so far there is no halfway house between being and not being a given individ-ual's mother, though with the birth, as I write, of the first 'test-tube baby' one can easily see how two women could in future reasonably disagree over which should count as someone's mother. (Is it the egg or the womb that is decisive?) It is not at all clear that the inventors of lexical decomposition intended it as a philosophical claim about the nature of human thought, or even as a useful practical descriptive tool outside the limited area for which it was designed.[3]

[1] This is not intended to call into question the special status of the 'truths of logic', such as *Either it is raining or it is not*. Unlike Katz I am inclined to accept the traditional view according to which 'logical particles' such as *not*, *or* are distinct from the bulk of the vocabulary in that the former really are governed by clear-cut inference rules. I shall not expand on this point here.

[2] F. G. Lounsbury, 'A semantic analysis of the Pawnee kinship usage', *Language*, vol. 32, 1956, pp. 158–94; W. H. Goodenough, 'Componential analysis and the study of meaning', *Language*, vol. 32, 1956, pp. 195–216.

[3] Even within that limited area, furthermore, the technical device of 'meaning-components' had already turned out to be inadequate by the time that Katz and

Katz's dispute with Quine over analyticity is the only real attempt I have encountered by a linguistic semanticist to answer the objections to the 'rule-governed' view of semantics that arise from the ideas of the philosophers mentioned above. (Chomsky, for instance, simply dismisses out of hand the possibility that the analytic/synthetic distinction might be open to question: 'There are no possible worlds in which someone was . . . an uncle but not male [etc.] . . . The necessary falsehood of "I found a female uncle" is not a matter of syntax or fact or belief.'[1] But in view of the above discussion of the sex-change operation it seems likely that one might be able to find a female uncle in the actual world.) We have already seen that Erdmann is wholly ignored by contemporary linguists, and the more recent philosophers fare little better. Wittgenstein is sometimes discussed in a desultory, uncomprehending fashion; Popper's name very rarely appears in linguists' writings.

For a time this neglect could be excused, since philosophy is not typically part of the training of the individual who finds himself attracted into the discipline of linguistics. When linguists first began to think about semantics, it is quite likely that many of them had only a dim awareness that the issues they faced had been discussed intensively by philosophers for many years (indeed, centuries) before them – this was my own case, for example. But new boys are entitled only to a limited period of grace. One of the worrying developments in the linguistics of recent years is that the phrase 'Linguistic Semantics', which was at first used simply to indicate such work on semantics as was being done by linguists, appears now to be turning into the title of a distinct discipline. 'Linguistic Semantics' is seen by many of its practitioners as a subject in its own right, properly independent of 'Philosophical Semantics'.[2] In fact the phrase is acquiring a use as a sort of

Fodor set out to extend it to the whole vocabulary; see F. G. Lounsbury, 'The structural analysis of kinship semantics', in *Proceedings of the Ninth International Congress of Linguists, Cambridge, Mass., 1962*, Mouton (the Hague), 1964, pp. 1088–90.

[1] p. 170 of 'Questions of form and interpretation', in Austerlitz, *The Scope of American Linguistics*.

[2] cf. the title of G. L. Dillon's *Introduction to Contemporary Linguistic Semantics*, Prentice-Hall, 1977, for instance, and notice the paucity of its references to philosophy.

institutional barrier, behind which linguists can cultivate their theories while refusing visas to awkward potential immigrant-ideas from the Philosophy Department. But this is intellectually indefensible; a belief cannot be protected by a name, only by argument. While linguists remain silent about the philosophical objections to essentialism, it is difficult to take seriously the pretensions of 'Linguistic Semantics'.

IV

In Chapter III we suggested that if the creative view of mind is correct there can be no such thing as a scientifically rigorous account of the semantics of a natural language, and we found that the objections to that conclusion which have actually been voiced by linguists are uncompelling. Let us now see whether the case for Linguistic Semantics can be strengthened by seeking more forceful objections to the thesis of Chapter III.

In the first place, the creative approach to language has implications that may seem unacceptable for our view of the relationship between figurative language, or metaphor, and literal usage.

One implication is that there should be no sharp distinction between the two. To use language figuratively is, I take it, to intend the hearer to treat as valid only some rather than all of the inference rules which standardly define the meanings of one's words. Thus, in Keats's lines

When by my solitary hearth I sit,
And hateful thoughts enwrap my soul in gloom

we are intended to treat the rule 'From *X enwraps Y in Z* infer *Z surrounds Y*' as operative but to ignore the rule 'From *X enwraps Y in Z* infer *Y is a physical object* and *Z is a plastic surface*' say – or, if 'ignore' is too strong, let us say that we are intended to 'demote' the latter rules in some way, so that they may still flavour our understanding of *gloom* with a suggestion of something like a blanket but we do not take Keats literally to be saying that gloom is a physical material which comes in two-dimensional sheets. We understand figurative language, presumably, by looking for the fewest 'demotions' of this kind that leave the discourse as a whole saying something non-contradictory, though if the writer is skilful the 'demoted' rules too will serve a purpose rather than simply going to waste.[1] Literal usage would be discourse in which all standard inference rules are fully 'operative'. But if the inference rules of literal language are themselves not a well-defined class, if individuals are constantly experimenting with new rules of inference and abandoning old rules as their experience grows, then it can mean very little to say that 'all standard rules are operative' for a given text – there is no 'standard' set of rules.

We might want to use the term 'figurative language' for language which forces us to demote inference rules which are relatively solidly entrenched, such as the rule 'From *father* infer *male*' and particularly when the same result could have been achieved by using other words that would not require the reader to demote any rules having that status; in that case we are likely to describe the former text as a figurative way of expressing the ideas that the latter text expresses literally. But the 'entrenchment' of a rule of inference is a matter of degree, and one that varies from individual to individual, so this way of understanding the terms 'figurative' and 'literal' makes the distinction between them very far from hard and fast. The creative view of language suggests, as it were, that all of us are using language somewhat metaphorically all the time; the thing about poets is simply that they take this tendency further than most of us. Such a conclusion may seem implausible to people who feel that they speak quite literally, and that metaphor is a specialist activity proper to Departments of English Literature.

As might be expected from the nature of their theories, the linguistic semanticists have tended to treat figurative language in this way as a 'cordoned-off' variety of linguistic behaviour. In a somewhat uncongenial metaphor of their own, they have described sentences involving figurative language as one category of 'deviant' sentences.[2] The question whether the distinction between figurative and literal usage is a cline or a sharp contrast is

---

[1] Cf. M. C. Beardsley, *Aesthetics*, Harcourt, Brace & World (New York), 1958, pp. 138–44; Max Black, *Models and Metaphors*, Cornell University Press (Ithaca, N.Y.), 1962, ch. 3.

[2] The treatment of metaphor by various theoretical linguists is surveyed in ch. 2 of S. R. Levin, *The Semantics of Metaphor*, John Hopkins University Press, 1977.

perhaps one that can be answered only in intuitive terms – I feel that the two shade into one another, but I must admit that there is nothing to stop a linguist imposing some sharp cut-off on the cline. There are no units of measurement in terms of which I could show that some of the usages on the 'figurative' side of the cut-off point are only infinitesimally further than some on the 'literal' side from the most orthodox use of a word. Since linguists' theoretical discussions of metaphor have been only programmatic, furthermore, there is a shortage of examples that one might use to make their postulation of a sharp figurative/literal distinction seem intuitively implausible.

What one can offer solid empirical evidence against, however, is the belief that recognizably figurative usage is a special activity of literary men, alien to the ordinary speaker in the street. Howard Pollio of the University of Tennessee, and his associates, have compiled fascinating statistics on the rate at which people use metaphor in various linguistic situations ranging from psychoanalytic interviews to televised debates between candidates for political office.[1] They could count, obviously, only turns of phrase which are sufficiently non-literal to be recognized as such (indeed their discussion of the problems of achieving agreement between experimenters with respect to metaphor identification[2] supports the view of the bounds of the literal as ill-defined); and they divided recognizable metaphors into 'frozen' examples (ones that have become institutionalized in the language, such as *mouth* used of a river) and 'novel' metaphors. Both categories turn out to occur at high frequencies in the various genres of spoken language they survey; novel figures at rates averaging about one and a half per hundred words, frozen figures at somewhat more than twice this rate. Projected over a lifetime's speaking, these rates suggest total production of millions of metaphors, which represents 'a lot of behavior in two language categories that often have been considered as esoteric rather than ordinary. . . . figurative language is not the special privilege of a few specially gifted speakers.'[3] The

[1] H. R. Pollio, J. M. Barlow, H. J. Fine, and M. R. Pollio, *Psychology and the Poetics of Growth*, Lawrence Erlbaum Associates (Hillsdale, N.J.), 1977.
[2] ibid., pp. 67–73.
[3] ibid., p. 9.

writers go on to suggest reasons for the ubiquity of figurative language in terms very similar to mine (and Erdmann's).[1]

One particularly interesting aspect of the Pollio study involved an examination of the frequency of figurative language in English essays by primary (in American terms, 'elementary') school-children. The authors find that, whereas university students produce metaphors in written compositions at rates comparable to those of (adult) spoken language, schoolchildren at ages 8–12 use far less figurative language in their writing. Furthermore, 'the rate of usage for novel figures (for children at the higher socio-economic and achievement levels) seems to decrease over grade level', while 'low socioeconomic low-achievement schools show an increase in use of novel figurative language over grades, so that by Grade 6 [i.e. age 11–12] children in these "poorer" schools have higher absolute rates than children in the "better" schools.'[2]

Pollio et al. regard this finding as 'surprising (and troubling)'. But is it so surprising? Literal language is language which respects the inference-relations, that is the pattern of beliefs, established in one's society; figurative language implies rejection of some en-trenched beliefs (whether the rejection is intended seriously or as a *jeu d'esprit*). The process by which an individual comes to grips intellectually with his world must always involve a tension between conformity to and rejection of the system of beliefs of his society; to treat every element of that system as questionable would prevent one deriving any benefit from the accumulated knowledge of one's predecessors, to treat none of it as questionable would be to fail to use one's own intelligence in order to improve on inherited wisdom. The time for questioning comes when one has mastered one's intellectual inheritance for what it is worth; the role of a primary school must surely be to equip its pupils with that inheritance, so naturally the overall ethos of a primary school must encourage intellectual conformity and therefore literalness in writing, whatever lip-service may be paid in English lessons to

---

[1] On the indispensable role of metaphor in scientific language (a genre commonly believed to be more literal than most) see E. R. MacCormac, 'Meaning variance and metaphor', *British Journal for the Philosophy of Science*, vol. 22, 1971, pp. 145–59.

[2] op. cit., p. 192.

'creativity'. The higher verbal creativity of 'low-achievement' pupils in poor schools could be taken as symptomatic of their more general unwillingness or inability to accept what primary school has to offer. If the children who succeed in becoming university students reach levels of verbal creativity which are so much higher by that stage, perhaps their extreme verbal conformism at primary school does them no harm in the long run. Formal education (at least in its early stages) teaches us to avoid such creativity, and Linguistic Semantics in effect over-estimates the degree to which we are affected by this training.[1]

A second point about metaphor is that, on the creative view of language, the ways in which a given word can be used metaphorically should themselves be unpredictable. If we invent concepts, i.e. ways of seeing entities as similar, then there is no knowing what concepts an individual will try taking as crucial for the use of a given word. Indeed, this point is relevant for 'literal' as well as 'figurative' language; it suggests that, even if we know rather precisely what a word means now, we cannot predict what changes of meaning it is likely to undergo in the future. What we recognize as a change in the meaning of a word must usually begin as a novel 'metaphorical' extension of the use of the word, which attracts enough imitators to become 'frozen' and finally not to seem figurative at all, if it ever did. (In many cases the extensions of meaning will proceed in small enough steps not to be noticed as figurative, though in other cases – as when *crane* was extended from the bird to the lifting machine – the figurative nature of the new usage must originally have been striking.) The linguists who set out to bring figurative language within the scope of their formal theories, on the other hand, maintain that the range of potential metaphorical senses of a given word is in principle predictable from its literal sense.

[1] In contrast to the findings of Pollio et al., Anglin (*The Growth of Word Meaning*) reports that adults are considerably more 'predictable' than children in their semantic reactions. One might perhaps argue that although children writing essays at school are more inclined than adults to conform to the standard semantic patterns of their society, adults are more familiar than children with abstract parts of those patterns and are therefore more able to conform to them in experiments such as Anglin's which are perceived as calling for exercise of this ability. When writing essays, as in the Pollio experiments, children could avoid areas of the inference-relation network where they felt unsure of the conventions.

It is hard to discuss this question by reference to particular instances of novel metaphorical usage, which are evanescent and often comprehensible only in the light of a particular context of circumstances; if the evidence went against them, linguistic semanticists might appeal with some plausibility to the notion of 'performance' diverging from 'competence'. A more promising approach might be to compare the frozen metaphorical extensions of the words for a given concept in various languages. The limited-minder should predict that if a set of words drawn from various languages are synonyms, their standard figurative senses should be identical or at least overlap heavily; the creative-minder will expect that, so long as the cultures to which the languages belong are independent of one another, the meaning-extensions that have become standard in the respective cultures will be quite diverse.

Only a small amount of work seems to have been published, unfortunately, on cross-language comparisons of figurative usage.[1] One interesting investigation has been carried out, however, by Solomon Asch.[2]

Asch examined a number of languages, widely separate geographically and culturally, in order to discover how far they resembled one another in extending terms for physical qualities to

---

[1] The reason for this deficiency is probably that most work on metaphor is done by literary specialists rather than psychologists, and the interests of the former are usually confined to one language or one culture. Richard Billow provides an up-to-date survey of psychologists' studies of metaphor that would make a useful starting-point for deeper investigation of the issues raised here ('Metaphor: a review of the psychological literature', *Psychological Bulletin*, vol. 84, 1977, pp. 81–92). One literary scholar who has briefly argued against the position I am defending here is Stephen Ullmann ('Semantic universals', in J. H. Greenberg, ed., *Universals of Language*, 2nd edn., M.I.T. Press (Cambridge, Mass.), 1966, §3.1.1).

[2] S. E. Asch, 'On the use of metaphor in the description of persons', in Heinz Werner, ed., *On Expressive Language*, Clark University Press (Worcester, Mass.), 1955; 'The metaphor: a psychological inquiry', in Renato Tagiuri and Luigi Petrullo, eds., *Person Perception and Interpersonal Behavior*, Stanford University Press, 1958. In the former of these articles Asch stated his intention of publishing a fuller account of his investigation in due course, but as far as I have been able to discover he has not done so. Asch's work may be compared with A. Sanvageot's 'A propos des changements sémantiques' (*Journal de Psychologie*, vol. 46, 1953, pp. 465–72), which takes a rather equivocal line with respect to the point at issue here.

cover psychological properties (as when we use *hard* to mean 'merciless').

Asch presents his findings as supporting the view that human thought is much the same from culture to culture, and certainly some of his examples do show striking constancy in their metaphorical sense: words for 'straight' and 'crooked' very generally have the psychological senses 'honest' and 'dishonest', respectively. Others, however, do not; thus 'the morpheme for "hot" . . . stands for rage or wrath (Hebrew), enthusiasm (Chinese, Malayalam), sexual arousal (Thai), worry (Thai), energy (Hausa), or nervousness (in Shilha, a Berber language . . .). . . . Similarly, the morpheme for "cold" . . . stands for self-possession (Hebrew), indifference or hostility (Chinese), loneliness (Thai), laziness or apathy (Hausa).'[1] There are similarities here, as well there might be (a language will not develop an extension to the sense of a word unless there is *some* connexion to be perceived between old and new senses), but these certainly do not amount to identity; it seems inconceivable that an Englishman might call a man 'cold-hearted', as the Thais apparently do, to mean that he is love-sick. Asch mentions that the 'straight'/ 'crooked' example is an unusually impressive case of shared meaning-extension.

Since Asch presents only excerpts from his data, it is difficult to know how far his evidence as a whole supports or undermines the creative view of language. But there are a number of reasons why Asch's suggestion that his data support the notion of universal psychology may overstate the force of his evidence against the creative view. First, Asch was to a large extent concerned to show simply that all languages have words with both physical and psychological senses – he certainly establishes this, but the creative-minder has no reason to predict the contrary. Secondly, Asch elicited only those secondary senses of his words which involved psychological properties. That is to say, a case comparable to the English use of *hard* to mean 'difficult', said of a problem or a task, would not have been picked up by Asch's methodology; so that Asch considerably reduced the possibility of discovering unique extensions of meaning by his choice of research technique.

[1] 'On the use of metaphor', p. 33.

The third point is that Asch explains away examples tending to refute the notion that figurative extension follows universal rules by appeal to an invalid argument. Thus, Asch mentions that words for 'colourful' have the sense 'cunning' in Homeric Greek and the rather different sense 'hypocritical in the religious sphere' in Biblical Hebrew (the words to which Asch refers are presumably ποικίλος and *ṣābhûaʿ* respectively), but he argues that this divergence is a consequence of the fact that the *literal* senses of the respective words are not identical as the gloss suggests: the Greek word (according to Asch) refers to change of colour, the Hebrew word to being painted over and thus showing on the surface a colour other than the underlying one. But this is just the kind of finding which the creative-minder expects. Something that is 'colourful' is so, often, because it has changed or regularly does change colour, but something that is 'colourful' is also often something to the surface of which an alien colour has been applied. An individual who picks out the former property in things which he hears referred to as 'colourful' may very naturally extend that word to mean something like 'shifty', hence 'cunning', while someone who notices the latter property may naturally extend the word to mean 'hypocritical'. There is no reason to expect the divergence in institutionalized aspects of meaning to occur only after extension from physical objects to psychological traits; such divergence may occur at any point.

Another objection which is sometimes made to the creative-mind approach to language is that it may seem to suggest that translation between the languages of different cultures should be impossible – which is manifestly false. I have already suggested, in Chapter II, that the degree of conceptual isomorphism between human languages is often greatly exaggerated by linguists familiar only with languages of modern Europe; but, that said, I am quite willing to admit that many, many concepts of modern English (particularly words referring to the natural world rather than human institutions) have quite direct translations in the languages of societies far removed in time or space. Yet, if we invent our concepts rather than having them thrust on us by our senses, and if this process of invention is not limited to a fixed range of potential concepts implicit in our minds, how does it happen that the same or very similar concepts are created independently?

The answer to this is that although our ideas are not *contained* in our experience, we try to make them *conform* to the world that we experience, and this world has definite properties. Both English and Chinese, say, contain a word for 'year', i.e. the cultures have independently evolved the concept that the changing pattern of weather, growth, and celestial phenomena reflect an underlying regular cyclicity in time; and the two cultures have evolved similar concepts because there really is such a regular cyclicity, which exists independently of whether there are human beings making conjectures about it – as we now know, it is caused by the fact that the axis of the Earth is not quite perpendicular to the plane of its orbit round the Sun.

The annual cycle of time is certainly not an immediate datum of sense; before men had changed from being food gatherers or hunters to agriculturalists there must surely have been a long period when they had not yet formulated the concept 'year', and would gaze out of their caves in winter morosely wondering whether the good weather they vaguely remembered would ever occur again. But to say that the notion 'year' is not part of our experience is not to deny that it corresponds to a real property of the world which generates our experience. We are never given a guarantee that our ideas mirror our world faithfully, but experience sooner or later winnows out those of our ideas which distort reality; it is not surprising that languages representing the outcome of many millennia of experience of the same world show considerable semantic similarity.

(A similar reply is appropriate in the case of an objection to the claim that words are extended to new instances in an unpredictable way. I have argued that we cannot know in advance how a speaker will analogize from a newly encountered thing to something for which he already knows a name, in order to extend the name to the new thing. In saying this I am doing no more than repeating the point made at length by Ludwig Wittgenstein a quarter of a century ago with reference to the word *game*.[1] This view is sometimes taken to imply that linguistic behaviour should

[1] *Philosophical Investigations*, Blackwell (Oxford), 1953, §65ff.

be much more anarchic than it is – we ought to find people calling what appears to us an ordinary sort of table, say, a 'tomato' or a 'motorway' rather than a 'table' on the basis of some resemblance apparent to them but not to us. Of course this does not happen, except when speakers or writers are consciously striving for literary effect;[1] but then a table is a thing with real properties, and if it is regularly called 'table' rather than 'tomato' or 'motorway' that is because it really is more similar to other things called 'tables' than to things called 'tomatoes' or 'motorways'. The properties of a thing are not simply components of our experience of the thing; we have to *reconstruct* a thing's properties from clues given in our experience of it, but there is a reality to which the reconstruction is more or less faithful.)

When we pass from words for natural phenomena such as 'year' to words for products or properties of the creative human mind itself, perfect or near-perfect translatability is less common because the realities as well as the ideas of the realities are to a large extent invented independently. If I were to meet a Confucian philosopher of the Han dynasty, I would expect to encounter extreme difficulty in explaining to him what I understand by the word *sport*, and conversely I do not fully understand what his contemporaries meant by the term *hsiu-shên*, or 'self-cultivation' as it is conventionally translated. Even in cases of these kinds, though, I agree that languages are not wholly mutually inscrutable; simple word-for-word translation is not adequate to convey the alien concepts, but by means of increasingly lengthy paraphrases one can bring about an ever better understanding of them by speakers of a language in which they do not occur. That is to say, although speakers of one language do not already know some of the concepts in another language, they can learn them – and this is what we would expect, since children growing up in the culture in question learned the concepts. The prediction of the creative view of mind is that no concepts will be wholly impenetrable to members of other speech-communities but that some will take much more learning than others, and that the most

[1] In the latter case, I. A. Richards suggests that virtually any word may be used for anything (*The Philosophy of Rhetoric*, Oxford University Press, 1936, pp. 125–6).

directly translatable concepts will tend to be concepts concerning aspects of the natural environment shared by both communities. This seems to be exactly right.

The prediction of the limited view is very different. As I have pointed out elsewhere,[1] if Chomsky believes that our biological endowment includes a complex, subtle structure of possible concepts, it is somewhat disingenuous of him to suggest that this inheritance is likely to be identical in all members of the species. To suppose this is to postulate a major difference of principle between the workings of biology in the mental and physiological domains, respectively, and the burden of Chomsky's argument is that we ought rather to assimilate our understanding of the two. In the physiological domain we do not find that complex organs are inherited in identical forms by all humans; rather, the structure of men's organs is broadly similar but with variation between the races of men and further variation between individuals of any race. If conceptual structure is inherited in the same way as physiological structure, we should expect that many words will be perfectly translatable between a pair of languages because they refer to concepts inherited by speakers of both languages, but that where there are problems of translation the problems will be wholly insuperable because absence of the concept in the thought of one community represents a biological rather than merely cultural deficiency. (Chomsky could, admittedly, argue that some word of language A lacks an equivalent in language B only because the speakers of language B have not yet consciously availed themselves of this particular element of their implicit conceptual inheritance – but in that case the translation problem would presumably require only a brief paraphrase in terms of more primitive concepts that do occur overtly in both languages, which is a much more straightforward procedure than is often demanded in practice by 'culture-specific' terminology.) Furthermore, the biological version of the limited-mind approach gives us no reason to expect that the wholly untranslatable concepts will be concentrated in the domain of human affairs – presumably they would be equally likely to occur in any part of the vocabulary. And finally, Chomsky's view suggests that an individual's difficulty in

[1] *Liberty and Language*, ch. 5.

mastering a novel concept should depend on his biological ancestry rather than on the structure of concepts to which he has been
exposed in his own lifetime. All these implications seem to fly in
the face of observable facts.

One point that may strike some readers as a difficulty in the
creative view of mind is the phenomenon of parallel invention of
ideas. If ideas are created *ex nihilo* rather than drawn from a fixed
set of possibilities, it might seem to follow that the likelihood of two
minds producing the same idea independently should be virtually
zero. Yet there are many cases in intellectual history where this
seems to have happened. One might suggest that if there is a
right answer to some problem posed by human experience, it is not
surprising that more than one creative mind should come up with
that answer at the same time. But, in the first place, I am not sure
that all cases of parallel invention of ideas are cases in which the
new idea turned out to be correct (although these are the cases in
which historians of thought are likely to be most interested). And
furthermore, the suggestion that experience poses problems to
which there is 'one correct answer' seems to imply a tighter
relationship between experience and thought than I have wished
to admit. If experience offers only fragmentary clues which the
mind must explain by hypotheses drawn from a literally boundless
range of possibilities, then perhaps it *is* surprising that two minds
should independently pitch on the same answer even if that
answer is right. And if even the process of learning from a teacher
or from books involves creative hypothesis-formulation about the
ideas lying behind the words of instruction, then the fact that
education is often a reasonably successful activity suggests that
parallel intellectual invention must be a rather common
phenomenon.

(Except for this last point, incidentally, the difficulty about
independent innovation offers an analogy – one of many –
between the creative view of mind and biological evolution; parallel evolution is a recognized difficulty for Darwinian theory.[1] We

[1] See e.g. E. C. Olson, 'Morphology, paleontology, and evolution', in Sol Tax,
ed., *The Evolution of Life*, vol. i of *Evolution After Darwin*, University of Chicago
Press, 1960, p. 538; and cf. pp. 481–3 of W. W. Bartley, 'The philosophy of Karl
Popper, Part i', *Philosophia*, vol. 6, 1976.

shall return to the analogy between intellectual and biological evolution in Chapter VII below.)

The issue just raised does seem to me to be a genuine difficulty to which I cannot offer a completely satisfactory answer. A partial answer would be to argue that cases of 'parallel invention' are not really as parallel as all that, that independently-invented concepts or theories are at most similar but never identical. In the case of formal education there is a good case for saying that when a pupil masters an idea, as opposed to merely learning to parrot the words of his teacher or textbook, what he acquires is not the teacher's or writer's idea but an idea of his own related more or less closely to the former idea.[1] The number of books published which consist of exegesis by one writer of a predecessor's ideas suggests that the transmission of thought is not as straightforward a process as one might expect it to be, if it involved merely finding a form of words to release in a reader's conscious mind a structure of ideas already implicit in the biological endowment shared by reader and writer. But this is perhaps a weak reply to a serious objection.

However, it is not altogether clear that the sort of limited-mind theory advocated by Chomsky is better equipped to meet the objection. The reason why parallel invention of ideas seems surprising on creative-mind assumptions is that those assumptions suggest that the number of potential ideas is indefinitely large, so that the probability of coming up with any particular new idea would be one in infinity, i.e. zero. But then Chomsky also does not believe that the range of possible ideas is *finite*; indeed he stresses that it is likely to be infinitely large, because there will be no limit to the complexity of the compounds that can be formed out of the primitive elements, and Chomsky insists only that the set of primitives and the rules for compounding them will be fixed and in principle specifiable.[2] In fact the kind of mathematicizing implied by the phrase 'one in infinity' has more relevance for Chomsky's

---

[1] 'What a luck in teaching! The tutor aims at fidelity, the pupil strives to learn, but there is never a coincidence, but always a diagonal line drawn partaking of the genius of the tutor and the genius of the pupil. This, when there is success, but that how capricious! Two precious madmen who cannot long conspire.' (R. W. Emerson, *Journals*, 1845.)

[2] Cf. Chomsky, *Reflections*, p. 124.

than for the creative view of mind. If ideas are compounds, of unlimited complexity, of a limited set of primitives, then the range of possible ideas is what mathematicians call 'denumerably infinite'. On the other hand, if ideas are original creations not drawn from a fixed range, then it makes little sense to say anything about the number of possible ideas.

One might argue that, even though possible ideas are infinitely numerous for Chomsky, the fact that they all conform to fixed rules of assembly means that there can be definite procedures for arriving at the 'right' new idea in given circumstances (which is impossible on the creative view, since a range of procedures implies a range of possible outcomes of applying them), and that this makes Chomsky's approach more compatible than the creative view with the fact of parallel intellectual innovations. Chomsky himself, however, rejects the notion of procedures for arriving at particular new ideas in particular circumstances. Chomsky believes that the *total range* of potential ideas is determinate and is a reasonable subject for scientific investigation, but that questions about how people operate within this range of particular occasions are much less or not at all accessible to investigation; for example, one can describe an individual's language rigorously at all levels including the semantic, but one cannot make predictions about which sentences of the language will be uttered when. Thus, contrasting 'problems' and 'mysteries' in the study of language, Chomsky argues that:

Roughly, where we deal with cognitive structures, either in a mature state of knowledge or belief or in the initial state, we face problems, but not mysteries. When we ask how humans make use of these cognitive structures, how and why they make choices and behave as they do, although there is much that we can say as human beings with intuition and insight, there is little, I believe, that we can say as scientists.[1]

If parallel evolution of ideas is a reality, then, it appears that Chomsky can make no more claim than the creative-minder to explain it; we must both leave it as a 'mystery'.

---

[1] *Reflections*, p. 138.

V

We have surveyed a number of arguments in favour of the limited-mind approach to semantics, and I have suggested that none has much force. The chief appeal of this approach, I believe, does not lie in any particular prediction it makes about observable facts, but rather derives from a deep-rooted, *a priori* reluctance to admit the creative view of mind as a possibility that can rationally be entertained. As W. W. Bartley points out, in a penetrating discussion of Popper's unique role in contemporary philosophy:

It is not surprising that [Popper's basic theme] should meet incomprehension and stark resistance, for it opposes the dominant watchwords of our philosophical tradition:
There is nothing new under the sun.
Nothing can be created or destroyed.
Ex nihilo nihil fit.[1]

Although the notion of 'creativity' or 'originality' is familiar and usual enough in the everyday discourse of the non-philosophical citizen, one must admit that it is a difficult concept when considered in depth. In the first place, one can never *prove* that minds are creative, in the sense that their future products fall outside any range of possibilities implied by their state at a given time. It is always possible in principle to construct a framework of 'potential concepts', akin to Fodor's 'language of thought', which allows for all the ideas that have emerged so far; and, whenever in the future an idea is produced which falls outside the framework, rather than having to give up the assumption that men are limited to a fixed framework of potential concepts one can always argue that there was a mistake in the particular framework proposed. This is not so very different, after all, from what happens in the case of theories about the physical world; every now and then one of these is

[1] W. W. Bartley, 'The philosophy of Karl Popper, Part II', *Philosophia*, vol. 7, 1978, pp. 675–6.

refuted, but rather than concluding that the physical world obeys no laws at all we try to construct an improved theory.

I would argue that there is a difference, however; new theories in the physical sciences commonly incorporate previous theories as special cases rather than discarding them outright, so that it is plausible to see physical science as moving fairly steadily in the direction of an ultimate (perhaps infinitely distant) truth. Predictive theories about possible human concepts, I believe, are destined to be merely overturned by later thought without any progress being discernible in the succession of such theories. Since the schemes actually put forward by linguistic semanticists have so far always been highly programmatic, one cannot point to this process happening now – but the very fact that the schemes are invariably only programmatic leads one to wonder why linguists are not yet ready to offer concrete, testable theories of the semantic structure of natural languages as they do in the domains of syntactic and phonological structure.

Once ideas have been created they acquire an aura of inevitability. Although we know intellectually that there was a time when the concepts of *insurance* or *picturesqueness* did not yet exist, we feel that there must then have been 'empty mental slots' waiting to be filled by these concepts. If a semantic system is a network of inference relations between words and between sentences, we might translate this feeling into the notion that the same network of inference relations existed in the minds of our predecessors as exists in our minds, but that at the earlier time certain pathways in the network were 'blocked-off', as it were, for lack of conventional phonetic shapes for the words to which they led. This feeling about 'empty mental slots' comes to seem illusory, though, when we try to detect such slots in our current framework of ideas. No doubt those who come after us will use concepts for which we have no words, but we do not find ourselves baulked in our thinking by lack of words to express particular ideas – our own vocabulary feels to us to be a self-contained system, and it is not at all apparent whereabouts in the semantic network new concepts are destined to emerge. It would surely be provincial to suppose that the semantic system of the language used by our ancestors 500 or 2,000 years ago was any less self-contained than ours, though it was very different from ours.[1]

More important than this natural tendency to see the thought of our predecessors as an imperfect approximation to our own is a propensity, deeply rooted in modern life, to reject the idea that there are limits to the domain of applicability of the scientific method.

I have argued that there is in the world a real phenomenon, namely human intellectual activity, which is not a mere myth like witchcraft or spiritualism but about which no scientific theory can be constructed. We can describe how humans have thought in the past, but we cannot make true predictions about how they will think in the future; and prediction is the essence of science. A predictive, scientific theory must specify some things which cannot happen, so that the theory can be tested by seeing whether the events it forbids do in fact occur. Creative human minds refuse to be constrained by such prohibitions.

Now many people hold that if mental activity is real it *must* be treatable by the scientific method. After all, the mind must be some sort of machine, even if a highly complex one (they argue), and in principle the workings of any machine can be specified (even if in practice the job is sometimes too big to be accomplished). There is, indeed, a whole discipline, that of Artificial Intelligence, devoted to constructing mechanical models to simulate the activities of the mind. The notion that some subjects can in principle be discussed only in the historical style of the humanities rather than the predictive style of the sciences seems to such people mere mysticism. Chomsky himself has made this view quite explicit:

Some intellectuals think that in certain fields of study all you can say is: I saw this and then I saw that and then I saw some other thing. They say that these fields are not subject to scientific investigation. But that's just a counsel of despair, and there isn't the slightest reason to believe it, particularly in the case of language. If our approach doesn't make sense, then there is no point in studying language at all.[2]

The last sentence quoted seems to be merely a remarkably

[1] Cf. R. G. Collingwood's *Autobiography*, Oxford University Press, 1939, p. 59ff.
[2] Quoted on p. 212 of Ved Mehta, *John is Easy to Please*, Secker & Warburg, 1971.

audacious attempt to claim a monopoly in linguistic scholarship. James Murray and his followers who constructed the *Oxford English Dictionary* did so on the assumption that they could only describe the vicissitudes of word-meanings over the centuries up to their own time, rather than make scientific predictions about future usage; can one seriously suggest that they ought to have concluded that there was 'no point at all' in their labours, in view of the enormous value of the *O.E.D.* as a tool of scholarship? Turning to the preceding passage, there surely is a reason – and by no means a 'slight' one – to believe that science may be inapplicable to the workings of the mind. Chomsky himself has given the reason, in remarks such as these:

... consider our near-total failure to discover a scientific theory ... to account for the normal use of language (or other aspects of behavior). Even the relevant concepts seem lacking; certainly, no intellectually satisfying principles have been proposed that have explanatory force, though the questions are very old. It is not excluded that human science-forming capacities simply do not extend to this domain, or any domain involving the exercise of will, so that for humans, these questions will always be shrouded in mystery.[1]

... as soon as questions of will or decision or reason or choice of action arise, human science is at a loss. These questions remain in the obscurity in which they were in classical antiquity.[2]

The fact is that, although psychology is about as ancient a study as any in the Western tradition, insofar as it has tried to go beyond mechanical aspects of human behaviour (such as the measurement of reaction times) to deal with categories of behaviour controlled by conscious thought and will psychology has signally failed to come up with successful scientific theories to explain the data. The contrast between the success of the scientific method when applied to the physical world and its failure when applied to human psychology is very striking.

Chomsky explains this contrast by arguing that in principle there are scientific explanations of all phenomena, but that the biological limitations on human minds prevent us constructing theories in certain domains, and it happens that the 'forbidden' domains include that of theories about our own mental activities.

[1] *Reflections*, p. 25.   [2] Chomsky/Magee interview, p. 435.

This seems a perversely roundabout way of interpreting the situation; surely it is simpler to say that human minds lie outside the domain of applicability of the scientific method than to posit a hidden range of theories which mysteriously combine the characteristics that we require of discourse we regard as scientific with the characteristic of being in principle incomprehensible by any human mind? It may be true that we cannot *prove* there to be phenomena to which scientific method is inapplicable (although, as we saw on p. 10 above, Popper argues that this can be proved). But we certainly cannot prove the converse thesis, that all phenomena can be described scientifically. The belief that science can be applied to all phenomena without exception is merely a prejudice (the prejudice of 'scientism', as it is called by Friedrich Hayek[1]); and, once we appreciate that it is no more than a prejudice, considerations such as those in the passages just quoted from Chomsky make it a highly implausible prejudice – if Popper's proof is satisfactory, perhaps a self-contradictory one. We all feel instinctively that human minds are a very 'special' component of the universe; even such an outspoken contemporary reductionist as the biologist Richard Dawkins finds it necessary to treat human thought as manifesting an entirely novel principle within the biological domain.[2] Those among us who suppose that the 'specialness' of mind cannot remove it from the field of application of scientific method do so for no better reason than that the temper of the times makes us feel obscurely that questioning the omnipotence of science is a symptom of unreason; but this feeling itself rests on no stronger authority than that of intellectual fashion.

Let me clarify what I suggest to be the situation by considering, in a little more detail than I have done so far, what a hypothetical successful scientific theory of the semantics of a language would have to be like. So far I have suggested that a theory of semantics would make predictions about the inferential moves people make from statement to statement, but clearly this is only part of the picture. In the first place many sentences (e.g. questions) are not statements and hence do not occur as premises or conclusions of

[1] F. A. Hayek, *The Counter-Revolution of Science*, Collier-Macmillan, 1955.
[2] *The Selfish Gene*, Oxford University Press, 1976, ch. 11.

inferences, but their meanings must also be described; more important, the drawing of a conclusion from premisses is a private, mental act, not a publicly observable event, so that a theory which makes predictions only about this category of action is not scientific. For a scientific theory of semantics we would need to supplement rules governing inference in a language with other rules relating the inferences a man draws to the external stimuli that impinge on him and to his own behaviour (both of which *are* publicly observable) in such a way that the theory as a whole makes predictions about correlations between these.

In principle it is fairly easy to see how one might set about doing this.

A central component of the enlarged theory would be a specification of the range of intellectual states potentially open to a speaker of the language being described – his possible structures of opinion and belief, at least insofar as these are articulated in language. One simple way of defining such a range would be to say that any (finitely or infinitely large) set of declarative sentences of the language counted as one of the potential intellectual states, so that a grammar of the language which defined the class of all possible declarative sentences would by the same token define the class of all possible intellectual states.

Secondly, one would specify the set of possible inputs to a speaker: any two patterns of momentary sense-input which are different enough from one another to receive different descriptions in the language would be different members of this set; and one would give rules spelling out how different inputs induce changes in intellectual state. If states are collections of sentences, inputs will presumably add new sentences to the state. Thus, the rules might imply among other things that 580-nanometre light entering an English-speaker's eye in a particular configuration will cause him to add the sentence *There is a yellow square in front of me* to his internal state. The stimuli of hearing utterances of various kinds would presumably cause the addition to the internal state of sentences such as *Bill is telling me that I am an idiot* or *John is asking me what time it is* – the fact that some sentences are not declaratives does not force us to say that speakers' internal belief-states contain anything other than declaratives.

A third component of the theory would specify how a speaker's intellectual state changes spontaneously, independently of the control of experience. This is the component which will subsume the kind of semantic description outlined in Chapter II; if states are collections of sentences then the obvious way to describe spontaneous changes of intellectual state is to specify rules, including at least the deductive rules of logic but possibly other rules having to do with the semantics of ordinary non-logical words, according to which states including particular sentences can come to include other sentences.[1] Thus, these rules might imply e.g. that, if a speaker's intellectual state includes the sentences *John is asking me what time it is* and *When someone asks me something I ought to answer him*, his internal state is liable to acquire the further belief *I ought to answer John*. The rules need not be deterministic; that is, for a given state they may permit many alternative successor states, and if the rules include those of deductive logic this will certainly be so (in constructing a logical derivation there are usually many alternative legal moves available at each point). For the theory as a whole to be predictive we require only that a definite range of possible alternative moves be specified for a given intellectual state.

Finally, a fourth component of the theory would define a range of possible 'outputs' – actions, including utterances, that the speaker can choose to carry out – together with rules relating intellectual states to particular outputs. Thus, these rules might provide that if the speaker's intellectual state acquires the sentence *I kick Bill* or the sentence *I tell John that it is ten to two*, the speaker kicks Bill or says 'It is ten to two'.

Taken together, these components would form an empirical theory of the semantics of a language, and so far as I can see only a system broadly similar to this could possibly count as such. The system permits us to make testable predictions about what people will do given particular histories of observable inputs. Such a theory is of course not only a theory of semantics – it covers also

---

[1] The reason why I say that the state-changing rules will only 'possibly' need to include rules concerning non-logical words is that rules such as 'From *bachelor* infer *male*' may be redundant, given that an intellectual state may include sentences such as *Bachelors are male*.

what is called 'pragmatics', and indeed rationality in general; but there is no way in which one could isolate the semantic aspects of the theory while retaining its empirical status.

In view of the (largely justified) criticisms made by contemporary theoretical linguists of Bloomfieldian 'stimulus-response' approaches to language, it is worth drawing attention to the fact that the kind of theory sketched here includes no direct links between inputs and outputs. The theory provides that behaviour is determined by internal mental state rather than by a particular input to the speaker. It is true that mental states are affected by inputs; but the state I am in now, say, insofar as it is determined at all, will be determined in a theory of this kind by the whole history of inputs to which I have been subjected throughout my life, together with the internal state in which I began life. Current mental state will not necessarily have an especially close relationship with the most recent inputs, so a theory of this kind in no way predicts that our actions occur as immediate responses to the stimuli of the moment (which in general they clearly do not).

Now there are two immediate provisos to be made about this account of what an empirical theory of semantics would be like. In the first place, clearly it would be fiendishly difficult actually to set up a test of such a system in practice, because any plausible model would presumably require a vast amount of knowledge about the history of inputs to an individual before it yielded any testable predictions about his actions, and in practice it would be virtually impossible to acquire such knowledge. But I am here concerned with the question of whether scientific theories of semantics are possible *in principle*, so I shall not use this practical problem in order to attack scientific semantics. Secondly, any theory which had a hope of being adequate would not be as straightforward as the kind I describe. In particular, I do not believe that an intellectual state could be simply a disconnected set of sentences with new sentences tacked on by experience; an intellectual state would have to be a coherent structure of some kind that would be modified by inputs (including heard sentences) in some fairly subtle way, rather than simply having 'raw' sentences added to it without 'digesting' them. (To quote just one reason for this: understanding a sentence involves working out the reference of any third-person pronouns it contains, so an intellectual state would need in some way to include elements corresponding to the things to which pronouns can refer, rather than including sentences with pronouns in them.) But, having made this point, I believe that for present purposes we would do well to focus on the simple version of the model, in which an intellectual state is simply a set of sentences to which new sentences are added. This model is relatively easy to think about, and the points I shall make about the simple model could readily be restated in terms of any subtler model of a semantic theory.

In fact, models of this general kind (and ones in which intellectual states are treated much more subtly than as simple sets of sentences) are already being constructed – although not on the whole by linguists, who show little interest in making their semantic theories testable. The construction and testing of models, or partial models, of this kind is precisely what is done in the discipline of Artificial Intelligence ('AI'), or at least in the central core of that discipline ('Category B AI' in the terms of the Lighthill Report[1]). As I understand it, as soon as Linguistic Semantics enriches itself in the respects needed for it to become an empirical subject, it coincides with AI. There are, admittedly, differences of detail in the ways that a linguistic semanticist and an AI researcher might typically be inclined to go about the task of putting flesh on the theoretical skeleton I have outlined. For instance, a linguist would probably tend to assume that the rules of my third component, governing spontaneous changes of intellectual state, are likely to be sensitive to quite small syntactic differences between sentences which are broad paraphrases of one another, whereas a number of AI researchers (though not all) prefer to abstract away from the details of syntax in order to concentrate on relatively gross features of the communicative import of utterances or propositions. But it seems reasonable to see these as alternative research strategies for attacking a common problem, rather than as indications that Linguistic Semantics and AI are trying to do two different things.

Now what I contend is that any explicit model of this general

[1] Sir James Lighthill et al., *Artificial Intelligence: A Paper Symposium*, Science Research Council, 1973.

sort must misrepresent the nature of human thought, and would be refuted if, *per impossibile*, it were to be tested. Consider the third component of the model, dealing with spontaneous changes of intellectual state. Some of the intellectual state-changes a person undergoes are cases where he comes to believe a new proposition by deducing it from his prior beliefs, and cases of this kind might well be described in terms of rules akin to logicians' rules of deductive inference. But not all our thought is deductive; we all commonly acquire new beliefs by induction from our obser-vations. New beliefs formed by induction are general statements; they are not mere reports of individual observations or conjunc-tions of observations, and they do not deductively follow from observation statements although observation statements follow deductively from them. In Popperian terms, beliefs formed by in-duction are unpredictable *guesses*. Take the case of the primitive men who have not yet understood the cyclical regularity under-lying the fluctuating phenomena of the climate: one day, the in-tellectual state of one of these men changed by the addition of a hypothesis such as 'There are seasons following each other regularly' (a hypothesis confirmed by subsequent experience), and nothing in the man's previous state could have allowed us to predict this as a possible hypothesis – this was the first appearance of the concept 'season' in anyone's mind.

Yet a semantic theory about this man's language which failed to predict his acquisition of the hypothesis would be refuted by observation of his behaviour, since this will certainly be influenced by his acceptance of the hypothesis; for instance the inference rules governing the use of the new concept 'season' may lead the man to make a point of gathering a stock of firewood in autumn now he knows that winter is sure to follow. Not only will the individual's novel concepts and hypotheses not be predictable in terms of the inputs to him; the nature of the inputs will be altered by the unpredictable changes in internal state, for instance a given pattern of physical stimulation will be perceived by the man who has formed a theory of seasons as a 'summer day' whereas his predecessor would have perceived it merely as a 'good day' or the like.[1] (Similarly, the structure of the internal intellectual state will

[1] Cf. N. R. Hanson, *Patterns of Discovery*, Cambridge University Press, 1958.

affect the range of possible behavioural outputs; e.g. it is possible
to decide to 'celebrate the winter solstice' only when one has
formed a theory of seasons.)[1]

Any Artificial Intelligence model, unless it restricts itself to
some peripheral area in which these questions do not arise, must
presuppose that the kind of unpredictable innovation described
here does not occur. Roger Schank's influential AI system, for
instance, is explicitly based on the assumption of a universal
'language of thought'; in terms of the discussion above, it presupposes that the range of possible intellectual states and the rules
governing state-transitions are fixed for all humans.[2] (Schank's
system lacks an 'eye' and a 'hand' – i.e. all its inputs and outputs
are linguistic – so that the possibility that ranges of possible inputs
and outputs might alter does not arise for Schank given his
assumption that various human languages all encode the same
conceptual content.)

One AI researcher who is much more sophisticated than most
about the issue under discussion is Yorick Wilks, whose
'Computable Semantic Derivations' system is expressly designed
to cope with the fact of linguistic creativity.[3] But Wilks's mechanical model can cope with creativity only because the task he sets
it (that of working out the 'gist' of sentences containing ambiguous
words, e.g. reducing *Our village policeman is a good sport really* to *A man
is a certain sort of man* rather than to *A man is a certain sort of recreational
organization*) does not require the system to 'understand' novel
concepts (it is irrelevant to Wilks's system what we mean by
calling someone 'a good sport'), and furthermore Wilks, unlike
some AI researchers, explicitly disclaims the ambition of producing a theoretically valid model of what human minds actually do.[4]

Certainly it is possible to make an AI system non-deterministic,
so that its individual changes of internal state, and hence outputs,
cannot be predicted. Chomsky's discussion of the contrast

[1] cf. Peter Winch, *The Idea of a Social Science and Its Relation to Philosophy*,
Routledge & Kegan Paul, 1958
[2] R. C. Schank, *Conceptual Information Processing (Fundamental Studies in Computer
Science*, 3), North-Holland, 1975; see p. 7ff.
[3] Y. A. Wilks, *Grammar, Meaning and the Machine Analysis of Language*, Routledge
& Kegan Paul, 1972; see pp. 17, 34, 128ff., 166ff.
[4] ibid., p. 104.

between 'problems' and 'mysteries' in the study of language suggests that he might argue that human minds are non-deterministic in this sense. But any explicit AI model must specify the *range of potential states* open to the device it describes, and its potential outputs; otherwise it fails to define any particular device. Chomsky makes it clear that he sees no problems of principle in this task; and it is this that I claim to be impossible when the 'device' under description is the human mind.[1] Minds do not merely make unpredictable changes of state; they enter states not belonging to a predictable set, and their ranges of possible inputs and outputs depend on their internal state.

One might, of course, argue that the range of possible mental states *is* in principle predictable, but that the prediction will involve concepts at a very different level from those with which linguistic semanticists and AI researchers work. Let me give an analogy. Someone familiar only with the flags of the chief nations of continental Europe might propose that there is some sort of natural law governing the range of possible flags: any flag must be an oblong made up of horizontal or vertical stripes in a selection of half a dozen primary colours. I could immediately refute this by showing him, say, the flags of Nepal and of the old Leeward Islands Colony, and arguing that the diversity of flags is limited only by the imagination of their designers and the need for distinctiveness. He might then reply that, although the law about stripes is clearly wrong, nevertheless there *are* constraints other than imagination and utility on the range of flags; any flag is an approximately two-dimensional arrangement of molecules of dye and cloth capable of flying from a pole, and chemists or physicists could in principle define a range of possible configurations of such molecules. This range would be inconceivably more numerous than the range permitted by the original theory about stripes, but it would nevertheless in principle be well-defined. It would even rule out some specifiable logical possibilities; thus there are presumably limits on the brightness of colours possible in a flag, and

---

[1] On pp. 193–4 of my *Form of Language* I argued that the above considerations might possibly be compatible with predictive theories about certain very restricted aspects of natural-language semantics. I now regard this as hopelessly optimistic.

on the fineness of graphic detail. Likewise, one might suggest, a particular structure of concepts and beliefs will ultimately, in principle, be reducible to an enormously complex configuration of cell-connexions in a man's brain, and again the range of possible brain configurations will in principle be definable – perhaps even changes of brain-configuration will ultimately be predictable.

Even if I were to concede this, it would do little to mitigate the case against Linguistic Semantics and AI. It is crucial to these disciplines that the primitive elements they work with are items that can be interpreted conceptually, and if the range of possible intellectual states is well-defined only in the sense just suggested then Linguistic Semantics and AI can say nothing useful about it; only neurophysiologists, at some very distant date, might be able to construct scientific theories about the data which linguistic semanticists and AI researchers are vainly trying to explain.

But in any case, I see little reason to concede the point in question. The analogy with flags is a poor one, because we in fact know a fair amount about the relationship between molecular structure and the gross appearance of things such as dyed textiles, whereas it is difficult to see how one could begin to explain ideas in terms of neurons and synapses. Unless one is committed to monism as an axiomatic faith, it seems more reasonable to hold a dualist view of the relationship between mind and body. To quote Popper, the alternative view

consists, essentially, of a . . . prophecy about the future results of brain research and of their impact. This prophecy is baseless. No attempt is made to base it upon a survey of recent brain research. The opinion of researchers who . . . started as identity theorists, but ended as dualists . . . is ignored. No attempt is made to resolve the difficulties of materialism by argument. No alternatives to materialism are even considered.[1]

One might also argue that the great majority of individuals are not constantly being creative in their thinking, and that, insofar as they are not creative, it is possible formally to model their thought-processes. I feel dubious about this; the idea that 'ordinary people'

---

[1] Popper and Eccles, *The Self and its Brain*, p. 97. Cautionary remarks about Popper's forthright dismissal of monism are made by John Beloff on pp. 271–2 of 'Is mind autonomous?', *British Journal for the Philosophy of Science*, vol. 29, 1978.

do not normally think creatively strikes me as a manifestation of the intellectual snobbery which is not uncommon among the university-trained. But again, even if I concede the point it does little to reduce the force of my criticism of Linguistic Semantics and Artificial Intelligence; the proviso 'insofar as they are not creative' seems to rob these disciplines of their theoretical interest. We could paraphrase the point by saying that Artificial Intelligence researchers can simulate just those aspects of human cognitive processes which do not display intelligence (since I take it that creativity is an essential component of behaviour that we think of as 'intelligent'[1]). Of course there may be *practical* goals for which this is adequate; not all AI research, by any means, aims at pure academic investigation of the workings of mind. Unlike AI, however, Linguistic Semantics has no applied branch; its practitioners justify its existence exclusively in terms of its status as a pure theoretical science. If many individuals really are intellectually uncreative for long stretches of their lives, then a linguistic semanticist's description of the language of a community might perhaps be justifiable as a rough-and-ready account of the intellectual states and state-transitions which are relatively likely to occur in the less imaginative members of the community at a particular point in its history; but such a description, though it would need to be considerably fuller and subtler than the kinds of semantic analysis actually produced by linguistic semanticists today, would have no theoretical status – it could not count as an empirical scientific prediction, because there can be no *guarantee* that any given human on a given occasion will be wholly unimaginative.

And, if semantic description cannot be scientific, then so far as I can see the complex apparatus of formal symbolism used by

---

[1] I do not suggest that creativity and intelligence are identical; M. A. Wallach and N. Kogan have demonstrated that they are distinct psychological traits (*Modes of Thinking in Young Children*, Holt, Rinehart & Winston, 1965). Intelligent behaviour, on the creative view of mind, requires both the production of novel hypotheses and their evaluation. Children could score highly on Wallach and Kogan's creativity tests by producing novel but quite inappropriate ideas; and conversely many I.Q. tests, including some used by Wallach and Kogan, provide the subject with a range of alternative hypotheses (in the shape of a 'multiple choice' of answers) and require him only to evaluate.

Linguistic Semantics serves little purpose. Formal symbolism normally functions in Theoretical Linguistics as a means of expressing a metatheory about linguistic universals; linguists define particular formal conventions for writing rules of grammar in order to claim that only rules which can be stated within those conventions are usable by humans.[1] But if there are no constraints on the semantic system of an individual speaker there can hardly be constraints on the diversity of semantic systems across languages. The job of giving approximate historical accounts of the most conventional usage of words at particular times does not require esoteric formalisms. It was already done, about as well as it could be done, decades before Linguistic Semantics was heard of – in the columns of the *Oxford English Dictionary* and its counterparts in other nations.

[1] cf. my *Form of Language*, p. 86ff.

VI

We turn now from the semantic aspect of language study to syntax, to see whether the objections to Theoretical Linguistics apply equally there.

Syntax is conceptually a rather easier subject to think about than semantics. Semantics is concerned with relationships, and rather subtle relationships at that, among the forms of a language, and between linguistic forms and the world in which the language is spoken. Syntax is concerned simply with the membership of a language, with specifying what counts as an example of the language. A syntactic description of a language – in linguists' parlance, a 'grammar' – is essentially a definition of the class of all and only those sequences of elementary units (words, or 'morphemes' – the roots and affixes which go to make up complex words) which count as sentences of the language. A grammar of English is a theory which predicts that, for instance, the sequence *The quality of mercy is not strained* is a well-formed, or 'grammatical', English sentence while, for instance, the sequence **Strained not is mercy of quality the* is not; and we judge a grammar by checking that the sequences it predicts to be grammatical correspond to the utterances actually used by speakers of the language. (It is conventional to mark with an asterisk sequences which are claimed to be ungrammatical.)

In practice, of course, syntax involves a rich system of concepts over and above the properties of grammaticality and ungrammaticality attributed to word-sequences. The grammar taught at school involves a categorization of words into parts of speech such as adjective, noun, and so on, sequences of words are categorized into various types of phrase (e.g. adjectival phrase, noun-phrase, and clause (e.g. relative clause, co-ordinate clause), and various syntactic relationships such as 'government' and 'concord' are recognized as obtaining between different elements within the same sentence. But these theoretical notions are ultimately justified (insofar as they *are* justified at all – traditional school grammar has its limitations as an account of English syntax, though the objectionable points are perhaps matters of detail rather than crucial flaws) in terms of the work they do in helping to specify the range of grammatical sentences.

Thus, we categorize *mercy* together with *humility, brightness*, and so forth as a single 'part of speech' (which, as it happens, we call 'noun') because, where one member of the category can occur in a grammatical sentence, other members of the category will be substitutable for it while preserving grammaticality. *The quality of humility is not strained*, or *The quality of brightness is not strained*, are just as much potential English sentences as the line that Shakespeare actually wrote. (True, not every noun could be substituted for *mercy* in that sentence; it is questionable whether one can regard e.g. *The quality of dog is not strained* as English. One can reply to this, first, that the traditional part-of-speech analysis taught in schools, according to which *mercy* and *dog* belong to a single category, is only a somewhat crude approximation – as already hinted – to the analyses evolved by modern linguistics; and, secondly, that membership of a common syntactic category implies not identity but only broad similarity between the respective environments in which various words can grammatically occur.) 'Noun-phrases' are sequences of words (such as article + adjective + common noun) which can substitute for free-standing proper nouns; if we know that *John is unwell* is grammatical, we know that *The young pianist is unwell* will be equally grammatical.

Likewise, 'relative clauses' are a range of word-sequences constructed according to a common principle, and which can be substituted for one another, preserving grammaticality, in a given sentential framework. Any relative clause can be thought of as the result of taking a declarative sentence, dropping one of its nounphrases, and replacing it by a relative pronoun in initial position. Thus *the postman gave Mary a kiss* is a declarative sentence; and *who gave Mary a kiss, whom the postman gave a kiss*, and *which the postman gave Mary* are relative clauses. The frame *The one . . . was sweet* becomes an equally good English sentence, whichever of these clauses is inserted in the blank.

Again, the statement that there is a relationship of concord with respect to number between, for instance, the word *man* and the word *walks* in *The old man walks unsteadily* means simply that if either one of these words is changed from singular to plural form the other must be changed to correspond, or the result will be ungrammatical; English-speakers do not say **The old men walks unsteadily*.

As speakers of a language, it is true, we do not commonly think of grammatical concepts such as those just mentioned as mere by-products of the process of distinguishing grammatical from ungrammatical word-sequences. Many of us are much more at home with notions like 'noun', 'relative clause' than we are with the idea of drawing a boundary between sequences such as *The quality of mercy is not strained* and **Strained not is mercy of quality the*. At school we are normally taught the former conceptual apparatus without the latter issue ever being mentioned. (In English lessons children are taught how to analyse the sentences that people actually do say or write, without their attention being drawn to the contrast between those sequences and others, such as the one just quoted, which lie outside the language.) This is because, for practical purposes, people are obviously more interested in characterizing what does occur than what does not. But, if one calls into question the grammatical apparatus used to characterize what occurs, the defence of this apparatus must appeal to the contrast between what occurs and what does not.

Syntactic analysis of a natural language, then, involves specifying the class of grammatical sentences of the language, in other words partitioning the class of all logically possible sequences of words of the language into a grammatical and an ungrammatical class. This goal was first made fully explicit by Chomsky,[1] and this is one of Chomsky's most noteworthy contributions to linguistics.

Now, clearly, the kind of objections I have made to the programme of semantic description of natural languages could quite conceivably be raised against syntactic description also. In the semantic case, I argued, it made little sense to try to specify rules which would predict whether or not a given consequent follows from a given set of premisses, because issues of that kind are not determinate in the real world which our scientific theories purport

---

[1] On p. 13 of *Syntactic Structures* (*Janua Linguarum, series minor*, 4), Mouton (the Hague), 1957.

to describe. Human beings infer not by rule but creatively, so that we modify the semantic relationships of our language in the act of using the language; a linguist may be able to describe anecdotally what has happened to semantic relationships in the past, but he will not be able to predict by general rules how the language will be used on occasions not yet observed. Similarly, one might feel, the membership of word-sequences in a language is not a determinate issue. We can examine the word-sequences that have been uttered in the past, and we will expect that new sentences uttered in the future will manifest *some* 'family resemblances' to those that have been uttered. However, the invention of ways of seeing previously unused word-sequences as analogous to sequences which have already been used (and thus as themselves worth using) may be a creative, open-ended activity; if so, there will be no set principles enabling us to divide the infinity of word-sequences that we have not actually encountered in use into 'grammatical' and 'ungrammatical' subsets.

My account, above, of the aim of syntactic analysis took for granted that grammaticality *is* determinate: I argued that *The quality of humility is not strained* is a 'potential' English sentence (although as far as I know I have never encountered it used in practice), while *Strained not is mercy of quality the* is not. But so much the worse, the reader may feel, for my account; perhaps all I am really saying is that I personally can see links between the former of these two sequences and sentences (such as the Shakespeare line) which I have met, and can accordingly see a possible use for the former sequence, while I cannot see any interesting or important way in which the latter sequence resembles utterances I have encountered, so that I cannot imagine how anyone might find a use for that sequence. This could be merely a matter of my limited imagination. The distinction between the two word-sequences might have no more to do with the nature of the English language, as an enduring phenomenon, than, say, the fact that one type of motor has already been invented by someone while another type still awaits its inventor has to do with the question whether they are efficient, useful kinds of machine.

This view of grammaticality as creatively indeterminate seems to me entirely coherent, and it has been held by one eminent

contemporary linguist, Charles Hockett.[1] However, I do not
myself believe it is correct. It is true that unstudied speech contains many bizarrely unconventional arrangements of words, and
Hockett lays considerable stress on this. Someone who reads the
transcript of a tape-recorded dialogue in which he took part often
finds himself wondering 'Could I really have spoken as ungram-
matically as that?' But in this case Chomsky's notions of 'competence' and 'performance' do seem applicable. It is very
plausible to treat the idiosyncratic concatenations of words that
occur in unplanned speech as resulting from failure to conform
perfectly to complex but nevertheless determinate conventions
that define what word-sequences are grammatical.

One reason why this view of the matter seems appropriate is
that, when people speak more deliberately or practise a speech to
themselves before delivering it, their output contains far fewer
syntactic unconventionalities. Likewise, the reaction of the man
who reads a transcript of his spontaneous discourse is that many of
his word-sequences were *wrong*, and this feeling is far too strong to
be explained away as an artefact of the rather sketchy training in
'correct usage' which many of us received in our schooldays.
Speaking, then, seems in its grammatical aspect to be somewhat
like playing a difficult piece of music on the piano: one may make a
hash of the piece, but it remains true that there exists an ideal
composition to which one's output is a poor approximation.
Notice how different this is from the case of metaphor. It would
surely be implausible, not to say insulting to many of our greatest
writers, to regard metaphor as a kind of 'mistake' which one could
weed out by careful attention to what one was saying. Likewise, we
saw that there was little justification for treating the difficulty

---

[1] C. F. Hockett, *The State of the Art* (*Janua Linguarum, series minor*, 73), Mouton
(the Hague), 1968, esp. §6.1; 'Where the tongue slips', in *To Honor Roman
Jakobson*, vol. ii (*Janua Linguarum, series major*, 32), Mouton (the Hague), 1967,
§§10–11; *Man's Place in Nature*, McGraw-Hill, 1973, ch. 8; and cf. p. 370 of Z. S.
Harris, 'Transformational theory', *Language*, vol. 41, 1965. I criticize Hockett's
argument on pp. 57–9 of my *Form of Language*. In earlier periods of the history of
linguistics this view of grammaticality as creatively indeterminate seems often to
have been taken for granted as a point scarcely needing to be argued; see e.g.
pp. 3–4 of August Schleicher, *Die Sprachen Europas in systematischer Uebersicht* (vol. ii
of *Sprachvergleichende* or *Linguistische Untersuchungen*), H. B. König (Bonn), 1850.

speakers encounter in distinguishing analytic from synthetic sentences as a mere 'performance' problem, since in this case too it is hard to see what one could point to as an indication that speakers have an underlying 'competence' to draw the distinction sharply.

The claim that syntax is determinate and uncreative does not require us to view grammaticality as a sharp yes-or-no affair. We saw in the case of semantics that the suggestion that inference might be controlled by probabilistic rather than absolute rules was quite distinct from the suggestion that inference is a creative activity. Likewise, we may well reject Hockett's view of syntax as creative in favour of Chomsky's idea that syntax is rule-governed, without necessarily agreeing with Chomsky that the criterion of grammaticality partitions the class of sequences of words of a language into two sharply distinct subclasses. A number of linguists in recent years have argued that grammaticality may be a cline, and have proposed ways of modifying techniques of syntactic description in order to allow grammars to predict varying degrees of grammaticality, and there appears to be considerable force in some of their arguments;[1] but they certainly cannot be taken to have shown that there is anything intrinsically wrong-headed about the enterprise of syntactic description, only that that enterprise is rather more complex than was once supposed.

To sum up, then, the task of constructing syntactic descriptions of the various natural languages seems to be an entirely appropriate goal for linguists to set themselves, and I have no quarrel with this aspect of the discipline. Chomsky's account, in *Syntactic Structures*, of how it is possible to give a finite definition of a natural language containing infinitely many grammatical sentences was in my view an important contribution to linguistics. A grammar of English can be just as much a predictive scientific theory as can a theory in physics or meteorology. (One can argue that the approach to this goal which contemporary linguists adopt in practice is an approach which renders their grammars unem-

---

[1] See particularly B. A. Mohan, 'Acceptability testing and fuzzy grammar', in S. Greenbaum, ed., *Acceptability in Language (Contributions to the Sociology of Language*, 17), Mouton (the Hague), 1977. With hindsight I now believe that my own rejection of 'probabilistic syntax' in *The Form of Language* (p. 53) may have been over hasty.

pirical and hence unscientific;[1] but that is a side-issue here – the point is that grammar-writing *can* be a scientific enterprise, and often it is.)

However, for the contemporary linguist, description of individual languages is by no means the ultimate purpose of his discipline. Grammar-writing is merely a means to an end: the end being a 'general linguistic theory', a scientific theory of the phenomenon of human *language*, of which individual *languages* are mere examples. The social structure of contemporary linguistics tends to assign to the 'data-oriented' scholars who do the work of describing particular languages a fairly lowly status compared to that of the theoreticians. Fortunately the number of linguists is too few and the degree of division of labour too limited for a rigid class structure to have emerged within the discipline, but the tendency is undeniable. The many scholars who publish both on syntactic analysis of an individual language or languages and on general linguistic theory make it clear that the former aspect of their work is subsidiary in their own minds to the latter. This situation is specifically a contemporary phenomenon; as mentioned above, linguists working in the tradition shaped by Franz Boas and Leonard Bloomfield had quite different priorities and saw 'general linguistics' as a tool to aid them in their primary goal of describing individual languages.

To say that a phenomenon is an appropriate subject for scientific theorizing is to say that the various instances of that phenomenon all obey some general laws, so that they resemble one another more than, logically, they need. If there is a true and non-trivial general linguistic theory, then all human languages must be in some sense cut to a common pattern. Another way of putting this would be to say that there must be universal properties of human language.

Someone who is attracted by the creative view of mind will incline to suppose that this is not so. Since languages are the products of human minds, the creative-minder will expect the languages of different human societies to develop syntactically as well as semantically in quite different and unpredictable ways. The creative-minder may be unworried by the observation, dis-

[1] Cf. my *Form of Language*, ch. 4; *Liberty and Language*, ch. 6.

cussed above, that the utterances produced by an *individual speaker* seem to be limited to a determinate set of syntactic possibilities, since he can explain this by pointing out that linguistic behaviour is normally social (soliloquy is an unusual use of language) and that the need to conform in order to be understood accounts for the fact that adults avoid syntactic creativity. (In the case of semantics, as we saw, it is impossible to go on applying a language to an unpredictable world without being creative; in the case of syntax nothing forces us to be continually creative, so we are not.) But the creative-minder will insist that nothing internal to men forces the languages of different *groups* of people to resemble one another syntactically, if those groups are linked by no social contacts. Even the creative-minder (or perhaps one should rather say 'the creative-minder in particular') accepts that there exists one kind of constraint on the products of human minds, namely that unsuccessful ones are weeded out in the light of experience. Languages have jobs to do, and if it can be shown that some kinds of language would be relatively inefficient at doing those jobs then the creative-minder will have no objection to a theory which predicts that such languages will not be used. But the creative-minder will not expect to find any universals of human language except universals which make languages fitter to perform their functions.

The attitude of the Descriptivists to language universals was much as this would lead us to expect – as witness the Joos quotation on p. 15 above, or compare Edward Sapir:

Speech is a human activity that varies without assignable limit as we pass from social group to social group, because it is a purely historical heritage of the group, the product of long-continued social usage. It varies as all creative effort varies.[1]

The grammars produced by these scholars emphasized the idiosyncratic, quirky features of the languages described, and they consciously strove to eradicate the provincialism which leads Europeans to imagine that all languages of the world will be structured more or less similarly to English, French, or Latin. The theoretical linguists of today approach language in just the opposite spirit. They recognize, of course, that languages do differ

[1] E. Sapir, *Language*, Harcourt, Brace & World (New York), 1921, p. 4.

in many respects, but for them the differences are relatively superficial and uninteresting matters which merely distract attention from strong underlying similarities. The central kernel of Chomsky's linguistic theory, in particular, is the claim that the syntactic structures of all natural languages can be observed to conform to common principles, and that these syntactic universals (which cannot be explained away as making the languages which possess them relatively 'efficient' or 'useful') constitute strong empirical evidence for the limited view of mind.

In Chomsky's pattern of thought, the semantic issues considered in earlier chapters actually play a quite peripheral role; Chomsky himself did not discuss semantics in his earlier writings, and he has written only a small amount about it subsequently (although he has said enough to make it clear that he approves of the general approach of Linguistic Semantics initiated by some of his followers). As suggested above, in the semantic domain linguists commonly presuppose, rather than citing evidence for, the view that there is a universal system underlying diverse human languages. It is in the case of syntax, which is Chomsky's central concern, that he and other linguists put forward serious claims to have discovered evidence in favour of the belief that the overall structure of language is innate rather than learned – that we are able to master the complex systems called 'English', 'Chinese', and so on, not because we are born with fertile, original minds endlessly ready to generate novel solutions for the endlessly unexpected problems with which the world confronts them, but because we happen to inherit complex psychological machinery designed specifically for processing languages of a particular structure (just as peacocks happen to inherit a particular complex kind of tail). Chomsky and other theoretical linguists make only occasional, fragmentary remarks about the notion that there are logically possible semantic systems which are unnatural for humans (cf. Chomsky's claim about the hypothetical word 'LIMB' discussed on p. 40 above, for instance). In the domain of syntax, on the other hand, Chomsky and his followers readily cite wide ranges of grammatical systems which are easy to define but which are not in practice used – because, the theoretical linguists claim, we are built so that we *cannot* use them, so that even if human infants were somehow to be exposed to such systems instead of those of their parents' languages they would no more be able to learn to use them than they could 'learn' to digest grass. It is this argument about syntactic universals which has caused linguistics over the last decade or so to come to seem enormously important to practitioners of subjects such as philosophy and psychology, and indeed to sections of the general educated public.

Chomsky himself would not agree that his theory of linguistic universals constitutes the *only* empirical evidence for the idea that linguistic structure is innate. He frequently suggests that this can be confirmed also by reference to the process of language-acquisition by children within any individual language-community. Chomsky argues, first, that children master their mother-tongue within a remarkably short period of time, and that this cannot reasonably be explained except on the assumption that they 'know' the broad outlines of syntax, which are common to all languages, before they begin, so that only details remain to be filled in from experience. Secondly, Chomsky suggests that the very fact that children invariably succeed in mastering their parents' language at all requires the nativist hypothesis, in view of the limited quantity and 'degenerate' quality of the data available to them. Adults' speech is distorted by the factors of 'perform-ance' – they speak in fits and starts, break sentences off in the middle, become tangled up in their own grammar, and so forth – yet children always manage to acquire a system matching their elders' 'competence', which suggests that they must begin with knowledge that allows them to recognize the imperfections of adults' speech as imperfections; and furthermore, even ignoring the 'badness' of the child's data, there just is not enough available to determine his elders' language uniquely. Thirdly, Chomsky claims that different individuals' degree of mastery of their mother-tongue does not vary with their level of general intelli-gence, which suggests that language is acquired by means of psychological machinery geared specifically to that purpose rather than as a particular instance of the general human ability to solve diverse problems by flexible thinking. 'Mere exposure to the language, for a remarkably short period, seems to be all that the normal child requires to develop the competence of the native speaker.'[1] 'The native speaker has acquired a grammar on the basis of very restricted and degenerate evidence; the grammar has empirical consequences that extend far beyond the evidence'.[2] 'We observe . . . that knowledge of language is . . . to a large extent independent of intelligence'.[3] 'To a very good first approximation, individuals are indistinguishable (apart from gross deficits and abnormalities) in their ability to acquire grammar'.[4] Similar remarks occur in many of Chomsky's writings.

However, these arguments seem to have very little force.

In the first place, the argument from the rapidity of language acquisition seems wholly empty unless we are given some quantification of 'maximum rate at which things in general can be learned' and of 'degree of overall complexity of a natural language' allowing us to calculate that children could not complete the task of language-acquisition in the observed time if they had to start from scratch. Chomsky makes no such proposals, and I doubt whether it is meaningful to think of reducing such matters to numbers. Putting the same point another way, this argument of Chomsky's dissolves as soon as one asks what particular period of time children would have to take to acquire their first language before Chomsky would be content to regard the non-nativist account of language-acquisition as plausible. Whether one thinks of first-language acquisition as a fast or a slow process has more to do, I suspect, with one's prior assumptions with respect to the creative- v. limited-mind issue than with any observable facts; I find it easy to see children as surprisingly slow at picking up their parents' language.[5]

---

[1] 'Explanatory models in linguistics', in E. Nagel, P. Suppes and A. Tarski, eds., *Logic, Methodology and Philosophy of Science: Proceedings of the 1960 International Congress*, Stanford University Press (Stanford, Calif.), 1962, p. 529.

[2] *Language and Mind*, Harcourt, Brace & World (New York), 1968, p. 23.

[3] ibid., p. 53.

[4] *Reflections*, p. 144.

[5] Chomsky says little to indicate at what age he thinks of the average child as having completed the task of grammar-acquisition, and this clearly depends on what one regards as essential to a language. One of Chomsky's most enthusiastic supporters among experimental psychologists, David McNeill, claims that the syntactic aspects of a mother-tongue are completely mastered by the age of four ('The capacity for the ontogenesis of grammar', in D. I. Slobin, ed., *The Ontogenesis of Grammar*, Academic Press, 1971, p. 17). I find this claim fantastic

On the second point, there is some dispute about how 'degenerate' the adult speech available to an infant really is; some studies
suggest that the child's data are better than Chomsky supposes.[1]
But, leaving this point aside, there appears to be a major paradox
in Chomsky's argument: if the data available to an individual
during his childhood are logically insufficient to determine his
parents' language uniquely, how can the data available to a
linguistic scholar about the language which that individual has
'internalized' by maturity be sufficient to show that the language
in question is indeed identical to that of his parents? The child has
to infer a language from samples of speech provided by his
parents; the linguist has to infer the languages of the respective
generations from samples of their speech, and then compare them.
Thus the linguist's task is actually greater than the child's, while
on the other hand the child will normally be able to devote himself
much more single-mindedly than a professional academic with
many calls on his time to the job of linguistic analysis. So the
linguist can never be in a position to know that the child has
inferred the 'correct' grammar from his data, and only if he did
know this would the fact that data underdetermine language be
evidence for innate knowledge of language.

As for the third point, namely the alleged uniformity of linguistic attainments as between individuals of very different levels of
general intelligence, I find this an odd view to be held by a
university teacher. Undergraduate students, after all, represent a
fairly narrow segment at the upper end of the spectrum of intelligence manifested by the population as a whole, yet even among
undergraduates there are great differences in the ability to use
(and, at least apparently, to comprehend – but it is harder to be
sure of this) the more complex of the various sentences allowed by
the grammar of English. Many people who are very far indeed
from the level of 'gross [mental] deficits and abnormalities' produce word-sequences to which it is impossible to assign an
interpretation, when the intrinsic complexity of their subject

unless Mc Neill counts many of the subtler points of syntax as not genuinely part
of the language, and it is not clear what could justify such a decision.
[1] See e.g. §1 of Susan Ervin-Tripp, 'An overview of theories of grammatical
development', in Slobin, op. cit.

forces them to go beyond the quite simple structures which are adequate for the majority of human purposes. (It is true that these differences may be evened out to some extent in the case of spoken language, where everybody goes wrong far sooner than in writing; but in the first place I do not think the differences are wholly absent even in speech, and whether they are or not there seem to be no good grounds for ignoring the evidence of written-language behaviour in this connexion.) I do not even believe that the syntactic differences between the usage of more and less competent users of language are restricted to the degree of complexity of sentences constructed in conformity to identical grammars; I have the strong impression that there are particular syntactic constructions, used relatively infrequently even by those who know them, which are mastered only by the more competent speakers of a language. (Is every adult English-speaker familiar – to give just one instance – with the construction exemplified by an adverbial clause such as *Surprising as it may seem?*)

If Chomsky intends his claim about indistinguishability of individuals with respect to their degree of linguistic competence to be understood as unrestrictedly as his words suggest, one wishes that he would quote some evidence for such surprising findings. If, on the other hand, Chomsky means merely that even individuals at the lower end of the normal intelligence range succeed in mastering the most frequently used syntactic constructions and employing them in sentences which do not involve a high degree of syntactic complexity, then one wonders whether this can really be taken as evidence for a sharp distinction between general intelligence and linguistic competence. The motive for an emotionally normal member of any human community to acquire the core abilities involved in using the language of his community is so immensely weighty that it seems predictable enough that even mentally handicapped persons would make that a high priority in the exploitation of what limited intellectual capacity they possess. There are surely very few other intellectual achievements which are anywhere near as worthwhile in terms of frustration eliminated as the achievement of joining the club of those who can communicate by means of a sophisticated language.

None of Chomsky's arguments from the facts of language-acquisition, then, seems to have a great deal of merit, and we shall not consider them further at this point (though we shall return to them in Chapter VIII, below). The argument from syntactic universals common to different languages, on the other hand, cannot be dismissed so lightly.

The claim that there are constraints on the syntactic diversity of natural languages is easily illustrated. One of Chomsky's favourite examples has to do with methods of forming yes/no questions. ('Yes/no questions' are questions such as *Is this the colour that Fiona wanted?* as opposed to '*wh* questions' – e.g. *Which colour did Fiona want?* – that cannot be answered by a yes or no.)

Different languages do vary considerably in their question constructions. In many languages, yes/no questions are produced by simply adding an interrogative particle to the end of the corresponding statement; in Chinese the word *ma* is enough to convert the translation of *This is the colour that Fiona wanted* into the question form. Other languages, and English is one of them, have more complicated arrangements. In English, the conversion of a statement into a yes/no question involves at least the following operations. First, pick out the finite verb of the main clause of the statement. Check whether it is a part of one of the verbs *do, be, have*, or a modal such as *can*. (This is itself not a trivial task; if we were programming a computer to carry it out, we would have to remember to specify that *is, am, were*, etc. are parts of *be*.) If the verb is one of these, move it to the beginning of the sentence. If it is any other verb, convert it to its infinitive form (e.g. *broke* is replaced by *break*), and place at the beginning of the sentence that part of the verb *do* which corresponds to the inflexion that the main verb has just lost (e.g. *did* if the verb was *broke*).

I do not mean here to imply that when we ask a question we first frame a statement and then convert it into question form. Having learned how to produce questions, no doubt an adult Englishman constructs them independently of statements, and certainly he does not consciously go through either the rules just quoted or any others; the words seem to come to his lips automatically. But, although we are no more conscious of the processes underlying our syntactic behaviour than we are conscious of the action of our liver, there must be some unobserved processes leading to the observable behaviour, and the detailed account of the relationship between statements and yes/no questions suggests how complex those processes must be. (In fact there are subtleties omitted above; thus if the word found in the first step is part of the verb *have* one must check whether it is acting as a main verb or an auxiliary, since in the former case it is pedantic to move it to the beginning of the sentence without inserting *got* in its original place; the verb *need* counts as a modal for the purpose of questions but not for affirmative statements – *Need John go?* v. *John needs to go*; and so on.)

Now, Chomsky argues, if natural languages resort to rules as subtle as these for forming constructions as basic as the yes/no question, one can easily imagine further hypothetical rules that might occur in other languages. For instance, some language might contain the rule that yes/no questions were mirror-images (with respect to word-sequence) of the corresponding statements; thus, if English used this rule, the question about Fiona would run *Wanted Fiona that colour the is this?* Obviously this rule is 'unnatural' in the sense that it is very different from the rule which is actually used in our own language, but Chomsky claims that the 'mirror-image' rule is unnatural in a deeper sense. According to him, no rule of this general kind is found in *any* language used by humans, and that is not just because there are only so many languages spoken in the world but because the 'mirror-image' rule runs 'against the grain' of human language, as it were. Yet what is wrong with the rule? It is intrinsically simple enough; as Chomsky rightly says, a mathematician who considered sentences purely as abstract sequences of arbitrary symbols would regard the mirror-image rule as very much more straightforward than the actual rule obeyed by English questions. And, if we were capable of learning to use the mirror-image rule, it would surely serve the purpose fully as well as the actual English rule. The only requirement about questions that seems to be imposed on a language by the tasks it carries out is that it contain *some* device for tagging the expression of a proposition as interrogative rather than declarative, and there seems to be no *a priori* reason why the device of reversing the order of words should not work as well as the device which we use in English.

One feels, intuitively, that we would find it difficult or imposs-

ible to learn to use the mirror-image rule in practice, even dis-
counting the fact that we have grown accustomed to a different
rule (thus, although it is in any case fairly hard for an adult to
master a second language, the task of acquiring fluency in a
hypothetical language incorporating the mirror-image rule would
surely be on an altogether higher plane of difficulty). In *this* sense a
language incorporating the mirror-image rule would be 'inefficient'. But this is exactly what Chomsky is saying: what makes
the mirror-image rule unnatural is a fact about the way human
beings happen to be built, which determines what they can and
cannot learn readily to do and to understand. Once one concedes
the claim that it is no accident that human languages lack rules
akin to the mirror-image rule (and I believe one should concede
this claim), then one has conceded that there are limitations on the
syntactic diversity of natural languages.

Here I have set out to render the existence of such limitations
plausible by citing one instance of a hypothetical phenomenon
which violates them. For what follows it will be more important to
indicate the positive syntactic properties which are claimed to
characterize all natural languages.

The core of the theory of 'linguistic universals' has to do with the
notion of *hierarchy*. The basis of the grammar of any natural
language will be a set of rules of the kind which Chomsky calls
'context-free phrase-structure rules' (I call them 'constituency
rules'), which are rules of the form 'An X is (or, "can be") a Y
followed by a Z followed by a W'. (A constituency rule can
mention any number of categories after the 'is' or 'can be' – my
example involves a sequence of three categories, but there may be
more or less than three. Conventionally, constituency rules are
expressed symbolically by means of an arrow notation – the rule
just given would be stated as '$X \rightarrow YZW$'.) Thus, English
grammar might incorporate rules such as 'a Sentence is a Noun-
Phrase followed by a Predicate'; 'a Predicate can be an Intransitive Verb, or a Transitive Verb followed by a Noun-Phrase'; 'a
Noun-Phrase can be a Pronoun, or a Determiner followed by a
Noun followed optionally by a subordinate Sentence'; 'a Noun can
be the word *colour*, or the word *cake*, or . . .'.

Rules of this general form build up a sentence as a hierarchical nesting of lower-level categories within higher-level categories, with the lowest-level categories being the parts of speech that classify individual words and the highest-level category being that of the Sentence. Thus, the statement *This is the colour that Fiona wanted* might be structured by the grammar in approximately this way:

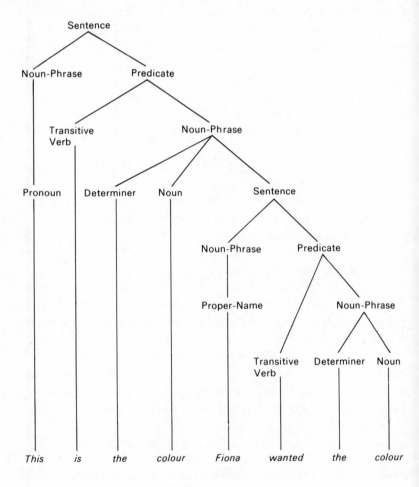

I do not suggest that all the details here are necessarily correct; for instance, if we set out to make the grammar more inclusive we would soon find good reason to distinguish copular verbs such as *be* from true transitive verbs such as *want*. But the details are not what matter; the theory of linguistic universals (or at least the relatively reliable 'hard core' of the theory) does not specify any particular categories to occupy the place of X, Y, Z in my definition of the notion 'constituency rule' (except that, by convention, the most inclusive category is always called 'Sentence').[1] The point is that the grammar of any natural language involves rules of this general type, so that any sentence of a natural language will be described as possessing a tree-structure akin to the one diagrammed opposite, though the particular trees associated with different sentences in a given language (let alone sentences of different languages) will be very different in detail.

In order to encompass the full range of syntactic possibilities found in a typical language, these constituency rules have to be supplemented with further rules (called 'transformational rules') which modify the structures produced by the constituency rules. For instance, the yes/no question *Is this the colour that Fiona wanted?* will be derived by applying a transformational rule to the structure diagrammed, turning it into a new tree-structure having the word *is* in the leftmost position; and Sentence elements, such as *Fiona wanted the colour*, which occur in relative clause position in the tree (that is, following a Noun within a Noun-Phrase) will be converted into well-formed relative clauses by applying another transformation as discussed on page 105: *Fiona wanted the colour* will become *that Fiona wanted*. These transformational rules are again centrally concerned with hierarchical structure; they convert word-sequences into new word-sequences in ways which depend crucially on the tree-structures associated with the sequences. In Chomsky's terms, transformational rules are 'structure-dependent'. Thus, our statement on p. 117 of the operations for forming English questions included the instruction 'pick out the finite verb of the main clause'. Translated into terms of the above

---

[1] In fact Chomsky has suggested that the individual syntactic categories are universal (*Aspects of the Theory of Syntax*, p. 28), but Hilary Putnam has shown this claim to be vacuous ('The "innateness hypothesis" and explanatory models in linguistics', *Synthese*, vol. 17, 1967, pp. 12–22, see p. 135 of the reprint in J. R. Searle, ed., *The Philosophy of Language*, Oxford University Press, 1971); cf. p. 187 of my 'Linguistic universals as evidence for empiricism', *Journal of Linguistics*, vol. 14, 1978.

tree diagram, this means 'pick out the Verb which is linked to the topmost Sentence node of the whole tree without an intervening Sentence node' – the word *wanted* is eliminated because of the subordinate Sentence node which dominates it in this tree (though there will be other declarative sentences in which *wanted* is the operative word for forming questions – *is* is chosen here not because it is the right sort of verb but because it is in the right place in the constituency structure). Again, the relative-clause-forming transformation has to pick out a sequence of words (to be replaced by a relative pronoun) which may be of very diverse kinds and lengths (in the case discussed, the relevant sequence is *the colour*), but the word-sequence chosen must always be traceable higher in the tree to a single node labelled 'Noun-Phrase'.

Now we see the basis for our feeling that the hypothetical mirror-image rule discussed above ran 'against the grain' of natural language. What is wrong with the mirror-image rule is that it operates on a sequence of words quite independently of the hierarchical structuring of the sequence. One can apply the mirror-image rule to *This is the colour that Fiona wanted* without needing to know anything about the constituency structure of the sentence – someone who knew no English at all could apply the mirror-image rule to the sentence quite successfully. In order to apply the actual English question rule, on the other hand, it is essential to know the grammar of the sentence so as to be able to pick out *is* as the operative word specified by the rule. The theory does not say that every rule of grammar of a natural language will depend crucially on hierarchical structure in this way – there will be some rules (such as the Chinese question-rule which runs 'Add *ma* at the end of the sentence') that are too simple to constitute tests of the theory. What the theory does say is that whenever a rule is more complex, so that it has a relatively 'global' effect on a word-sequence, it will be complex in a particular way – the way summed up in the term 'structure-dependence'.

The observation that syntax is hierarchical is by no means original to modern linguistics, of course. Constituency structure, and structure-dependent transformational rules, have been taken for granted (though not under those names) in discussions of language for centuries. What is new is, first, the observation that there is nothing logically necessary about this central role of hierarchical structure (one can perfectly easily define hypothetical 'languages', i.e. batteries of word-sequences, whose principles of well-formedness have nothing to do with hierarchy – though it is very difficult to imagine what it would be to use such a system as one's mother-tongue);[1] and, secondly, the construction of an explicit, formal theory which purports to demarcate in a precise and therefore testable way the boundary between those batteries of word-sequences which are potentially usable by humans as their mother-tongue and the unnatural languages which are not.[2]

It is important to be clear about the logical structure of the argument by which linguists infer their biological limited-mind theory from universals of language. The argument runs, in essence, as follows: 'All known human languages possess certain common syntactic properties. Attribution of these properties to languages is not tautologous – there is nothing in the meaning of the word "language" which implies that anything called a "language" must necessarily have the features in question. If we suppose that humans inherit certain complex, fixed mental structuring, it would follow very naturally that this structuring would impose rigid requirements on the languages that humans could use, so that we would expect to find that the various human languages share common structural features. In the absence of alternative explanations for the linguistic universals, we should infer that this hypothesis of innate mental structuring is the correct explanation.'

Clearly this argument is vulnerable in several respects. Most obviously, it fails immediately if one can show that the alleged linguistic universals are not in fact universal – that some actual human languages fail to conform to them. More subtly, it fails if one can demonstrate the universals to be in some way logically necessary; that is, if one can show that, independently of the

---

[1] For examples of hypothetical, syntactically 'unnatural' languages see pp. 41–2 of my *Form of Language*.

[2] Chomsky's general theory of syntax is formalized in his *Logical Structure of Linguistic Theory* (written 1955; published by Plenum Press, New York, 1975) – on which see my review article 'What was transformational grammar?', *Lingua*, vol. 48, 1979, pp. 355–78.

creative-mind v. limited-mind issue, one would want to understand the term 'language' in such a way that a hypothetical system failing to conform to the universals would not be recognized as a 'language' no matter what similarities with actual human languages it might manifest in other respects. By far the most important respect in which the argument is vulnerable, though, is that it fails if one can find an alternative explanation for the linguistic universals. As Hilary Putnam puts it, the argument depends on a rhetorical 'What else?': it offers one explanation for the universals and asks 'What else could account for the observations?'[1]

The first point, that the linguistic universals must be genuinely 'universal', can be dealt with fairly briefly; I do not believe it leads to real problems for the limited-mind argument. Certainly there have been various false claims made by linguists about linguistic universals, but I have seen no evidence tending to suggest that the 'hard core' of syntactic universals having to do with hierarchy fail to hold true for any human language. Linguists' detailed proposals about just what phenomena can and cannot occur in natural languages are constantly being modified as linguistic research continues, but no one has ever suggested that some natural languages might not structure their sentences hierarchically at all, so that notions such as 'phrase' and 'clause' would be inapplicable; and, although the extent to which structure-dependent transformational rules are needed in various languages is debated, the claim that there are no clearly structure-*independent* rules in natural languages (apart from rules which are too simple to test the theory of structure-dependence) has as far as I know gone completely unchallenged.

What of the second vulnerable aspect of the argument – that the universals may be logically necessary? Here, much depends on how one interprets the word 'language'. Theoretical linguists work with a very abstract definition of 'language'; for them, a 'language' is simply a class of sequences of elements drawn from a finite

---

[1] 'The "innateness hypothesis"', in J. R. Searle, ed., op. cit., p. 133. Putnam objects to the 'What else?' character of Chomsky's theory primarily in connexion with his argument from the alleged rapidity of language acquisition, discussed above.

vocabulary. Thus the English language is equated with the class of those sequences of English words or English sounds which constitute grammatical English sentences. Given this definition it is clearly not a logical truism that all actually occurring languages are hierarchically structured, since it is easy to define hypothetical classes of word-sequences which are not; for instance, the class of all and only those sequences of English words within which the words occur in alphabetical order is a 'language' in the defined sense whose 'grammar' has nothing at all to do with hierarchy (and of course it is a 'language' which no human community uses as its mother-tongue, as predicted by the theory of universals).[1]

But it is clear that in everyday usage the word 'language' carries more meaning than this; there are things which would count as 'languages' under the above definition which we do not think of as languages in real life. Consider for instance the finite set of elements such as 'switch on ignition', 'shift into first gear', and so on, constituting the separate actions which one performs in driving a car. (We had better leave out movements of the steering wheel, since these vary continuously rather than discretely.) Now we could think of a car trip as the 'utterance' of a long sequence of these units, and we could treat drivers as people competent in a 'language' whose sentences are such sequences. Some sequences will be 'ungrammatical' in this language: for instance, any sequence containing a shift into reverse immediately after a shift into top. I do not know whether or not the 'language' consisting of all and only the 'grammatical' sequences will be hierarchically structured in the same way as a language like English; but what is quite clear is that, if it is not, theoretical linguists would not regard

[1] A number of linguists have argued that Chomsky's linguistic universals are logically necessary in the sense that there are mathematical proofs showing that any set of word-sequences that can be defined at all (including e.g. the set just defined in terms of alphabetical order) can be defined by a Chomskyan 'transformational grammar'. Whether this is true depends in part on exactly what counts as a transformational grammar, and it is demonstrably *not* true for one relatively plausible version of the theory of transformational grammar (P. S. Peters and R. W. Ritchie, 'Nonfiltering and local-filtering transformational grammars', in K. J. J. Hintikka, J. M. E. Moravcsik, and P. Suppes, eds., *Approaches to Natural Language*, Reidel (Dordrecht), 1973). But in any case the point seems to be a red herring, for reasons discussed in my 'The irrelevance of transformational omnipotence', *Journal of Linguistics*, vol. 9, 1973, pp. 299–302.

their theory as refuted by the fact that many humans 'speak' this 'language'. Rather, they would say that their theory makes predictions about the category of phenomena exemplified by English and Chinese, and that driving does not fall under that category and hence cannot be used to test the theory. But it is left to our intuition to decide whether or not a given phenomenon counts as a 'language' for the purposes of testing linguistic theory; the question is whether, when we try to spell out what further characteristics a 'language' in the abstract sense has to have in order to count as a 'language' for these purposes, we may not find that hierarchical structure has been smuggled into the definition. In that case, the theory of linguistic universals would be a mere tautology.

To define the essence of the word 'language' as used in everyday speech is as difficult a task as defining any other everyday word exhaustively, and I shall not attempt to do the job completely here.[1] Concentrating on the crucial point thrown up by the example of driving, presumably the most important difference between English, Chinese, etc. on the one hand and the 'language of driving' on the other, is that the former serve for communication while the latter has a quite different function – we drive in order to transport ourselves and others, not in order to tell people things. A 'language', then, is a class of sequences used for communication.

This still allows a number of phenomena to count as 'languages' which in everyday speech would be thought of as 'languages' only in a loose, derivative sense. The 'language' whose 'sentences' are symbolic representations of games of chess, for instance (I mean the system which generates sequences such as '1 P–Q4 Kt–KB3 2 P–QB4 P–K3 . . .', and so forth), is used for communication between chess enthusiasts; yet I cannot imagine a linguist being very happy about abandoning the theory of universals if this 'language' should turn out to be non-hierarchical. We might deal with this by specifying that only the most inclusive communication system of a community counts as a language (English is more inclusive than chess notation in the sense that all utterances

---

[1] cf. C. F. Hockett, 'The problem of universals in language', in J. H. Greenberg, ed., *Universals of Language*, 2nd edn., M.I.T. Press (Cambridge, Mass.), 1966.

in the latter can be translated into the former while only a small minority of utterances in the former have any translation in the latter). In fact I suspect that the grammars of these 'sub-languages' such as chess notation probably *are* hierarchical insofar as they are complex enough to test the theory at all, so that the issue is unimportant in practice; I shall not pursue the definition of 'language' any further.

We are left with the point that languages serve for communication. 'Communication' is also a fairly vague word, though. Is there anything about the notion of communication which guarantees that any system serving this function must necessarily be hierarchical?

Stephen Toulmin suggests an affirmative answer to this question, by pointing out that the syntactic structures identified by linguists in natural languages are devices serving to give tangible expression to the 'logical forms' of propositions as discussed by logicians. Thus, he writes:

it is a matter of sheer communicative efficiency to distinguish those symbols that draw attention to what we are talking about – 'indexical' terms – from those other symbols that say something about the subjects so indicated – 'descriptive' terms. A language lacking any such functional differentiation would be needlessly ambiguous and confusing. . . . This is only the first, and simplest, step in a very much longer story.[1]

Certainly it is true that 'hierarchy' and 'structure-dependence' of rules are highly salient in the formal systems worked out by logicians – the formulae of such systems rely heavily on bracketing to represent hierarchical structure, and Chomsky's notion of 'transformational rule' was consciously modelled on the rules which logicians use to specify relationships between their formulae. But to suggest that linguists have no need to explain the

---

[1] S. E. Toulmin, 'Brain and language: a commentary', *Synthese*, vol. 22, 1971, p. 386; cf. Toulmin's *Human Understanding*, vol. i, Oxford University Press, 1972, pp. 467–8, and my 'Can language be explained functionally?', *Synthese*, vol. 23, 1972, pp. 477–86. Toulmin suggests that the 'longer story' is essentially contained in Karl Bühler's *Sprachtheorie*, Fischer (Jena), 1934. I cannot see that either Bühler or Toulmin succeed in explaining in 'functional' terms the syntactic universals to which Chomsky's nativism appeals; however, the other points made by Toulmin about Chomskyan linguistic nativism are very apposite.

ubiquity of hierarchical structure in the syntax of natural
languages because it is a natural consequence of the ubiquity of
hierarchy in logic is to miss the point – why should formal logic be
hierarchical?

The fact is that the various systems of logic that have been
worked out over the last hundred years or so can be interpreted as
attempts to formalize and render explicit the meaning content of
natural languages, shorn of the various irregularities and redundancies which all natural languages contain. It is perfectly easy to
invent artificial systems of formal logic whose formulae are defined
non-hierarchically and whose rules of transformation are independent of structure; logicians do not work with such systems,
because they have no relationship with natural languages and are
therefore uninteresting.[1] Of course it is no accident that our
natural languages and our formal logics share the same basic
principles of structure, but we are left in need of an explanation as
to why those principles should be what they are. Why do we not
find humans in distant parts of the world who speak languages
conforming to quite alien syntactic principles, and who have
worked out similarly alien systems of formal logic?

Another way in which one can attempt to flesh out the notion of
'communication' is to say that it involves the exchange of symbols
which correlate in some way with aspects of the world; a message is
in some sense a picture of the things or states of affairs with which
it is concerned. Clearly, pictures tend to share structural properties with their subjects, but this principle will certainly not explain
the universality of hierarchy in natural language; the world that
we use language to discuss contains entities of all conceivable
structures and of no structure at all. It is not that sentences dealing
with armies exhibit hierarchical syntax while sentences about
undisciplined mobs are syntaxless jumbles. *All* sentences are hierarchically structured (except for utterances such as *Hello!* which
are too simple for the notion of 'structure' to have any bite), and

---

[1] cf. my 'Empirical hypothesis about natural semantics', *Journal of Philosophical Logic*, vol. 5, 1976, pp. 209–36. Oddly, Chomsky himself seems to have mis-understood this point; see his 'Some empirical issues in the theory of trans-formational grammar', in S. Peters, ed., *Goals of Linguistic Theory*, Prentice-Hall, 1972, p. 75; cf. my *Form of Language*, pp. 164–5.

the particular structure found in a given sentence is quite independent of the subject-matter of the sentence; the latter is reflected
by the choice of vocabulary rather than by syntax. The argument
from linguistic universals to the limited mind cannot be defeated
by suggesting that it is tautologous to attribute the universals in
question to language; it is not tautologous to assert that all natural
languages possess those properties, unless one chooses to *make* this
a tautology by redefining 'language' in such a way that a hypothetical communication-system lacking the properties would
thereby cease to count as a language. To make this move with no
better motive than a desire to defeat the limited-mind argument
would not be playing the game.

There remains, however, the third problem: the limited-mind
explanation for the linguistic universals may fail because some
better explanation for them is available. Our discussion on
pp. 40–41, above, of Chomsky's claims about semantic universals
suggested a degree of blindness on his part to this possibility;
Chomsky stressed that the alleged universality of the features he
mentioned is not *logically* necessary, as if to suggest that it follows
that they constitute evidence for innate mental structuring. There
are other places in Chomsky's writings[1] where he makes it clear
that he does realize that his limited-mind argument is vulnerable
to the possibility of alternative explanations for the universals, but
his discussion of semantic universals suggests that the problem
may be one which he is inclined to overlook when he is not
explicitly addressing himself to it.

Many writers who have examined Chomsky's ideas have
realized that they are potentially vulnerable to alternative explanations of the universals, and have set out to provide such an
alternative. Hilary Putnam, for instance, suggests that the existence of linguistic universals could well be explained if we suppose
that the various natural languages of recorded history all
ultimately descend from a single ancestral language which just
happened to have one kind of structure rather than another.[2]
However, to my mind the various counter-explanations that have
been put forward in the literature are all fairly clearly inadequate.

[1] e.g. *Problems of Knowledge and Freedom*, Fontana, 1972, pp. 42–3.
[2] 'The "innateness hypothesis"' in J. R. Searle, ed., op. cit., p. 136.

In the case just mentioned, for instance, it is quite true that we cannot disprove the hypothesis of a single historical origin for all languages of the world (it is unlikely that we shall ever have data that would be decisive either way as to whether language emerged once or on many independent occasions in the history of our species), but even if we accept the hypothesis for the sake of argument we are not thereby relieved (as Putnam seems to think we are) of the need of an explanation for the universality of hierarchical structure in languages of the present time. If all languages have a common origin, then they have undergone enormous changes in the meantime in many respects (since the phonological structures and vocabularies of contemporary languages, for instance, are often very different from one another); so why have none of the descendant languages ever changed with respect to the syntactic properties identified by general linguistic theory? If the 'linguistic universals' were an assortment of un-related and fairly trivial properties, one might be happy to adopt Putnam's explanation and say that, of all the properties possessed by the *Ursprache*, this particular subset had purely by chance been left unaffected by linguistic change in any of the lines of descent. But the 'linguistic universals' are not like this; they are central, fundamental organizing principles.[1] To explain their ubiquity as due to 'chance' is to throw up one's hands and abandon the search for truth altogether – one might as well suggest that it is a matter of 'chance' that all the dropped objects we observe happen to obey the so-called law of gravity rather than adopting diverse motions.

One might, I suppose, suggest that it is the very centrality of the properties claimed to be universal which makes them resistant to modification over time; people can modify their vocabulary and

---

[1] It often seems unfortunate that theoretical linguists describe themselves as discovering 'linguistic universals', since the plural suggests the kind of ragbag of separate properties that one might well dismiss as happening by chance to be universal. In fact the well-founded hard core of 'constraints on the diversity of natural languages' that have been established by Theoretical Linguistics are not disconnected elements, but are rather related parts of a single whole. When linguists have proposed universals unconnected with the hierarchicality of syntax, these have tended to be either rash extrapolations from very restricted data or else easily explainable from considerations other than alleged innate psychological structure.

details of their grammar piecemeal as generation succeeds generation, but perhaps a hierarchy-based grammar cannot evolve into
a grammar based on some other organizational principle, no
matter how arbitrary the original adoption of the hierarchical
principle may have been, just because the change would be too
radical and abrupt. Compare our arithmetical habits: people can
and often do abandon the English way of writing sevens in favour
of the Continental form with a crossbar, but it seems inconceivable
that we could ever give up decimal arithmetic for a duodecimal
system even though the latter would probably be more efficient –
such a change could of its nature only be abrupt rather than
gradual, and since the decimal system was established it has
acquired too much momentum to be overthrown in practice.

But I cannot believe that this is all there is to it in the case of
language. In the arithmetical case, after all, there are many traces
in the cultures of the world of counting systems not based on tens,
and it seems certain that some cultures would have chosen wholly
non-decimal counting if it were not for the factor of our ten fingers.
In the case of language there is no hint of non-hierarchical syntax
reported from any culture, yet no outward, tangible factor akin to
our possession of ten fingers seems to be predisposing us towards
hierarchical grammar.

In ch. 6 of my *Form of Language* I surveyed the various suggestions, such as Putnam's, that have been made in the literature
concerning non-nativist explanations for the linguistic universals,
and I found that none of them stood up.[1] At that time I concluded

---

[1] F. W. Householder has responded to my discussion in *The Form of Language* by
suggesting a new explanation for syntactic universals, namely the need for
sentences to be 'improvisable'; very roughly, sentences are 'improvisable' if their
endings are not heavily dependent on their beginnings, so that one can decide
what to say as one goes along and still get the grammar right. (See Householder's
'Innateness and improvisability', in R. J. di Pietro and E. L. Blansitt, Jr., eds., *The
Third LACUS Forum, 1976*, Hornbeam Press (Columbia, S.C.), 1977.) If it were
true that the natural languages coincided with the languages whose sentences are
'improvisable' in Householder's sense, his explanation of Chomsky's universals
might be a good one; but it is far from true. On the one hand, the artificial
'languages' defined on pp. 41–2 of *The Form of Language* are 'improvisable' but
quite unnatural; on the other hand, natural languages often contain features
(such as the selection by different German past participles of auxiliaries *haben* or
sein) which quite gratuitously make for 'non-improvisability'.

that we were bound to accept Chomsky's limited-mind explanation of the universals. I still find the alternatives that I
examined in 1975 unsatisfactory, but I no longer believe in the
limited-mind account of the syntactic universals. Since writing
The Form of Language I have encountered an explanation for the
universals which is not just equally adequate but much better than
Chomsky's explanation, and which not merely does not require us
to accept Chomsky's view of linguistic structure as innate but is
actually incompatible with that view. I discuss this explanation in
the chapters that follow.

VII

The explanation for Chomsky's theory of syntactic universals which I believe to be the correct one is based on a discussion by Herbert Simon (of the Carnegie-Mellon University) of the mathematics of evolution.[1]

Simon begins his discussion of evolution with a parable about two watchmakers, Hora and Tempus. Both make equally good watches, but Hora's business prospers while Tempus's fails. The reason for this has to do with the structure of their respective watches. Each contain roughly the same number of elementary parts – say, a thousand. Tempus must assemble all thousand parts in a continuous operation to produce a solid watch; if he has to put down a partly assembled watch to attend to an interruption, it falls apart into its component pieces and he must begin again from scratch after the interruption. Hora's watches, on the other hand, consist of ten hundred-part sub-assemblies which are solid in themselves; if Hora is interrupted in the middle of assembling the ten sub-assemblies into a complete watch, after the interruption he has to reassemble only the ten sub-assemblies rather than all thousand elementary parts. Each sub-assembly, similarly, is made up of ten independently-solid sub-sub-assemblies each containing ten basic parts. The result is that, when Hora is interrupted, he loses at most eight individual assembly operations performed before the interruption, whereas Tempus may lose anything up to 998 operations; and therefore Hora produces complete watches very much more rapidly than Tempus. If each carries out individual operations at the same rate, and if they are interrupted at the same average frequency, say once per hundred

[1] H. A. Simon, 'The architecture of complexity', *Proceedings of the American Philosophical Society*, vol. 106, 1962, pp. 467–82; my page references are to the reprint in H. A. Simon, *The Sciences of the Artificial*, M.I.T. Press, 1969. The following discussion of the implications of Simon's work for linguistics draws heavily on my 'Linguistic universals as evidence for empiricism', *Journal of Linguistics*, vol. 14, 1978, pp. 183–206.

operations, then, Simon shows, Hora will complete almost 4,000 watches for every one completed by Tempus.

The essential difference between the two kinds of watch is that Hora's watches are hierarchically structured while Tempus's are not. The two designs can be represented abstractly by means of diagrams in which nodes represent units that are stable, or 'solid' as I put it above (i.e. capable of enduring as units); I have simplified the diagrams by using threes rather than tens:

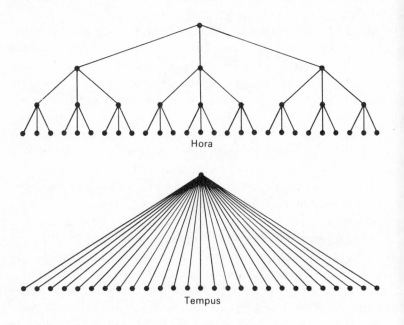

Hora

Tempus

Each tree has a single 'root' node, representing the completed watches, which are stable in both cases, and each tree has the same number of 'leaf' nodes representing the elementary parts from which the watches are constructed, which are stable because they are not made up of smaller parts. Tempus's design has a single non-leaf node, the root node, with a 'span' (i.e. number of immediately dominated nodes) of 27 (in the example worked out in the text, 1,000) while Hora's design has a number of non-leaf nodes each with a span of three (in the text, ten). Other things (including, in particular, the number of leaves) being equal, a design with a low average node-span can be produced in a much shorter time than a design with a high average node-span; the difference will increase very rapidly with increase in rate of interruptions.

The point of the parable is that it shows, according to Simon (and I believe he is right), that complex entities produced by any process of unplanned evolution, such as the Darwinian process of biological evolution, will be hierarchical as a matter of statistical necessity, even if hierarchy is not logically necessary to them.

An evolutionary process can be thought of as one in which elementary building-blocks of some kind are constantly shuffled together in varying combinations, and some particular combinations which happen to be stable – 'fit' is the Darwinian term – survive as units in the shuffling process. ('Shuffling' is represented in the parable both by the watchmakers' actions in bringing parts together and by the interruptions which cause them to fall apart unless they form a stable whole.) In the case of biology, for instance, think of various molecules floating past one another in the 'primaeval soup' within which life is supposed to have begun some three or four thousand million years ago. They would have constantly come together in diverse chance combinations, and some of these combinations would have fitted together as stable ensembles which then took part as units in the continuing process of shuffling – so that, as time went on, the soup would contain organisms of increasing complexity. (Let me mention in order to avert misunderstandings that the particular threshold beyond which certain fairly complex ensembles acquired the ability to reproduce their kind, though all-important in most discussions of biology, is not very relevant to our present discussion. Self-replication is simply one means by which a *type* of organism can endure through time.) Intuitively it is easy to grasp the idea that a complex organism stands a far better chance of being translated from possibility into actuality if it can be built up in many stages, each of which is independently viable, than if all its many ultimate components have to happen to come together in the right way simultaneously.

Notice that Simon is *not* saying that hierarchical organisms are necessarily 'fitter' or stabler than non-hierarchical organisms.

Tempus's watches were just as good as Hora's once they were completed. What Simon is saying is rather subtler. Suppose that there exist two logically possible organisms which are equally complex in the sense that they are composed of the same number of elementary building-blocks, and equally fit to fill some environmental niche, but one is structured hierarchically while the other is not. Then, Simon is saying, it is a statistical certainty that the former will be thrown up by the evolutionary process as a *candidate for survival* long before the latter organism gets a look in. (The important point about the Hora/Tempus parable is not that Hora completes watches 4,000 times as frequently as Tempus but the corollary that, if the two begin making watches at the same time, Hora can expect to complete his first watch 4,000 times sooner than Tempus's first watch is completed.) If the two possible organisms are equally fit, the fact that the hierarchical one is given the earlier chance is quite sufficient to guarantee that the hierarchical rather than the non-hierarchical organism will fill the environmental niche; as evolutionists put it, 'prior arrival pre-empts survival'. In other words, Simon is arguing that there might well be complex non-hierarchical organisms which would in principle succeed, if given a chance, just as well as the complex hierarchical organisms actually found after an evolutionary process has reached an advanced stage; but the nature of the process by which new types of organism come into being guarantees that the non-hierarchical ones never will be given their chance. This cannot fail to remind us of Chomsky's argument that hierarchical grammar is not logically necessary to language, and that one can conceive of systems similar to languages except that they are not structured hierarchically; yet no such systems are actually used by any human communities.

Before we consider how far Simon's argument can in fact be used to explain linguists' syntactic universals, let us examine its application to the areas with which Simon is more centrally concerned.

The obvious example of an evolutionary process is biological evolution, and Simon argues that his discussion can be used to explain observable facts about biology. Thus, all complex biological organisms are made up of cells, and cells were originally independent organisms. While biology is the best-known example of an evolutionary process, though, it must be said that it is not a specially good example for Simon's purposes – a point which Simon himself does not altogether recognize. In the first place, Simon predicts that complex organisms will have a *lot* of layers of hierarchical organization, yet it is not clear that familiar biological species contain intermediate levels of hierarchy, in his sense, between the level of cells and that of complete individuals. Simon writes that 'we find cells organized into tissues, tissues into organs, organs into systems'.[1] But these latter categories of biological component surely are not descended from independent organisms; there never was a time when the ancestors of, say, circulatory system, respiratory system, and skeleton chanced to encounter one another and from then on evolved jointly as a symbiotic unit.

Simon fails, in fact, to distinguish two rather different processes by which hierarchical structure may be created. On the one hand organisms which were previously independent may contract a permanent symbiotic relationship with one another, thus becoming a single larger organism; if this happens repeatedly, and the units which came together retain some sort of identity within the more inclusive organism, the result is hierarchy of what we may call the 'symbiotic' variety. This is the kind of hierarchy predicted directly by the watchmaker parable. On the other hand, a very salient feature of biological development is that hierarchical structures are created by the repeated splitting and differentiation of what begins as a *single* unit. This is well-known in the case of ontogeny, the development of an individal of a species: a man, composed of a billion or more cells, is the outcome of repeated division of a single fertilized egg, and the kind of hierarchy indicated by Simon's 'tissues, organs, and systems' corresponds to the successive divisions into different lines of descent that specialize in different directions. In this respect as in many others, 'ontogeny recapitulates phylogeny' not necessarily in exact detail but broadly; a complex species such as Man has been produced not by the coming-together in successively larger aggregates of what were originally a very large number of different kinds of protozoon, but by failure on the part of the descendants of one

[1] op. cit., p. 88.

single-celled ancestor species to drift apart after splitting. We may call this latter kind of hierarchy 'endogenous'; it is much less clear that the watchmaker parable can be used to predict that the products of an evolutionary process must contain endogenous hierarchy, yet that is the kind of hierarchy most noticeable in biology.

However, at another level of biology than the one just discussed Simon's predictions have in fact been borne out in a way that is all the more striking in view of the fact that the relevant biological theories were worked out only after the publication of Simon's article. (Whether it should be so or not, a theory which makes true predictions about facts unknown to its author is always more impressive than one which succeeds only in explaining facts that the theorist already knew.) To the layman, the cell sounds like a very elementary sort of unit, but this impression is quite fallacious; G. G. Simpson stresses that 'if, as must almost necessarily be true short of miracles, life arose as a living molecule or protogene, the progression from this stage to that of the ameba is at least as great as from ameba to man.'[1] In discussing the biological application of his thesis about hierarchy, Simon wrote vaguely that 'well-defined subsystems – for example, nucleus, cell membrane, microsomes, mitochondria, and so on – have been identified in animal cells.'[2] More recently it has come to be widely accepted that the evolutionary history of 'eukaryotic' cells (i.e. cells with nuclei, including protozoa such as amoebae, and the cells of all higher organisms – all living things are or are made up of eukaryotic cells except for bacteria and blue-green algae, which are 'prokaryotes') involves a series of cases of symbiosis between previously-independent organisms, just as Simon leads us to expect. As Lynn Margulis reconstructs the sequence of events, first an anaerobic host bacterium teamed up with a number of smaller, aerobic bacteria, which developed into the original mitochondria; then a number of spirochaete-like bacteria attached themselves to the surface of the resulting organism, evolving into the spindle apparatus for mitosis; while this ensemble was the ancestor of the animal and fungus kingdoms, in another line (or other lines) of

[1] G. G. Simpson, *The Meaning of Evolution*, Yale University Press, 1949, p. 16.
[2] op. cit., p. 88.

descent it in turn formed a symbiosis with blue-green algae to produce the kingdom of plants.[1]

Once the symbiotic relationships became established, of course, the partners developed in such a way that they ceased even potentially to be independent organisms; one cannot remove a mitochondrion from a eukaryotic cell and grow it as an isolated bacterium. There is no analogue for this in the watchmaker parable – cogwheels and the like remain what they are and do not develop spontaneously; but the point does not damage the force of Simon's argument, it means merely that we must understand him to be predicting that the products of evolution will be hierarchical in the sense that they are made up of components, sub-components, etc., which are *or which descend from units that once were* independent organisms.

Although the 'endogenous' type of hierarchical structure is less obviously related to Simon's analysis, it may well be indirectly explicable in the same terms. Too little is yet known about how a genetic programme determines the structure of an organism for the issue to be discussed authoritatively. But one reason for the apparent lack of relationship between endogenous biological hier-archy and Simon's argument seems to be a fallacious view of genetics. Since we identify ourselves much more with our bodies than with the sets of genes which control the development of our bodies, it is very natural that we think of biological evolution as a process which creates new species in the sense of new sorts of body, and that we think of chromosomes and their constituent genes merely as part of the means by which bodies replicate themselves with modifications. As Richard Dawkins has pointed out, how-ever, this is an egocentric attitude;[2] theoretically it makes much better sense to think of biological evolution as a process which creates new sorts of *gene* and retains those that are fit (i.e. capable of perpetuating large numbers of copies of themselves), and in which bodies are merely devices that have been selected for their use in keeping sets of genes more secure and better able to replicate than they were when they were molecules floating independently in the primaeval soup.

[1] L. Margulis, *Origin of Eukaryotic Cells*, Yale University Press, 1970.
[2] *The Selfish Gene*, Oxford University Press, 1976.

Seen in this light, endogenous biological evolution becomes much easier to assimiliate to Simon's account. Reproduction is the shuffling together of nucleotides into new combinations through meiosis and occasional mutation. Of course we do not, in the higher species, find symbiotic evolution in the sense that a horse which rolls in burrs becomes the ancestor of a race of horses with prickly lumps on. But we do find symbiotic evolution in the sense that nucleotide sequences which have succeeded in becoming common in a gene-pool are constantly shuffled into new longer sequences, a few of which themselves turn out to be highly 'fit' as units. Simon would then be saying something like this: logically it is entirely possible that a highly fit organism could emerge from a reshuffling which destroyed the unity of the various sub-sequences of nucleotides already established as successful (the processes of meiosis and mutation occur at random with respect to the 'semantics' of a chromosome); statistically, however, it is sure that fitter organisms must emerge through slight modifications to and new combinations of nucleotide sequences which had proved their worth in ancestor-organisms (which is why it is appropriate to think of the nucleotides along a chromosome as grouped into 'genes'). Little is yet known in detail about the relationship between particular nucleotide sequences and the structure of the bodies they manufacture, but it seems not implausible that the 'endogenous' kind of anatomical hierarchy is connected with Simon's statistical argument via considerations such as these.

Furthermore, even if this argument that endogenous biological hierarchy can be assimilated to symbiotic hierarchy is inadequate, Simon's thesis would not be refuted by the absence (or, at least, limited incidence) of symbiotic hierarchy above the cell level in biology. Simon does not predict that all complex products of evolution must be hierarchical; he predicts only that, where hierarchical and non-hierarchical organisms would both in principle be fit for survival, the more hierarchical organisms will be the ones that actually occur. If animals and plants contain little symbiotic hierarchy above the cell level, this may be because there are no logically possible fit organisms resulting from such symbiosis – which is quite compatible with Simon's argument. (Even Tempus's watch business would succeed if no hierarchical design akin to Hora's were possible for a watch.)

Whether or not Simon's argument achieves much with respect to anatomy above the cell level, it is worth noting that Richard Dawkins finds Simon's principle to be one of first-rank importance for another branch of biological theory, namely ethology.[1] Dawkins suggests that Simon provides the intellectually satisfying explanation for a characteristic of animal behaviour widely noticed by ethologists (Dawkins gives a wealth of references), and that this is an achievement comparable to Darwin's use of the notion of natural selection to account for the diversity of species.

Moreover, although the term 'evolution' has come to be associated primarily with Darwinian biological evolution (presumably because that application of the evolutionary principle was so emotionally disturbing in its day), biology is of course by no means the only domain in which evolutionary processes occur. Indeed, despite the currency of the term 'Social Darwinism' to describe the ideas of men such as Herbert Spencer, a phrase which suggests that evolutionary ideas were borrowed into sociology from biology, the truth is that historically the direction of intellectual influence was rather the reverse. Spencer's evolutionary approach to the origin of social phenomena was first propounded shortly before the publication of Darwin's *Origin of Species*;[2] but Spencer was only one of the last and best representatives of a long tradition of sociological analysis in evolutionary terms. According to Friedrich Hayek, during the late eighteenth and early nineteenth centuries evolutionary concepts developed first among students of social phenomena (particularly law) and were borrowed from them by biologists; Hayek argues that the evolutionary approach to the understanding of society has been unjustly slighted by the swing of intellectual fashion in recent decades.[3]

---

[1] Dawkins, 'Hierarchical organization: a candidate principle for ethology', in P. P. G. Bateson and R. A. Hinde, eds., *Growing Points in Ethology*, Cambridge University Press, 1976. Cf. also H. H. Pattee, ed., *Hierarchy Theory*, George Braziller (New York), 1973.

[2] In Spencer's 'Progress: its law and cause', 1857, reprinted in *Essays on Education and Kindred Subjects* (*Everyman's Library*), Dent, 2nd edn. 1976.

[3] See e.g. Hayek's *Constitution of Liberty*, Routledge & Kegan Paul, 1960, ch. 4, esp. §3.

The development of human societies, as Simon points out, seems to conform rather well to the pattern he predicts. In the early history of our species, men can hardly have belonged to social groups much larger than the bands of a score or so individuals observed in related species – lack of technology would have ensured that no regular social relationships could be maintained across distances of a hundred miles or more, and one band would have had only sporadic, chance contacts with others. The growth of technology (in the broadest sense) both permitted the emergence of wider social units (by facilitating communication) and provided a motive for such developments (that of taking greater advantage of the division of labour). So far as can be inferred from the data available for the historical period, the growth of increasingly inclusive social organizations has built up hierarchical systems from smallest to largest just as Simon suggests: several extended families group themselves into parishes or similar units, parishes later group themselves into wapentakes or the equivalent, wapentakes into counties, counties into nations, nations into empires. The precise natures of the units at different levels, and indeed the number of intermediate levels, vary from place to place in the world; that is expected. The watchmaker parable gives no reason to predict that evolution-generated hierarchies will be regular, with the same number of branches between each leaf and the root (Simon made the hierarchical structure of Hora's watches regular only in order to simplify the calculation). The parable predicts only that the average span of nodes will be low and that the pattern will be a true hierarchy, with no 'ambiguities of dominance' (i.e. upward branching). To assert that social institutions show a strong tendency to be hierarchical in this way seems a mere truism; but it is not a necessary truth, as is shown by the fact that in a few special situations the pattern does not hold and 'ambiguities of dominance' are found. Thus, in contemporary Britain, one aspect of government is organized by regions that cut across the boundaries of (the rest of) local government: namely, the management of water resources. The reason is obvious; it would be hopelessly inconvenient if the organization of this particular resource failed to respect natural geographical watersheds. In other words, in this particular case a perfectly hierarchical society would be relatively 'unfit', and the greater fitness of the slightly non-hierarchical arrangement has outweighed the general tendency towards hierarchy (again, this is permitted by Simon's argument).[1] Social institutions contain plenty of endogenous hierarchy, but they also conform to Simon's theory by manifesting a great deal of symbiotic hierarchy.

In society as in the biological realm, once a unit is absorbed into a superordinate organism it may gradually evolve into something very different from what it was when independent. A modern English county council is quite unlike what governments must have been when county-sized territories were independent political units. (A county council, most obviously, has no department of defence.) But, as Simon points out, in the social sphere as in biology the units commonly retain their identity as units for periods, often very long periods, after they have lost their independence.[2] Simon refers to the fact that the empire of Alexander the Great resolved itself after his death into some of the same components from which it had earlier been formed. Likewise, Scotland is now seeking a measure of independence centuries after being absorbed into a single political entity with England; nobody finds this very surprising, whereas we would be more startled to hear that, say, Co. Durham, Northumberland, and South-East Scotland wanted to go it alone as a new unit.

In many societies known to history an account of the governmental structure, from emperor, king, or president down to the family unit, would be a virtually complete account of the whole social organization. Some fortunate societies have arranged to restrict the spheres of life in which government is allowed to play a role, so that activities in other spheres are carried out by entities such as commercial firms, universities, etc., which function independently of any tier of government. But these again, as Simon

---

[1] This example is not ideal, since the modern system of Regional Water Authorities did not emerge from a gradual process of blind evolution of novel social structures, but rather was imposed consciously from above by national government. However, it serves to make the point that the hierarchicality of government is not a truth of logic and that its near-ubiquity therefore stands in need of an explanation – such as Simon's.

[2] op. cit., p. 98.

points out,[1] show considerable internal hierarchical structure. Large firms very frequently result from mergers of a number of smaller concerns, which may in turn be the successors to groups of lesser firms again; very often the subordinate firms retain an identifiable individuality as components of the conglomerate long after they have lost their independence, though at the same time they will often have changed a good deal since they were taken over.

A final example of a domain in which Simon's argument can be applied is one more closely related to the linguistic issues with which we are concerned here: namely the domain of complex intellectual products, such as scientific theories or novels. As Simon points out,[2] a book, whether a novel or an academic treatise, will be divided into chapters, the chapters into sections, the sections into paragraphs, the paragraphs into sentences. (These divisions are marked by various typographical conventions, but they are not, of course, *purely* typographical; the hierarchical structure of continuous prose is manifested in many ways in the wording, and in most books the structure could be reconstructed with reasonable success from a text printed continuously.) In the treatise the various elements may correspond to different steps in an argument, different aspects of the topic being expounded, or the like; in the novel they may correspond to different episodes and related sequences of episodes in the plot. In neither case is it at all clear that hierarchical structure is logically necessary. Real life does not on the whole proceed in discrete episodes, and dividing up a big subject into separate aspects for expository purposes can often be a fairly artificial procedure, in the sense that it forces the writer to make many arbitrary decisions. Logically speaking there might seem to be no good reason why we should not often encounter books consisting of continuous sequences of sentences not grouped into any higher-order units. One practical reason why we do not may perhaps be that readers could not cope with such books if they did exist, and Simon's argument seems to have nothing directly to say about that. But it seems likely that another reason why books are hierarchical is that this is the only way they

[1] ibid., p. 88.
[2] ibid., p. 90.

can be written. Writing a book is very much a process of trial-and-error evolution. (There are said to be prodigies who sit down at their typewriters and rattle off the finished work from scratch, but even they must presumably go through long processes of experimentation in their heads before putting the result on paper.) If so, then Simon predicts that books must be built up step by step, with lower-level units worked over and improved before they are incorporated into higher-level units; and the finished book will reflect this hierarchical aspect of its composition. We may expect that books which approximate to the unstructured-sequence-of-sentences model will be ones which have undergone relatively little revision and polishing, whether in the writer's head or on paper, before publication.

The distinction between symbiotic and endogenous hierarchy is somewhat difficult to draw in this case. A clear instance of symbiotic hierarchy would be where a don 'cannibalizes' a group of his published articles in order to incorporate them in a book; some of the articles may in turn have been worked up from published or unpublished notes on individual points, and it may well be that, when the articles were written, the more general idea with which the book is concerned had not yet emerged into the writer's consciousness. As in the case of symbiotic evolution in biology or sociology, so here the sub-components will commonly be modified when they are incorporated into the greater whole, but their identity as units will still be discernible. On the other hand, the hierarchical structure of many books is reached by an opposite process more akin to endogenous evolution. One starts with the overall 'message' of the book, understood in a fairly simple way; one then picks out a number of distinct points all of which need to be argued in order to make good this overall thesis; consideration of the separate points reveals each of them in turn to raise a complex of considerations; and so on, until down each branch of the argument one reaches a point at which the reader may, with luck, allow one to rest one's case. However, I would suggest that the symbiotic process is the means whereby one attains a new belief for oneself; the endogenous process is characteristic of a situation in which one sets out to persuade others of a belief already established in one's own mind.

What of the hierarchicality of language discussed by theoretical linguists? Simon does not discuss this, though he includes a brief allusion which seems to imply that he draws no distinction between this issue and the issue just dealt with about the hierarchicality of texts. (When Simon points out that books are divided into chapters, sections, paragraphs, and sentences, he continues the list with clauses, phrases, words, and morphemes.[1]) To conflate these two cases of hierarchy is a mistake. The internal hierarchicality of sentences, which is what theoretical linguists discuss, is essentially a characteristic of a *language* as a repertory of potential sentences, rather than of a text. Many of the constituents of a sentence are not marked off in any overt way – subordinate clauses are often delimited by intonation, represented in writing by commas, but most constituents have no overt boundary-markers. For the most part, the hierarchical structure we assign to a particular sentence is a theoretical construct produced as a by-product of the search for a maximally elegant grammar which defines the range of all and only the sentences of the language in question. On the other hand sentences, by definition, are the longest sequences within which syntactic co-occurrence restrictions apply; it would make no sense to write a grammar to generate well-formed sequences of sentences, since there are no rules prescribing how sentences may or may not be chained together and it is up to the individual language-user's ingenuity to find whatever sequence of sentences best serves his rhetorical purpose.[2] The hierarchical structure of a text is a property of the individual text, not of the 'repertory of possible texts'. Thus the fact that sentences are hierarchically-structured is not a mere corollary of the fact that texts are.

Nevertheless, I believe that Simon's thesis can be used to explain the universals of sentence structure to which Theoretical

---

[1] ibid., p. 90.

[2] It is true that much recent work by German-speaking linguists has been devoted to so-called *Textgrammatik*, but the point made above remains valid, in my view. Of course it is possible to say that what is criterial for the unit 'sentence' is that it begins with a capital letter and ends with a full stop or equivalent punctuation mark, in which case it is an open question whether or not there are co-occurrence restrictions between sentences; but I believe that as a matter of empirical fact the maximum domains of syntactic co-occurrence restrictions are identical or near-identical to 'sentences' in the orthographic sense.

Linguistics draws attention, and that this application of the general thesis is actually more satisfactory than the applications which Simon himself considers and which we have surveyed in the foregoing pages. The reader may be inclined to feel that Simon's argument has by now turned out to be sufficiently problematic that little respect needs to be accorded to it at this point, so that it is more or less irrelevant whether or not the predictions the argument makes about linguistic structure coincide with the universals discovered by linguists.[1] But the difficulties I have raised have not been problems about the statistical properties of evolutionary processes considered abstractly, as illustrated by the watchmaker parable. This was a matter of simple mathematics, and it would be hard to quarrel with. Rather, the difficulties arose from the fact that Simon's thesis seemed redundant in some of the domains to which he applied it, since the hierarchical structure which certainly is present in these domains often seemed to be adequately explained independently of that thesis. For one thing, much of the hierarchy found in these domains is the outcome of endogenous evolution, to which the thesis is not always clearly relevant. Furthermore, particularly in the sociological case of governmental structures, it is very plausible to argue that hierarchy itself makes for fitness – divided authority destroys the efficiency of a social organization. In linguistics, on the other hand, hierarchy is claimed to be in need of explanation; linguists vehemently deny that hierarchical syntax can be explained as making languages more efficient, unless one supposes that we have innate mental machinery that requires hierarchical syntax. So, if Simon's thesis is capable of accounting for the syntactic data without this latter postulate, it certainly cannot be dismissed as redundant. Linguists argue that a limited-mind theory must be adopted for lack of any alternative explanation of the linguistic universals; if Simon's argument can be used to construct an alternative explanation, it will be very much to the point. And indeed it can.

In the first place, nothing is more plausible *a priori* than to

---

[1] Chomsky refers in correspondence to a criticism of Simon's thesis by Chomsky's M.I.T. colleague David Berlinski, but I answer Berlinski in n. 2, p. 191 of my 'Linguistic universals as evidence for empiricism'.

suggest that languages of the complex kind we know today arose through an evolutionary process from simple beginnings. Presumably we shall never have any direct evidence about the birth of language, but it seems almost banal to suggest that men began with one-word utterances (as infants do today), and that complex syntax grew up gradually as various sorts of sequences of words, at first concatenated more or less at random, proved useful in practice and thus achieved a recognized place in the linguistic repertory. At first, say, *Up, Mountain, John* would be unclassifiable 'holophrastic utterances', i.e. one-word-sentences, each of which would be used in a very broad range of situations. 'Up' might mean that someone had gone up something, that the honey was high up on the ledge, that the rock needed lifting up, etc. etc.; and similarly for the other 'word-sentences'. An utterance might consist of more than one word-sentence, but it would be for the speaker to string them together as he saw fit, as we string sentences together without following set rules. In due course it might turn out that 'discourses' of the pattern 'Up . . . Mountain . . .', 'In . . . Cave . . .' were so commonly useful that the pattern would be learnt as a fixed model, along with the individual words – and the 'prepositional-phrase sentence' would be born. (While the words were still independent sentences, no doubt people would on one occasion say 'Up . . . Mountain' and on another occasion 'Mountain . . . Up', depending on which aspect of the global situation presented itself most immediately to their minds; originally chance alone would dictate that small short-term differences in frequency between these two orderings would cause one tribe to regularize the former pattern and evolve a prepositional language such as English, while another tribe adopted the latter pattern and evolved a postpositional language such as Japanese.) Later still, discourses such as 'John . . . Up-mountain', 'Mary. . . . In-cave' would be recognized as commonly useful, and one kind of subject-predicate structure would become a learned feature of the language; and so on.

Partly because of the impossibility of acquiring hard evidence about the prehistory of language, the topic has been rather markedly unfashionable in recent linguistic discussion. (According to Jane Hill, in the recent past 'the juxtaposition of linguistics and evolution theory was felt to be slightly improper'.)[1] For this reason, many linguists are likely to feel suspicious or scornful of the inevitably speculative remarks I am making here. I should therefore emphasize that the logic of my argument by no means requires me to show that the origins of language must have conformed to the scenario I have sketched; I need argue only that my opponents cannot demonstrate that it did not. Theoretical linguists claim that linguistic universals force us to posit fixed innate mental structure, since no alternative explanation for the universals is available; I am arguing that there is an alternative which is at any rate equally plausible on its face. (I have not yet begun to show that my alternative is actually preferable; this will be done in Chapter VIII.) The speculative nature of my discussion here in no way differentiates it from the linguistic theory of innate mental structuring, since we have not a scrap of direct observational evidence of such structuring despite the fact that brains are available to us for inspection (admittedly under strong ethical constraints) while the first speakers have long vanished into the past. (Linguists, indeed, often lay considerable stress on the fact that their nativist explanation of syntactic universals cannot be correlated with any neurophysiological findings that have emerged so far or that are likely to emerge in the near future;[2] they appear to feel, surely rightly, that if the two programmes of research did overlap in this way linguistics would rapidly be eclipsed and public attention granted exclusively to the relatively 'hard-nosed' researches of the neurophysiologists.)

Other linguists, I suspect, will be happy to accept, at least for the sake of argument, that my scenario is a reasonably plausible one, but will urge that I am providing no alternative to the limited-mind explanation for linguistic universals since the very terms in which my scenario is stated take that explanation implicitly for granted. In describing the growth of language as an

---

[1] 'On the evolutionary foundations of language, *American Anthropologist*, vol. 74, 1972, p. 308.

[2] 'Neurophysiology is in too primitive a state now to find the mechanism [of universal grammar]. For them, it's just a dream. We linguists hope to show the neurophysiologists what to look for.' (Quoted from Chomsky in Ved Mehta, *John is Easy to Please*, Secker & Warburg, 1971, p. 211.)

evolutionary process I am treating 'usefulness for communication' as the property analogous to 'stability', or 'fitness' in Darwinian theory, which causes some momentary concatenations of utterances to become permanent features of the language while other utterance-combinations that someone hits upon on one occasion are forgotten as soon as the occasion is past. But, it may be objected, the view that certain kinds of word-combination are inherently 'useful for communication' while others are not already embodies the assumption which I am claiming to argue against, namely that the nature of human thought imposes particular structural characteristics on any language which is to succeed in communicating it from one human mind to another. Further, I suggested above that in the initial stage of linguistic evolution a single word such as *up* 'might mean that someone has gone up something, that the honey was high up on the ledge', or the like. Again, my opponent may suggest, this wording presupposes that the speaker who says 'Up' has 'in his mind' some particular proposition of the complex kind that present-day languages are adapted to express, and that he fails to articulate it only because he and his community have not yet evolved a recognized means of doing so. In that case the nature of the complex languages which are eventually used will be determined by the need to provide means of symbolizing the various elements of the propositions which were already 'in people's minds' before language began – which is just what I claim to be arguing against.

I reject this objection. When I suggested that a one-word sentence such as 'Up' might 'mean' any of a number of different things, I did not imply that a speaker of such a language had a particular one of those things 'in his mind'. Rather, I intended to suggest that a speaker of a holophrastic language could have been motivated to say 'Up' by any one of a number of different circumstances, which would stimulate a speaker of *English* to utter diverse English sentences such as *John has gone up the mountain*, *The honey is up on the ledge*, and so forth. It is essential to the picture of language-development being sketched here that the speakers are *not* to be thought of as evolving forms of words to express complex ideas which were 'in their heads' all along; rather, in evolving new syntactic forms they are creating for themselves new patterns of thought (just as, I argued in earlier chapters, the invention of a new word commonly represents the creation of a new concept rather than merely a means of expressing a concept implicit in people's existing mentality). To make syntax is, literally, to make sense.

Some linguists, in my experience, find this way of looking at the growth of syntax intuitively ungraspable, and they dismiss it as incoherent. I do not find it intuitively difficult, for one thing because there is an experience that one can undergo nowadays which offers a speeded-up subjective analogue for the hypothetical creation of syntax over many generations: namely, the experience of trying to make oneself understood in a language of which one has not studied even the barest rudiments. One picks up somehow a handful of isolated words, and with these one thrashes about in the search for ways of using them that will release one's pent-up urge to communicate. Some combination of words that one tries out, though no doubt hopelessly ungrammatical in the language as it is actually spoken, nevertheless succeeds in 'getting through' to the hearer; one remembers such combinations and incorporates them into subsequent attempts to say more complicated things.

Of course this situation is in some ways very different from the hypothetical birth of language as I describe it. For one thing, the speaker in this case certainly has got complex ideas already 'in his mind' in the sense that he is already the master of a full-scale language such as English, though it happens that his hearer does not know that particular language. A linguist attracted to the limited view of mind may well be inclined to interpret the foreign-language situation as one in which the speaker is trying to guess what sequence of known words in the other's language will come closest to expressing the content of a *particular* sentence in the speaker's own language (or in Fodor's neutral 'language of thought'). In some cases, where the motive for communication is very specific, this is quite accurate; one's wife says trustingly 'Ask him how much those peppers are', and one tries desperately to guess what might be the Hungarian for 'How much are those peppers?' But often one wants to communicate with a friendly foreigner as much for the sake of communication as because there is some specific thing one needs to say, and my own introspection suggests that in such circumstances one does not first think of articulate propositions and then guess how to convert them into a language in which one does not know how to be articulate, but rather works within the alien language as best one can without reference to a familiar language. (This kind of thing may depend partly on personality; there are people who feel embarrassed about speaking a language they have not learned properly, and I suspect that such people will be relatively unlikely to recognize the experiences sketched here. But clearly that particular kind of inhibition would not have been relevant for speakers of an *Ursprache* in which nobody had yet evolved sophisticated syntax.)

Again, in the foreign-language situation my opponents might be inclined to say that what makes one's fumbling attempts at self-expression 'fit' or 'unfit' is their degree of resemblance to well-formed utterances in the foreign language as it is actually spoken, a criterion for which there is no analogue in my hypothesis about the creation of an *Ursprache*. But my own impression is that, in the real-life 'inarticulate foreigner' situation, successful communication does not depend purely on the speaker's pitching on arrangements of words which are identifiably similar to those that are grammatical in the hearer's language; provided the hearer is not too mentally inflexible he will often succeed in guessing the speaker's intention without referring his output to any particular grammatical form of words. The speaker and hearer will to some extent *invent* a shared language which may be quite unlike either of their mother tongues, given only a quite meagre foundation of a few vocabulary elements.

This process of language-creation will not normally be taken very far; if the people in question are going to be doing a lot of talking to one another, then one of them will probably start to learn the other's language properly. But that is not always true; sometimes 'languages' created in much this way become enduring systems of communication used by numbers of people, in which case they are called 'pidgins' or, if they acquire native speakers of their own, 'creoles'. (According to Derek Bickerton, it is noticeable that actual instances of pidgins and creoles have fewer syntactic rules than maturer languages.)[1] And even when the process of

[1] 'Some problems of acceptability and grammaticality in pidgins and creoles',

'language-creation' I have portrayed is an affair of only a few hours on a holiday afternoon, while it lasts it offers a small-scale model for the route our ancestors may have taken towards articulateness.

However, I realize that those who find the limited-mind approach to language convincing will have no difficulty in re-interpreting my account of the 'inarticulate foreigner' situation in conformity with their own view. I included that account not to try to demonstrate by analogy that my hypothetical description of the origin of language must be admitted as coherent, but to render that description more intuitively graspable and realistic for those readers who are prepared in abstract intellectual terms to concede that it is a coherent possibility. There is no need for me to argue that the hypothesis is coherent in the sense that it is not *logically* inadmissible, because the linguistic theorists whose views I am opposing themselves implicitly concede this. To say that my account of the birth of language is incoherent would be to say that the invention of novel syntactic constructions can be construed only as the invention of devices for expressing patterns of thought that already existed in the speaker's mind, that relative 'fitness' of a syntactic structure can mean only relative directness of corre-spondence to fixed mental structures which any human language must express. In other words, to treat my account as incoherent would be to treat the limited-mind theory of fixed innate mental structure as an axiomatic truth. But the argument of the theor-etical linguists with which we are concerned asserts that we must adopt the theory of fixed innate mental structure because there is good evidence for it. To make this assertion is to concede that the theory of fixed innate mental structure is *not* an axiomatic truth but an empirical issue; it is an elementary principle that if obser-vations of any kind count as evidence for a given assertion then that assertion cannot be a truth of logic. So it must be common ground that the idea of men creating their patterns of thought in creating their patterns of speech is logically coherent, and the question is whether the empirical evidence favours this view, or whether, as linguists argue, it rather supports the view that the

in S. Greenbaum, ed., *Acceptability in Language* (*Contributions to the Sociology of Language*, 17), Mouton (the Hague), 1977.

invention of language was merely the invention of outward clothing to fit predetermined internal thought-patterns.

It is quite true, of course, that there are many respects in which the hypothetical evolution of languages is a very different sort of process from the evolution of biological species. Thus, a biological species consists of a class of individuals each of which will on the whole be structurally very similar to all the others. In Man there are differences between the sexes, but these differences are fairly small in comparison to the anatomical resemblances between men and women. Some species, such as ants, exhibit greater intra-specific differences (a queen ant is *very* different from a worker), but again there will be only a small number of different types within the species (in the case of ants, essentially three types). The sentences of an evolved language, on the other hand, are structur-ally extremely different from one another; we find everything from one-word sentences to highly complex periods containing many layers of subordination, and it is moderately unusual in practice to encounter two structurally-identical sentences differing only with respect to their vocabulary. Again, one of the most salient facts about biological evolution is that individuals of a species descend from pairs of other individuals of the species; but, given a particu-lar sentence of English, we cannot identify other English sentences as its 'parents'. It would not be difficult to think of further dis-analogies between biological and linguistic evolution,[1] and such disanalogies may seem to make Simon's argument irrelevant to language.

What is wrong with this objection is that it ties the notion of 'evolution', to which Simon's argument appeals, too closely to the particular features exhibited by the biological example of evol-ution. Certainly there are disanalogies between the hypothesized evolution of languages and Darwinian biological evolution, as there are disanalogies between biological evolution and the evolution of social institutions, or of books. This does nothing to

---

[1] For instance, linguistic evolution must presumably be what Stephen Toulmin calls 'coupled' (*Human Understanding*, vol. i, Oxford University Press, 1972, pp. 337–40) – new forms are produced as responses to a felt need, whereas in biological evolution mutations occur at random with respect to ecological pressures. Like Toulmin, I see little significance in this distinction.

hinder us in using Simon's argument as an explanation for the
linguistic universals, unless the small number of characteristics of
'evolutionary processes' which are relevant for Simon's thesis turn
out to include any which are inapplicable in the linguistic case.
But that is surely not so. All that Simon's thesis requires of an
'evolutionary process' is that novel species emerge as the output of
a shuffling together of smaller constituents which are such that a
few of the potential products of shuffling are stable while the
majority are not. For Simon's statistical argument to succeed it is
quite irrelevant whether what we identify as a 'species' is a class of
similar individual organisms connected up with one another by
the parent/child relationship, or is an entity of some quite different
category. In the social sphere we can (and often do) apply the
notion of evolution in such a way that the 'species' are patterns of
complex behaviour – for instance we can discuss the evolution of
games such as chess or draughts; here the 'individuals' of the
species (particular instances of chess-playing behaviour) are
related to other instances not as children to parents but by the
relationship of imitation. (I assume, without specialized knowledge, that chess and draughts, and a number of other somewhat
similar board games, share a common ancestry, but obviously *not*
in the sense that two games-boxes got together in the drawer and
spawned a succession of slightly modified progeny.) This offers a
much closer analogy for the evolution of language. There could
even be cases of 'evolution', conforming to Simon's thesis, in which
the individual/species distinction was wholly inapplicable
because the entities which were modified over time were themselves individual physical objects. (I cannot quote an example,
but this is only because I cannot think of a category of physical
objects capable of spontaneously forming stable combinations in a
small number of ways but subject to being shuffled into a much
larger range of combinations.) Even within biology it would be
quite provincial to think of sexual reproduction as an essential
property of evolution; there are plenty of biological species in
which new individuals are created by other mechanisms. For the
general argument about evolution with which we are concerned,
the creation of new *individuals* of a species is a red herring; we are
interested in the way that new *species* come into being. In the case

of language, utterances of sentences are the individuals and languages are the species. Theoretical linguists discuss the question why all *languages* share certain common structural properties; they do not argue that there are unexpected consequences of the fact that all *sentences* uttered by a member of a given language-community reveal structural relationships with one another. It would surely be much more remarkable if a given speaker's sentences did not reveal common traits.

The fact that the individual sentences of a language are so diverse (while nevertheless being related in ways that make it possible to speak of them as belonging to 'one language'), whereas the individuals of a biological species are very similar to one another, is certainly an interesting issue. It is to be explained, presumably, in terms of what makes for 'fitness' in the respective domains. A language is 'fit', i.e. suitable to be adopted as a medium of communication, if it is useful to speakers, and for a speaker it is useful, not to say essential, that the repertory of utterances available to him be distinguishably different from one another – it is only the fact that our sentences contrast with one another that enables them to convey different meanings. A biological species is 'fit', on the other hand, if its members can maintain themselves alive long enough to produce progeny, and for this it is not essential that the individuals of the species be very diverse. One man in one place uses his legs and arms to hunt one piece of game; another man living elsewhere uses *his* legs and arms to hunt another piece of game, and the fact that both men have the same complement of limbs does nothing to diminish the success of either of the separate hunts. Thus the relationships between individuals and species are very different for these two cases of evolution; but this difference between the two domains is quite irrelevant to the applicability of Simon's thesis, which does not deal with individuals but only with species.

In one respect, furthermore, language offers a better analogue of biological evolution than do the other 'evolutionary processes' discussed by Simon. A common objection to 'social Darwinism' is that it ignores a problem about small numbers. Biological evolution deals with almost astronomical numbers of individuals succeeding one another over aeons of time, so that the great majority of innovations which occur can be weeded out as unfit and yet those which remain can still cumulate into the major differences between species which we observe to occur. When we turn to the 'evolution' of social institutions – say, commercial firms – on the other hand, it can be argued that so few individuals will be competing within a society at a given time that there is no good reason to ascribe to the survivors any intrinsic 'fitness' or 'efficiency' – they may well just be lucky. The biological analogue of this is called the 'Sewall Wright effect' or 'genetic drift'; Wright is taken to have shown that in small populations the law of natural selection is effectively suspended.[1] How far the 'Sewall Wright effect' is a reality is a matter of controversy within biological theory.[2] But even if the argument from small numbers should be valid as against various aspects of 'Social Darwinism', it seems to have no force against an evolutionary account of the creation of language. A man utters sentences much more frequently than members of most biological species produce offspring. There is no difficulty in postulating 'competitive pressure' as heavy and as long-drawn-out as one is likely to want in applying evolutionary theory to the case of language.

In another respect language is a much *more* appropriate domain than biology for the application of Simon's thesis. We saw that Simon overlooked the distinction between symbiotic and endogenous evolution. His argument directly explains only evolution of the former category, and there is only a limited amount of this in the biological domain – perhaps because above a certain level there are few or no *potential* combinations of biological organisms which lead to stable ensembles. (Protozoa and blue-green algae are claimed to have merged into stable entities which became the first plants, but, as already pointed out, a horse which rolls in burrs will not produce a race of quadrupeds with prickly lumps on; the burrs will soon be rubbed off, and the genetic material of horse and burr has no chance of being linked together

[1] See e.g. Sewall Wright, 'Fisher and Ford on "the Sewall Wright effect"', *American Scientist*, vol. 39, 1951, pp. 452–79.
[2] See E. Mayr, *Animal Species and Evolution*, Harvard University Press (Cambridge, Mass.), 1963, p. 203ff.; G. G. Simpson, *This View of Life*, Harcourt, Brace & World, 1964, p. 75.

by such an event.) In the case of words, on the other hand, if some novel combination of previously-independent units proves useful, there is no barrier to the linking becoming a regular feature of the linguistic repertory. The linguistic analogue of the biological fact that higher organisms are contained in tough skins which prevent individuals merging their identities would presumably be some phonetic difficulty in pronouncing as a sequence utterances that had previously been used in isolation, or a difficulty in remembering novel utterance-sequences once they had been used, but such difficulties do not occur. Nothing is physically easier than stringing words together in any way one chooses, and humans have good general-purpose memories.

Far from regarding the extension of Simon's argument to the case of language as a dubious enterprise, then, I would suggest that language *if anywhere* should be the domain in which Simon's thesis applies.

And, if we agree that the hypothetical origin of language fulfils the conditions required for it to count as an 'evolutionary process', then the predictions made by Simon's thesis seem to match the observed syntactic universals very well. The thesis will predict that complex sentences should be hierarchically structured, with the sub-sentential units of the hierarchy being elements that have independent uses as utterances – or which, at least, derive historically from units which once were independently useful. This is precisely what we find.

The hierarchical structure of sentences is the characteristic represented within Theoretical Linguistics by the claim that a 'constituency grammar' plays a central role in the definition of each natural language. Chomsky frequently makes a point of the fact that the constituency base component of the description of a natural language is 'recursive', i.e. that the category Sentence occurs to the right of the arrow in some of the rules, thus allowing for subordinate clauses and hence for an unlimited variety of sentence-structures. In other words, some subordinate nodes in a sentence will themselves dominate sentences, which are by definition potentially independent utterances. By no means all the nodes intermediate between leaves and root in the constituency-structure of a sentence will be labelled 'Sentence', of course. One of the commonest other labels is 'Noun-Phrase'. We are brought up to think of noun-phrases, such as *John's uncle, both books, that big one*, as 'not complete sentences'; at school we are taught that it is improper for such expressions to appear in isolation in our writing. But everyone knows that bare noun-phrases do occur constantly in speech for purposes such as identifying people or things, drawing attention to things, summoning people, and the like; in other words, this category of sentence-constituent is observably useful as an independent utterance even though it is no longer the most inclusive category. A noun-phrase preceded by a preposition makes a prepositional phrase; I have already suggested that it is plausible to see this rule as a reflection of syntactic evolution, and certainly one often hears prepositional phrases such as *on the ledge* used as complete utterances.

Some categories of sentence-constituent are not commonly used independently; it seems to be rare to hear a common noun such as *dog* in isolation, although a noun-phrase such as *the dog* is a usual enough utterance. My application of Simon's logic requires that *dog* must once have been a likely utterance. But there is no difficulty here. Now that the category of noun-phrases including articles has evolved, the extra precision attained by using these prefixes no doubt outweighs the small effort of pronouncing the one or two additional phonemes they comprise, so the simpler utterance *dog* has become near-extinct. We have no reason to believe that such utterances were not found useful before the category of grammatical articles had evolved; judging by the speech of young children, and by the many languages of the modern world lacking any equivalent of *a* and *the*, such utterances clearly are useful to individuals who have not mastered the system of articles.

I shall not attempt to go through all the categories of sub-sentential constituent proposed for English. One general point is worth making, however. If we find some syntactic category which seems inappropriate to serve a purpose as an isolated utterance, we need not necessarily conclude that the Simonian explanation for constituency structure is wrong; it may instead be that our syntactic analysis is mistaken. If we allow ourselves to resort to this escape-route too freely the appeal to Simon's thesis will become empty, but the move would be relatively unobjectionable if there are independent reasons to question the validity of the particular syntactic constituent.

An interesting case in this regard is the category 'Predicate', or 'Verb-Phrase'. Sentences have traditionally been divided into 'subject' and 'predicate', and in their early work Chomsky and his associates took it for granted that this traditional analysis should be reflected by including as the first rule of a constituency grammar the formula 'Sentence $\longrightarrow$ Noun-Phrase Verb-Phrase' (commonly abbreviated as 'S $\rightarrow$ NP VP'). The latter node would then be expanded by rules such as 'VP$\rightarrow \left\{ \begin{array}{c} V_i \\ V_t\, NP \end{array} \right\}$' (where 'V$_i$' stands for intransitive verbs such as *sleep*, 'V$_t$' for transitive verbs such as *love* – the braces indicate that 'VP' is expanded as *either* 'V$_i$' *or* 'V$_t$ NP'). But 'verb-phrases', or 'predicates', seem quite uncommon and odd as independent utterances, at least in contemporary English. I can hardly imagine a situation (ignoring the very special case of headlines in American newspapers) in which someone would be likely to say *Loves the countryside*, for instance.

However, of the various syntactic categories mentioned in the rules quoted above, it happens that 'Verb-Phrase' is much less well motivated than the others. It seems very likely that the rule 'S$\longrightarrow$NP VP' might be the *only* rule in the grammar of English in which 'VP' appears to the right of the arrow; and, it if it *is* the only rule with this property, then it would be more economical to merge the two rules quoted into one by writing 'S $\rightarrow$ NP$\left\{ \begin{array}{c} V_i \\ V_t\, NP \end{array} \right\}$ ', abandoning the VP node. (By contrast, the category 'Noun-Phrase' is quite secure, since it will undoubtedly need to occur on the right-hand side of a number of different rules of grammar – which implies that it would be uneconomical to dispense with the category.) As general linguistic theory developed, the validity of the category 'Verb-Phrase' came to be called into question for a number of reasons, all of which were entirely independent of the evolutionary approach to syntax discussed here.[1] If it turns out that the only constituents which seem implausible as indepen-

---

[1] See e.g. J. D. McCawley, 'English as a *VSO* language', *Language*, vol. 46, 1970, pp. 297–8.

dent utterances are also the ones whose status as syntactic constituents is most doubtful, the persuasiveness of the Simonian account of syntactic universals will be strengthened rather than the reverse. (Clearly, the issue deserves a more comprehensive investigation than I have space for here.)

I pointed out, above, that many of the constituents of a sentence will themselves be labelled 'Sentence', these being what we know as 'subordinate clauses'. (I ignore the case of *co*-ordinate clauses here, since the grounds for grouping these into single complex sentences are very weak.[1]) Some subordinate clauses are indistinguishable from sentences which occur as independent utterances; the italicized clause in 'I know *John is here*' is a case in point. Many other subordinate clauses, however, would not be found occurring as isolated utterances; we say e.g. 'This is the book *that my brother lent to Mary*', but we would not use the relative clause 'That my brother lent to Mary' on its own as a statement. In linguistic theory, this situation is described by the device of transformational rules, already discussed; the subordinate clause is said to have the 'underlying' form 'My brother lent that to Mary' or 'My brother lent the book to Mary' (these being word-sequences which *could* occur as independent sentences), and it is modified by the Relative Clause Formation rule when it occurs in a certain position as a constituent of a larger sentence. In a Simonian account of linguistic evolution, transformational rules will be interpreted historically as processes by which sentence-constituents come to change their form after being incorporated into larger constructions. Once, we may suppose, our ancestors would have said something like 'This is the book; my brother lent the book to Mary'. It turned out frequently to be convenient to make a noun-phrase used in one sentence more precise by adding a second sentence saying something else about the object in question, so that in due course such pairs of sentences became a recognized type of utterance. Since the whole point of these sentence-pairs was that the words (here, *the book*) occurring as antecedent were equally applicable in the second sentence, they were redundant there and were dropped or replaced by a short

[1] cf. my 'Against base co-ordination', *Foundations of Language*, vol. 12, 1974, pp. 117–25.

relative pronoun. For our own language family such a course of development can be only guessed at, but syntactic evolution of very much this kind has been observed in detail in a contemporary creole.[1]

One might suggest that the trick of moving the relative pronoun to the beginning of the relative clause could have been introduced in order to make it more obvious which of the noun-phrases of the relative clause referred to the antecendent in the main clause; or perhaps there was a general rule by which the psychological topic was placed first in any clause, and the present differentiation between main and relative clauses has resulted from abandonment of this principle in *main* clauses in order to allow word-order to reflect logical relationships consistently.

All this is quite analogous to the situation in biology whereby an organism changes its nature after it has been absorbed into symbiosis with another organism. What we would expect is that parts of the subordinate organism which no longer have a function within the new organism will atrophy – thus words in relative clauses which merely repeat the antecedent are deleted; while the subordinate organism develops new features permitting it to collaborate better with the more inclusive organism it has become part of – this is paralleled, perhaps, by the device of moving relative pronouns to the front of their clause in order to mark their relationship with the antecedent.

I believe that the Simonian approach to language succeeds very well in predicting just the kind of syntactic features which are observed to be common to all natural languages. What Simon has in effect shown is that, even if we accept Chomsky's argument that there is nothing logically necessary about the syntactic universals (and I have argued that we should accept this, though it is a point that many people have found difficult), we nevertheless know that

---

[1] Gillian Sankoff and Penelope Brown, 'The origins of syntax in discourse: a case study of Tok Pisin relatives', *Language*, vol. 52, 1976, pp. 631–66. In contrast with the situation in phonology (where the historical data are much fuller) there has been very little discussion in the syntactic domain about whether the transformational rules posited by linguists describing contemporary languages can be seen as reflecting the history of the respective languages; however, see R. A. Jacobs, *Syntactic Change: A Cupan (Uto-Aztecan) Case Study (University of California Publications in Linguistics, 79)*, University of California Press, 1975.

any complex language which actually emerges from the gradual process of evolution is sure to share these universal traits – not because possession of them makes a language 'better' or more 'efficient', but simply because the mathematics of evolution favours such properties so long as they are not positively disadvantageous. It might be, as Chomsky suggests, that a language based on some quite different structural principles could in theory serve the communicational needs of some hypothetical organism; but, given that the language is gradually evolved rather than adopted 'all in one go', the theoretical possibility cannot be realized in practice. (Indeed, one can illustrate this last point by an actual example. Computers are a kind of 'organism' which can be described, without distorting the meanings of words very far, as accepting and emitting 'messages' expressed in complex 'languages', and the 'native languages' – in computer jargon, 'machine codes' as opposed to 'programmer-oriented languages' – of digital computers are not based on hierarchical grammar.[1] The significant fact is that computers, obviously, do not gradually evolve their machine codes by trial and error from simple beginnings; the codes are built in as finished systems by the designers.) Since Simon's thesis permits us to predict the syntactic universals without postulating fixed innate mental machinery, the universals cease to have any force as evidence in favour of a nativist account of mind.

I have encountered one strategy which challenges this, as follows. Nativists such as Chomsky claim that the nature of human languages is determined by the nature of human beings. I have shown that the nature of human languages follows from the nature of evolution. Therefore, the challenge runs, I have not contradicted the nativists but merely expanded on their account of how language is determined by filling in an intermediate link in the causal chain: human nature being what it is, any of our complex cultural products must result from evolutionary processes, and evolutionary processes being what they are, any of *their* complex products must be hierarchical. If this counts as nativism, then I have no quarrel with the nativists. But it is quite clear that

[1] cf. my *Form of Language*, p. 131.

limited-minders such as Chomsky mean that human nature determines linguistic structure in a much directer sense than this. They do not claim merely that human nature is such that our complex cultural products evolve gradually from simple beginnings – this is a banal commonplace. Rather, they claim that human nature imposes a particular logically arbitrary structure on our languages (and presumably, by the same token, on our thought) just as it imposes a particular logically arbitrary number of fingers on our hands; and it is this quite surprising claim which has turned Theoretical Linguistics into the focus of intellectual attention which it is today. Chomsky has been fairly scathing about the value of the theory of evolution as an 'explanation' of anything.

There is in fact a beautiful irony in Chomsky's attitude to Darwin. Chomsky has dismissed the biological theory of evolution with some scorn as an empty tautology, in the sense that it permits us to make no predictions about 'what will happen next'. Darwin asserts that relatively fit organisms will survive, but he gives us no criterion of fitness other than the fact of survival; looking backwards we can always point to any particular past biological innovation and claim that it survived because for some reason it increased the fitness of its possessor, but we decide that an innovation is on balance advantageous only because we know that its possessor did survive. This general point about Darwin's theory has often been made.[1] Some scholars have taken it to demonstrate that a theory can have other virtues than the ability to generate testable predictions;[2] but Chomsky takes a shorter way with Darwin.[3] What Simon has shown is that Darwinian evolutionary theory does after all lead to one rather general kind of prediction, namely that (other things being equal) its products will be highly hierarchical. Many people have supposed the fact that organisms of various categories are hierarchically structured to be a mere truism not standing in need of explanation; Chomsky's predecessors in linguistics, though well aware of the hierarchical struc-

---

[1] See e.g. Michael Ruse, *The Philosophy of Biology*, Hutchinson, 1973, p. 38ff.

[2] Michael Scriven, 'Explanation and prediction in evolutionary theory', *Science*, vol. 130, 1959, pp. 477–82; and cf. W. B. Gallie, 'Explanations in history and the genetic sciences', *Mind*, new series vol. 64, 1955, pp. 160–80.

[3] Chomsky, *Language and Mind*, Harcourt, Brace & World, 1968, pp. 59–62, 83.

ture of sentences, took that fact absolutely for granted and never dreamed that things might, logically, be otherwise. It is specifically Chomsky who has been at pains to argue that hierarchicality in this domain, however familiar in practice, is *not* a logically necessary feature of language. In other words, despite his dismissal of Darwinian theory, it is Chomsky who argues that the consequences of Darwinism for language are a true empirical prediction rather than an empty tautology. And in making this prediction, and thus destroying the case for a nativist explanation of syntactic universals, Darwin removes the foundation-stone on which Chomsky's theoretical edifice is supported.

VIII

In the previous chapter I argued that, if we assume languages to have evolved gradually during Man's history from simple, holophrastic beginnings, then Simon's thesis explains the fact that complex modern languages all share the kind of hierarchical structure identified by theoretical linguists. However, defenders of Chomskyan nativism have a fairly obvious strategy available for rebutting my objection. As an attempted refutation of linguistic nativism (the rebuttal runs) my argument for Simonian evolution in syntax simply misses the point. What I have done is to show that the properties common to the languages of various speech-communities are explained if we assume that the communities have evolved their languages over long periods rather than somehow acquiring them as complete systems overnight. But Chomsky (the objection continues) is not concerned with the phylogenesis of language but with its ontogenesis – not with how the language of a speech-community comes to be as it is, but how an *individual* of any community succeeds in acquiring his mother-tongue on the basis of the limited range of examples available to him.

As we have seen, Chomsky argues that the data about the syntax of his mother-tongue which are typically available to an infant learner are very meagre and 'degenerate', yet the infant always induces from its elders' speech a grammar which, except possibly in a few trivial respects, is identical to theirs. (It is important to bear in mind that children learn their mother-tongue not by being given theoretical instruction in it but purely by reconstructing it from the large but finite set of examples to which they are exposed.) An account (such as my Simonian account) which purports to explain how a language comes during its history to acquire the properties discussed by theoretical linguists is quite useless, my opponents may suggest, as an account of how those properties are transmitted from one generation to the next.

(Compare the case of biology: Darwin's theory of natural selection shows how species have come to be adapted to a range of
diverse ecological niches, but does nothing to explain how species
breed true – the mechanism of this is a quite separate issue which
biologists have only recently begun to understand.)

Chomsky argues that we can explain the phenomenon of accurate transmission of language between the generations only by
postulating that the *individual* contains inborn mental structures
which determine the grand design of any language learnable by
the individual, and which leave only relatively peripheral matters
of detail to be filled in from experience. Then we can suppose that
the data available to the infant *are* normally sufficient to decide
these limited matters of detail which genetic inheritance leaves
open (and cases where the data leave one of *these* issues undecided
will lead to the modifications to syntax which do occur over the
centuries).

What I have really shown (according to this objection) is that
the linguistic mechanisms innate in the minds of contemporary
men must have evolved gradually, by the small genetic mutations
postulated by orthodox neo-Darwinian biological theory, rather
than having appeared full-blown in our species by a sudden,
un-Darwinian genetic saltation – as a 'typostrophism', or 'sys-
temic mutation', of the kind advocated by the unorthodox biologists O. H. Schindewolf and Richard Goldschmidt.[1] It is true
that I wrote about the steps in this evolutionary advance as if they
were intellectual rather than genetic developments – that is, as if
the occurrence of a new syntactic construction were akin, say, to
the composition of a new poem (which does not correspond to any
modification in the poet's genes) rather than to the growth of a
new organ. But this manner of speaking is a red herring (the
objector maintains), because even if individuals did evolve syntactically sophisticated languages through intellectual developments
such languages would 'fall apart', as it were, as the individuals
died and were replaced by younger individuals who would have
heard too limited a range of examples to be able to reconstruct the

[1] O. H. Schindewolf, 'Darwinismus oder Typostrophismus?' *A Magyar
Biológiai Kutató Intézet Munkái*, vol. 16, 1945, pp. 104–77; R. Goldschmidt, *The
Material Basis of Evolution*, Yale University Press, 1940.

particular type of grammar their parents had evolved. The only way that a linguistic advance can not merely occur but endure over the generations is for it to be a genetic development; intellectual linguistic advances would vanish as fast as they arose until they happened to be mimicked by genetic mutation.

The use of Simon's thesis to demonstrate that the phylogenesis of language must have consisted of a gradual cumulation of small genetic mutations rather than one big sudden saltation is valid (the objector might add), but it does not go against Chomsky's theory; Chomsky does not address himself to this question, and often claims to be agnostic about the phylogenetic origin of language.

I suggested in Chapter VI that the arguments Chomsky bases on the speed and accuracy of children's acquisition of language and the 'degenerateness' of the data available to children suffer from logical difficulties. Let us suspend our scepticism at least temporarily, however, and consider what force the objection just outlined would have if Chomsky's arguments from the success of language-transmission between the generations should be valid.

One answer to the objection is that Chomsky is not really quite so agnostic as suggested. Chomsky's poor opinion of Darwinism makes him reluctant to think of language as having evolved genetically through the kind of long series of small random mutations which that theory postulates as the general mechanism of species formation, and here and there in his writings Chomsky drops hints that in general he favours the 'typostrophist' view of biological evolution.[1] But this is a side issue, and certainly Chomsky has not been very explicit on the point. The truly fatal flaw in the objection just described is that it seriously underestimates the force of the Simonian argument against Chomsky, as I shall now go on to show.

Chomsky treats the acquisition by a child of his first language as a matter of hypothesis-formulation, very much akin to the work of a scientist who discovers a theory to account for some series of laboratory observations. In both cases the data are a finite set of examples, but what is induced from the data is a general system (a theory in the scientific case, a grammar in the linguistic case)

[1] *Language and Mind*, p. 83, and p. 88, n. 26.

which allows for an infinitely large range of potential examples including those which have actually been observed as particular cases. Once the scientist has succeeded in working out the correct theory of the phenomenon in question, he goes on to apply it by making predictions about new cases, different from those on the basis of which his theory was formulated. (There is of course a question about whether scientists ever discover ultimately correct theories, but let us ignore this point.) Likewise, we know that a child has mastered the syntax of his parents' language when he spontaneously produces word-sequences different from those he has heard but which nevertheless are grammatical in the language – this shows that the child has succeeded in inducing the general rules exemplified by the particular data he has observed.

Some find this an odd way of thinking about the language-acquisition process. D. W. Hamlyn criticizes Chomsky on the grounds that (as an obvious truism not needing to be supported by argument, so it seems) 'the child is not like a little scientist putting questions to nature and attempting to elicit answers; such a view would make no sense'.[1] There is, certainly, one major difference between the two cases: the scientist is normally rather explicitly conscious of the hypotheses he formulates and of the tests to which they are submitted, whereas the child presumably is not consciously aware of his grammatical hypotheses or their relationship to his data. (Even for the adult linguist it is a difficult task to formulate explicitly the grammar of his own language.) Indeed, the child *could not* be explicitly aware of these matters unless we accept Fodor's notion of a 'language of thought', since, otherwise, the child has as yet no language to be explicit in.

But this difference between the case of the scientist and the case of the language-learning infant is not important for present purposes. It is easy to give examples from adult experience of wholly unconscious theory-formulation. Thus, every time one sees a new three-dimensional object one must induce a hypothesis about its shape from a two-dimensional pattern of retinal stimulation which is logically speaking quite insufficient as a basis for the decision – the stimuli will always be compatible with an infinitely

---

[1] D. W. Hamlyn, *Experience and the Growth of Understanding* (*International Library of the Philosophy of Education*), Routledge & Kegan Paul, 1978, p. 11, and cf. p. 35.

numerous range of three-dimensional objects other than the
one actually being seen, and sometimes we are made aware of this
when further observation forces the realization that the object is
not in fact what we originally saw it as.[1] Normally we are quite
unaware of the process of hypothesis-induction – we just see the
world three-dimensionally, and it is not easy to appreciate how
sophisticated an achievement this is; and commonly it would be
quite impossible for us to articulate our perceptual hypotheses
explicitly, because we will often have no exact names for complex
shapes. Inducing a three-dimensional world from a two-
dimensional pattern of stimulation is, obviously, a very much
more rapid process, and one in which fewer wrong turnings are
taken, than inducing a language from a series of utterances, but
that is a merely quantitative difference. The case of perception
serves to establish that the notion of unconscious theory-
formulation and theory-testing makes good sense.

(A further reason why one might be unhappy about assimi-
lating the activity of the child acquiring a language to that of a
scientist discovering a theory is that empirical research on everyday problem-solving behaviour suggests that the average human
is really quite bad at applying the scientific method of hypothesis-
formulation and testing; for instance people commonly persevere
with refuted hypotheses.[2] But this does not in fact seem to create a
disanalogy between the activities just mentioned. On the one hand
it has often been observed that children persevere with linguistic
forms – say, *sheeps* – which have been corrected by their parents,[3]
though if they were perfect little Popperians they should presumably drop such mistaken usages at the first whiff of counter-
evidence; and on the other hand philosophers of science such as
T. S. Kuhn have shown that real-life scientists do not in practice
behave as 'scientific saints' would.[4] If children nevertheless

[1] R. L. Gregory, *The Intelligent Eye*, Weidenfeld & Nicolson, 1970.

[2] P. C. Wason and P. N. Johnson-Laird, *Psychology of Reasoning: Structure and Content*, Batsford, 1972; cf. A. Tversky and D. Kahneman in R. E. Butts and J. Hintikka, eds., *Basic Problems in Methodology and Linguistics*, Reidel (Dordrecht), 1977.

[3] See e.g. M. D. S. Braine, 'On two types of models of the internalization of grammars', in D. I. Slobin, ed., *The Ontogenesis of Grammar*, Academic Press, 1971.

[4] T. S. Kuhn, *The Structure of Scientific Revolutions* (*International Encyclopaedia of Unified Science*, vol. ii, no. 2), University of Chicago Press, 1962.

invariably succeed in mastering their mother-tongue, this can surely be explained by saying that their motive for doing so is so overwhelming that they persist until they succeed despite their incompetence as scientists.)

It can certainly be said against Chomsky that he blurs the distinction concerning conscious awareness that holds between language-acquiring infant and adult scientists. The effect of this is that Chomsky advocates a very strange methodology for linguistics, in which one is encouraged to treat native speakers of a language as possessing reliable conscious knowledge about theoretical issues on which their opinions, if they have any, are in reality frequently no better founded than those of the linguist coming to the language in question for the first time. However, we are not concerned here with the methodology of linguistic research but rather with the logical relationship between data and the mental structures which are formed in response to those data, and in this respect Chomsky seems to be right in treating the scientist and the language-learning infant as on a par with each other; their data underdetermine their theory, but their theory is formed nevertheless.

Now, the creative-mind approach to theory-construction in any domain, which is the approach that Chomsky is concerned to argue against in the case of language-acquisition (and indeed more generally), is that since we begin with no reliable knowledge at all we must develop what ultimately becomes a complex, sophisticated theory through a gradual process of formulating fallible hypotheses, testing and refuting many of them against the data of experience, formulating further fallible hypotheses which are at a 'higher level' in that they exploit concepts established by those earlier hypotheses which have survived testing, and so on. In other words, on creative-mind assumptions the growth of knowledge (within the individual, or within a society) is itself a Simonian evolutionary process, in which the analogue of 'stability' is the ability of ideas to stand up to testing against experience. It follows that, even if the experiential data about some complex phenomenon that are available to a learner or learners are logically compatible with various non-hierarchical mental representations of that phenomenon, the general nature of learning as an activity guarantees that the representations actually arrived at will be hierarchical.

In the case of language we may well concede to Chomsky that there will be non-hierarchical grammars compatible with the totality of linguistic data available to an infant. The reason why such grammars are not the ones acquired, however, is not that they fail to fit our innate psychological machinery but that, as hypotheses, they would have to be formulated and tested 'all in one go' or not at all. A non-hierarchical grammar will make predictions about *sentences* but, by definition, not about sub-sentential constituents (if a grammar is defined in terms of sub-sentential constituents it is a hierarchical grammar). In the case of a real language such as English it is open to the infant to formulate and test out low-level hypotheses, e.g. about the identity of parts of speech, before beginning to think about higher levels; the child can establish a class of nouns before investigating the structure of noun-phrases, and do the latter before considering the shape of sentences as wholes.[1] Given that this gradual sort of grammar-formulation process is *possible* for the data available, Simon's thesis guarantees as a statistical certainty that this is how children will in fact acquire their mother tongue – the probability of their guessing one of the non-hierarchical grammars also compatible with their data before they master the data in the gradual way is so remote as to be negligible. In other words, the grammars internalized by children will be hierarchical, even if non-hierarchical grammars are available for their data, and despite the fact that nothing in the architecture of their minds makes non-hierarchical grammars unthinkable for them.[2]

---

[1] I do not claim that this exact sequence is characteristic of children's acquisition of syntax, but that a process of this general kind is. An up-to-date survey of evidence for universals of syntax-acquisition is given on pp. 352–4 of Heidi Feldman et al., 'Beyond Herodotus', in A. Lock, ed., *Action, Gesture and Symbol*, Academic Press, 1978; the references quoted there hardly seem to suggest greater invariance in the syntax-acquisition process than Simon's argument would lead us to expect.

[2] Stephen Stick argues that this is not an adequate answer to Chomsky's attack on empiricist accounts of language-acquisition, because it is necessary to explain not merely why each child formulates a grammar conforming to the linguistic universals but how each child manages to discover the *right* grammar

As has already been suggested (pp. 149–54), a limited-minder may seek to dismiss this account of syntactic development by claiming that the creative-mind approach is no genuine alternative to his own view; he may hold that the ability to formulate syntactic hypotheses presupposes an antecedently given range of possible hypotheses from which new ones are drawn by the child as earlier ones are refuted. As we have seen, the creative-minder denies that his approach involves such an assumption. But, to restate the point made before, this objection is not available to linguistic limited-minders such as Chomsky, since the objection amounts to claiming that only the limited view of mind is tenable as a matter of logic; anyone who argues that universals of language constitute *evidence* for the limited view of mind thereby concedes that the creative view is a tenable alternative. Certainly it would be open to a limited-minder to concede the force of Simon's thesis against the claim that the overall hierarchical framework of grammar is innate, but to argue that although the framework is learned from scratch the elements to be fitted into that framework are given in advance. But what Chomsky actually argues is precisely the contrary: he claims that the grand design of grammar is what is built in at birth, and that what an infant has to learn are the particular details that fit into the innate framework. (This perhaps overstates the role that Chomsky allots to learning; if the 'details' include the words of the child's mother-tongue then, as we have seen, Chomsky and his followers do claim that these are drawn from an innate stock of 'possible words', but we saw also that this is a gratuitous assumption rather than a conclusion for which evidence is cited.) If the hierarchical 'grand design' of grammar were innate, it would be a remarkable coincidence that it is just the structure that would be created by a learner who had to evolve a grammar of his mother-tongue from scratch.

Chomsky often discusses a thought-experiment in which one attempts to teach infants an 'unnatural', non-hierarchical language by exposing them to numerous examples of it as infants

conforming to the universals ('Between Chomskian rationalism and Popperian empiricism', to be in the *British Journal for the Philosophy of Science*). But this falls foul of the paradox already discussed on p. 115 above (cf. my 'Popperian language-acquisition undefeated', ibid.).

are ordinarily exposed to examples of their parents' language.[1] Such an experiment would, as Chomsky recognizes, be quite impractical, in the first place for moral reasons but also because, since by definition no adult humans speak 'unnatural' languages, it is unclear how the ordinary circumstances of language-acquisition could be simulated for such a language. However, we can perhaps imagine a hypothetical experiment along these lines, and the prediction that Simon's thesis would make about such an experiment is clear: provided the artificial language to be learned was as complex in its own way as natural languages are in their way, then if the infants succeeded in inducing any grammar at all from the data it would be a hierarchical grammar. For the non-hierarchical grammar to be tried out as a hypothesis it would have to be formulated 'all in one go' or not at all, and the chances of hitting on a highly complex hypothesis all in one go from scratch would be negligible. On the other hand, in a large quantity of data exemplifying an unnatural language there would surely be material that could be taken as partial confirmation of various simpler hypotheses of the kind that the learner would have a good chance of coming up with from scratch. Therefore, given a strong desire to learn the language, an infant would in all probability be able to make evolutionary, step-by-step progress towards a hier-archical grammar which would actually (from the experimenter's point of view) be wrong. For the infant the difference between this and the normal language-acquisition situation would be that here the data would have to be treated as very corrupt (but then, Chomsky argues that the data available in the normal situation are rather corrupt anyway).

If infants in such a situation actually began to induce a hier-archical grammar from data exemplifying a non-hierarchical language, Chomsky would undoubtedly take this as a very strong vindication indeed of his claim that humans are constrained, in their intellectual response to experience, by fixed innate mental structuring. (In his own discussions Chomsky limits himself to the less ambitious predictions that the children would fail to learn anything at all, or would eventually learn the unnatural grammar with immense difficulty as a conscious puzzle.) But in view of the

[1] E.g. *Reflections*, p. 29.

discussion above it seems that Chomsky would be wrong to take such results as support for his nativist views; these results would actually be evidence against innate mental structure and in favour of the view that we construct our mental models of reality freely and on a basis of initial ignorance.

Here I may seem to be going further than my argument warrants. I have shown that the nature of the evolutionary processes guarantees that languages would have to share common structural features if they were created and learned step by step from scratch; but I have accepted Chomsky's argument that the hypothesis of complex and fixed innate mental machinery for language-processing would also imply common traits in all human languages. So it may seem that we have reached stalemate; the observation of syntactic universals is predicted by both of these contrasting approaches to mind, and therefore does not permit us to choose between them.

This is an error. The evidence cited by Chomsky decisively favours the creative view of mind as against his own view.

The point is that, although the hypothesis of innate mental structuring leads to the prediction that there will be *some* structural universals of language, it gives us no way of predicting what the universal features will be. The hypothetical observation that hierarchy played no role in the structure of our languages, for instance, would be just as compatible with the limited-mind hypothesis as would the actual observation that hierarchy is all-important. Hierarchy would not be produced by evolutionary learning processes, because the structural universals would not be learned. If linguistic universals were explained nativistically, the specific nature of the linguistic universals would depend entirely on the nature of the innate mental structures, and since we have no direct knowledge about the latter we would have no grounds for predicting the former. (Notice that Chomsky and other theoretical linguists invite us to infer the existence of innate mental structures from the existence of linguistic universals, from which it is clear that we are not in a position to predict anything about linguistic universals from independent knowledge of innate mental structures.)

If another species of animal, or a race of hominoids on another planet, were discovered also to use complex languages, the nativist approach gives us no means of predicting what their languages would be like; provided the speakers were biologically unrelated to us, we would not expect their linguistic universals to coincide with ours. On the other hand, the hypothesis that we know nothing about language when we begin life and therefore have to acquire all aspects of our linguistic competence in a step-by-step, trial-and-error fashion leads to the prediction that human languages will share certain *specified* common traits, and just those traits are in fact observed. If any other species anywhere in the universe has languages which are transmitted culturally rather than geneti-cally, we can be sure that their languages will share the same common traits as ours.

It is a cliché of the philosophy of science, and an axiom which we take for granted in our everyday lives, that stronger theories, i.e. theories which make relatively specific predictions, are preferred to weaker alternatives. Suppose we hear that the computer pro-gram which controls the flow of money on the books of a bank contains some obscure flaw which has led to payments having gone astray for years past. We perhaps feel sorry for the program-mer whose work has turned out to be so unsatisfactory. Then we are given the additional information that the effect of the flaw was to divert payments which should have gone elsewhere into the programmer's own account; and our feelings about the program-mer change. Logically, we are not forced to revise our previous opinion that he was honest but incompetent. But that hypothesis predicts only that the program will contain *some* flaw, whereas the hypothesis of dishonesty predicts a flaw of a very specific type, and just that type of flaw is observed. Who, in such circumstances, would continue to believe in honest oversight? In a law court the fact that the honest-oversight interpretation is logically tenable might possibly suffice for it to prevail; but an accused theory, unlike an accused citizen, is entitled to no presumption of innocence.

The more ways of making mistakes *other* than self-enriching ones there are open to the programmer, the harder it becomes to believe in his innocence if the 'mistake' he makes is in fact a self-enriching mistake. Likewise, the more Chomsky stresses that numerous hypothetical alternatives to the natural languages can easily be constructed, the more decisively we must conclude, from the fact that the common features of natural languages are those which would be expected if linguistic competence were evolved from scratch, that Chomsky's nativist explanation for those features is too implausible an alternative to take seriously.

To summarize: an argument from linguistic universals to innate mental structure might well be a sound argument so long as no alternative explanation were available for the universals in question. But *the particular universals cited by Chomsky are evidence against, rather than for, the nativist account of language-acquisition.*

I might use this opportunity to make amends for a mistake of my own. Several scholars have argued that Chomsky assumes too hastily that linguistic universals correspond to innate contents of the human mind, ignoring the alternative possibility that they could be a by-product of the language-acquisition process. M. D. S. Braine, in particular, has constructed quite extensive models of the alternative views.[1] In my *Form of Language* I maintained that this contrast between 'process' and 'content' explanations for the linguistic universals was a distinction without a difference;[2] I was wrong.

Let me return to the question of limited-mind versus creative-mind accounts of the linguistic universals. I have argued that the creative-mind account must be preferred if it predicts the specific identity of the linguistic universals while the limited-mind account predicts merely that there will be some or other universals. But, it may be objected, the prediction of the limited-mind account need not be unspecific. True, Chomsky does not show that his postulate of unobserved innate mental structures enables us to predict the particular constraints on the diversity of natural languages that

---

[1] Braine, op. cit.; cf. D. I. Slobin, 'Comments on "Development psycholinguistics"', in F. Smith and G. A. Miller, eds., *The Genesis of Language*, M.I.T. Press, 1966, pp. 87–8; D. McNeill, 'The capacity for the ontogenesis of grammar', in Slobin, *The Ontogenesis of Grammar*, p. 38ff.; B. L. Derwing, *Transformational Grammar as a Theory of Language Acquisition* (*Cambridge Studies in Linguistics*, 10), Cambridge University Press, 1973, p. 53ff.; Jean Aitchison, *The Articulate Mammal*, Hutchinson, 1976, ch. 7.

[2] *Form of Language*, p. 129.

are observed, and in view of Chomsky's leanings towards biological typostrophism it is quite appropriate that he does not – if the innate structures had emerged typostrophically no predictions would follow. But biological development of the ordinary, non-typostrophist, Darwinian kind is a paradigm case of a Simonian evolutionary process. Therefore someone who is unimpressed by the claim that the data available to an individual infant are meagre (and who therefore sees no room for an explanation of how individuals acquire hierarchically-structured languages once it is given that their communities have evolved such languages) will return to the objection, already discussed, that all I have done is to make the relatively uncontroversial point that a biological explanation of the linguistic universals would have to be Darwinian rather than typostrophist. Simon shows that gradual evolution of theories within an individual who starts with no innate knowledge would lead to hierarchical mental structures, but he shows equally (the objection runs) that gradual evolution of inherited mental machinery over the generations would lead to similar structures, so the linguistic universals really are neutral as between limited-mind and creative-mind accounts of linguistic competence.

But again this is wrong. The creative-mind approach holds that individual humans inherit no 'knowledge of language', so that they succeed in mastering the language spoken in their environment only by applying the same general intelligence which they use to grapple with all the other diverse and unpredictable problems that come their way. (It would be ludicrous to suggest that *all* our intellectual achievements are facilitated by innate mechanisms specific to themselves; how could an ability to diagnose faults in motors, for instance, have been produced by biological evolution?) If this approach is correct then we should predict that universals of human language will be limited to just those features which follow from the general nature of the evolution of complex knowledge, since there is no mechanism which could impose uniformity in other respects (given that there are or have been many culturally-independent linguistic communities in the world). If, on the other hand, the use of language is made possible by complex innate mental machinery, then certainly that machinery will be hierarchical (provided it evolved in the species gradually rather than emerging by sudden typostrophism), but it will have some *particular* hierarchical structure rather than another. On this view, Simonian hierarchicality would have to be only a trivial part of what human languages share in common. An elephant and an oak-tree both begin life programmed to develop a physical structure which, arguably, is hierarchical; but they inherit not just hierarchicality in general but *particular*, and very different, hierarchical structures – it is our knowledge of those structures that enables us to tell an elephant and an oak-tree apart.

To say that the diversity of natural language is constrained by the need for it to fit inherited mental machinery, and, in answer to a question about the identity of the constraints, to reply that they are identical to the constraints which would exist if there were no such inherited mental machinery, would be self-evidently ridiculous. But the fact is that natural languages *are* very diverse; they all have hierachical grammars, but that does not mean that they all have the same grammar. Some languages have enormously complex systems of inflexion, others have no inflexion at all. Some languages allow words to be permuted fairly freely within a sentence, others have rigid (and quite diverse) rules for word-order. And so on. If the only well-established linguistic universals are characteristics explained by Simon's thesis, we must prefer the creative-mind to the limited-mind account of linguistic competence.

The last point we must consider, then, is the question whether or not the observed linguistic universals really are restricted to the properties which Simon's thesis allows us to predict.

IX

I have little doubt that proponents of linguistic nativism will have become fairly impatient with the way in which I identify the 'linguistic universals' discussed by theoretical linguists with the notion of 'hierarchicality', and that they will have felt that this trivializes what they see as a rich and detailed system of shared features going far beyond anything that follows from Simon's thesis. I believe this reaction is mistaken. As already suggested, the notion that the 'linguistic universals' form a heterogeneous assortment of many independent characteristics, each of which is found to recur in all human languages that have been inspected, seems to me to misrepresent the true state of play in linguistic research. I have argued elsewhere that there are reasons, having to do with aspects of the methodology currently fashionable in linguistics, why linguists tend at any given time greatly to over-estimate the number of hypotheses about general linguistic theory that can be regarded as reasonably firmly established.[1] In order to resolve the question, we must now survey the various well-established universal findings and check what relationship, if any, they have with Simon's argument.

Since it is Chomsky who has done most to urge the limited-mind implications of linguistic universals, the obvious way to begin is to take the various writings in which Chomsky has argued at length for this position, and to check the various items of evidence that he cites in its support. I have examined the published versions of three public lectures by Chomsky (his second Beckman Lecture given at the University of California in 1967, first Russell Lecture at Cambridge, 1971, and third Whidden Lecture at McMaster University, Hamilton, Ontario, 1975) which include the fullest expositions known to me of Chomsky's nativist argument.[2]

---

[1] *Schools of Linguistics*, ch. 6.
[2] See Chomsky, *Language and Mind*, Harcourt, Brace & World, 1968, Ch. 2; *Problems of Knowledge and Freedom*, Fontana, 1972, ch. 1; *Reflections on Language*, Temple Smith, 1976, ch. 3.

It is not altogether straightforward to distil from these sources a clear-cut set of universal claims. In places it is unclear whether Chomsky is making claims about language in general or merely about English; at other points Chomsky leaves the explanation for cited data as an open question; and universal claims made in the earlier works are modified considerably in the later ones, so that for instance what in 1967 was called the 'A-over-A principle' is replaced by the rather different 'subjacency principle' in 1975. To make these points is not to criticize Chomsky; these characteristics of his writing are to a large extent signs of his honesty and willingness to revise his opinions. They have the consequence, however, that it is difficult for me to be certain that the issues I deal with below exhaust the range of alleged syntactic universals that Chomsky has in mind; nevertheless, I believe my treatment is close to if not completely exhaustive.

In the first place, the syntax of all human languages is defined by constituency rules together with 'structure-dependent' rather than 'structure-independent' transformational rules operating on the output of the constituency base.[1] As we have seen, these points follow immediately from Simon. If a language develops (within a community and/or within the individual) by gradual evolution, then the smallest elements will come into existence first; at successive steps, the community and/or the infant will come to form larger units by assembling units of the kinds they have already acquired. It follows that the outcome will be definable by constituency rules. When a species of complex unit is established, however, it may itself evolve (under the pressure of economy of effort, or for other reasons); but such evolution will naturally manipulate the elements which have just been assembled into the new whole rather than re-opening the question of how lower-level (i.e. long-established) constituents are constructed, thus transformations will be structure-dependent.

Transformations, or some of them, apply 'cyclically'; that is to say, the sequence of transformations applies first to the lowest-level clauses in a complex sentence, then re-applies to the immediately-superordinate clauses, and so on until the sequence

---

[1] *Language and Mind*, p. 27; *Problems*, p. 29.

of transformations has been applied to the main clause.[1] Naturally that will be so. Once the unit 'clause' has become established and has undergone some independent evolution, a new generation will learn to make the appropriate adjustments when putting lower-level constituents together to form clauses; and if they subsequently learn to form larger clauses by fitting together constituents some of which are themselves clauses, then the learners will use for this purpose clauses as they know them, not the unevolved clauses which their ancestors used. Not all transformations are cyclical; there are also 'post-cyclical' transformations which apply only to a sentence as a whole and not independently to its subordinate clauses. In other words, while sentences were originally merely clauses that were not being used as constituents of larger clauses, the species 'sentence' has undergone some evolution of its own, in addition to the evolution of the species 'clause'; since the two species are logically quite distinct, fulfilling different communicative functions, this is not unexpected.

Until recently, 'Sentence' nodes alone were regarded as 'cyclical categories' – that is to say, a series of transformations would apply to a subordinate clause and also to its superordinate clause, but would not apply separately to any intermediate constituent, of a category (such as noun-phrase) other than the clause. Probably few transformations constitute crucial tests of this, but the Simonian prediction is clearly different. Any sub-sequence of a sentence which is historically a constituent ought potentially to be a cyclical category; thus there should be no bar to noun-phrases undergoing independent development, and if they did the transformations reflecting that development would cycle on 'Noun-Phrase' nodes. Sure enough, in more recent theorizing the notion of 'cyclical category' has broadened to include 'Noun-Phrase'.[2] If it has not been necessary to recognize the prepositional phrase as a cyclical category this is presumably because the concatenation of a preposition with a noun-phrase is so very simple a construction as to allow little scope for endogenous evolution; while the fact that 'Verb-Phrase' is not a cyclical category would be explained by

---

[1] *Language and Mind*, pp. 38–40.
[2] This is Chomsky's position in *Reflections*, for instance.

arguing that it is not a constituent at all, as discussed on p. 160 above.

Again in Chomsky's recent theorizing, all transformations obey a principle of 'subjacency', and there are no unbounded transformations; that is, any given transformational cycle cannot affect an element which was in the domain of a cycle earlier than the immediately previous one.[1] Thus it is permissible (not to say stylistically desirable) to transform [*the only one* [*that I like*]] *of Tolstoy's novels* into *the only one of Tolstoy's novels that I like*, but one may not transform [[*the only one* [*that I like*]] *of Tolstoy's novels*] *is out of print* into **The only one of Tolstoy's novels is out of print that I like*. (To my judgement this last sentence is not so absolutely un-English as Chomsky seems to suggest, though it is certainly rather clumsy; I prefer to avoid quarrelling with Chomsky on questions about grammaticality-data, however.) The evolutionary approach to syntax seems to entail a principle very like this in the same way as it entails that transformations will be structure-dependent: once a behaviour-pattern has become thoroughly established, it will tend to be treated as a fixed given when used as a constituent of a more complex, later-learned behaviour-pattern. Strictly, the implication of Simon's thesis would appear to be not that a transformation can 'look downwards' for a distance of one and only one cycle, as Chomsky's principle says, but rather that the 'further down' a hypothetical transformation looks the less likely that transformation is to occur in a natural language. It is not clear to me that the data cited by Chomsky are sufficient to decide between these formulations of the general principle (my parenthetical demurral, above, from Chomsky's ungrammaticality-judgement, if justified, may suggest that my formulation corresponds better to the facts). Both formulations agree in ruling out as unnatural 'unbounded transformations' which manipulate constituents irrespective of the depth at which they are embedded. Such transformations have often been proposed by linguists, so it is interesting to find Chomsky claiming that they are never in fact needed.[2]

---

[1] *Reflections*, pp. 85ff.; 92–3.

[2] Chomsky's claim is by no means universally accepted by theoretical linguists, so that the empirical adequacy of the evolutionary account of syntactic

A related point is the claim that natural languages permit 'upgrading' transformations (which move a constituent out of a subordinate clause into a superordinate one) but not 'downgrading' transformations (which do the reverse).[1] For Chomsky this is an entirely arbitrary finding; *a priori* it could equally well have turned out that downgrading rules occur and upgrading rules do not. In evolutionary terms, however, the finding is fully predictable. An upgrading rule corresponds to a case in which a community created a new utterance-type by manipulating the elements of lower-level units already established in their language. A downgrading rule would correspond to a case in which the community creates an utterance-type by manipulating the elements of a larger construction yet to be invented by their descendants, which is an obviously nonsensical idea.[2] Similarly, many theoretical linguists have claimed (although Chomsky does not discuss the point in the works cited) that while natural languages include 'post-cyclical' transformations they never contain 'pre-cyclical' transformations though these are, logically speaking, equally conceivable. In evolutionary terms, a pre-cyclical transformation would reflect a development that occured after the complex sentence had emerged (since, to be seen as 'pre-cyclical', a transformation must apply to a constituency structure containing subordinate clauses) but before the simple

universals may be vulnerable at this point. See e.g. Joan Bresnan, 'Variables in the theory of transformations', in A. Akmajian, P. Culicover, and T. Wasow, eds., *Formal Syntax*, Academic Press, 1977. E. Bach and G. M. Horn ('Remarks on "Conditions on Transformations"', *Linguistic Inquiry*, vol. 7, 1976, pp. 265–99) suggest that Chomsky's subjacency condition may follow from a more general constraint on grammars according to which 'the subsentences formed at the end of each cycle must underlie possible grammatical sentences in their own right' (op. cit., p. 297). This latter constraint is a clear prediction of the Simonian approach to syntax: it translates into the statement that whenever a community creates a new sentence-type using smaller sentences as building-blocks, those smaller sentences must actually exist in their language.

[1] *Reflections*, p. 107.

[2] Chomsky argues (*Reflections*, p. 109) that the distinction between upgrading and downgrading transformations is a special consequence of a more general constraint on anaphora. I am not clear whether this affects the status of my remarks above, because I am not sure whether the 'trace theory of movement rules' to which Chomsky appeals constitutes an empirical claim about linguistic universals or a methodological decision about techniques of syntactic analysis.

sentence had evolved (since it is *pre*-cyclical) – this is a contradiction.[1]

Certain of the universals referred to by Chomsky seem explainable without recourse to evolutionary considerations. Thus, Chomsky argues[2] that there are constraints (which he does not claim to be able to state precisely) on the operation of deletion transformations, so that elements may be deleted only when they are in some sense identical to elements which remain, and certain syntactic relationships must obtain between the deleted and nondeleted members of the pair of identical constituents. If economy of effort is one of the pressures influencing the evolution of complex syntactic units, then it is very natural that deletion transformations should arise; but such transformations would be efficient only if the suppressed elements could be 'understood' by the hearer, and this is unlikely to be the case unless deleted elements are synonymous with specifiable undeleted elements. Chomsky makes some play with the fact that identity of meaning rather than merely of form is necessary for deletion; since the hearer is concerned to recover the speaker's meaning, it seems natural that this will be the relevant variable.

One point that might well prima facie seem wholly arbitrary and unpredictable (and therefore suitable as the premiss of an argument for linguist nativism) is that indefinite noun-phrases are 'transparent' with respect to extraction of elements but definite noun-phrases are not; thus *Who did he see a picture of?* versus **Who did he see the picture of?*, **Who did he see John's picture of?*[3] But this distinction follows rather naturally from considerations already introduced. Simon's argument suggests that transformations

---

[1] An alleged syntactic universal rather different in kind from those discussed above is Chomsky's claim, on pp. 42–4 of *Aspects of the Theory of Syntax* (M.I.T. Press, 1965), that natural languages contain optionality phenomena but not rotary relationships between syntactic elements – I leave the reader to consult Chomsky's book for elucidation of these terms. My colleague James Hurford has argued that this claim may be vacuous ('The significance of linguistic generalizations', *Language*, vol. 53, 1977, pp. 574–620); but, as Hurford has pointed out to me, if the claim has any content it is predicted by the theory that syntax is the outcome of a process of symbiotic evolution.

[2] *Language and Mind*, pp. 28–30, 47–9.

[3] ibid., p. 46.

applying in the construction of an element at a given level will tend to avoid interfering with the internal structure of independently-stable elements at lower levels; and an element is 'independently stable' if it has or once had a use as a complete utterance. I suggested on p. 159 above that noun-phrases have many uses as complete utterances; but the functions I quoted (drawing attention to things, identifying people or objects, summoning people) are all normally fulfilled by definite noun-phrases, and it is surely true that indefinite noun-phrases are much more rarely useful in isolation. It is very plausible to suppose (though, admittedly, quite unprovable) that the category 'definite noun-phrase' is historically older than the category 'clause', but that indefinite noun-phrases arose only as parts of clauses, and the occasional utterance of an isolated indefinite noun-phrase (e.g. Richard III's *A horse! A horse!*) is a phenomenon post-dating the evolution of the clause. If so, then definite noun-phrases alone ought to be opaque to extraction, as Chomsky finds. This principle accounts equally for the second pair of examples with which Chomsky illustrates what he calls the 'specified-subject condition'.[1]

The definite/indefinite principle, further, predicts the difference between *I didn't see pictures of many of the children*, which is ambiguous (the negation may apply to *see* or to *many*), and the unambiguous *I didn't see John's pictures of many of the children*.[2] *John's pictures of many of the children* is a definite noun-phrase, therefore it has a meaning of its own which will not vary with the context in which it may be embedded, so that if that context includes a

---

[1] See *Problems*, p. 36. The first set of facts which Chomsky uses to motivate the specified-subject condition, namely the derivability of *The candidates expected to defeat each other* from *The candidates each expected to defeat the other* versus the impossibility of deriving *The candidates expected John to defeat each other* from *The candidates each expected John to defeat the other*, are not explained by a distinction between definite and indefinite noun-phrases; but this problem could easily be dispelled by, say, deriving *The candidates expected to defeat each other* not from the source suggested by Chomsky but from *The candidates expected [each to defeat the other]* instead. This seems equally plausible syntactically, since *each* is commonly a pronoun; and the semantic fact that the proposed underlying form implies a paradoxical belief by the candidates which is not suggested by the surface form can hardly be used as an argument against the analysis, since it is well-known that transformations involving quantifiers such as *each* do not normally 'preserve meaning'.

[2] ibid., pp. 37–8.

negation that negation cannot be understood as applying to *many*; the same sequence without *John's* is indefinite, and therefore the words of which it is composed do not form an independent meaning-unit but are interpreted only within the context of a whole clause, which in this case leads to uncertainty about the application of the clause-element *not*.

In some cases the category 'noun-phrase' is realized as a clause of some kind, preceded by a 'complementizer'. Although the definite/indefinite distinction familiar in simple noun-phrases is not normally applied to complement noun-phrases, these resemble indefinite noun-phrases in lacking a use as independent utterances. *My seeing Mary, John's drinking beer* (with *'s* as genitive rather than reduced *is*), or *(For) John to drink beer* would hardly be heard in isolation. On the other hand, it is also possible to use a sequence having the internal structure of a definite noun-phrase, which can in general occur in isolation, to express a proposition: *John's excessive drinking of the beer*. It follows that the last, but none of the earlier three, sequences should be 'opaque' to extraction when embedded in a longer sequence; just this point is made by Chomsky.[1]

I believe that the preceding paragraphs cover all the syntactic universals referred to by Chomsky in the cited works.[2] It may be that I have overlooked one or two points because of the difficulties of interpretation mentioned earlier, and the reader may perhaps feel that my Simonian explanations for Chomsky's claims are less compelling in some cases than in others. Even if that were so, I hardly think it would be reasonable to accept Chomsky's nativist account of mind on the grounds that there exist a few loose ends in my non-nativist, evolutionary explanations for his data; provided

[1] *Language and Mind*, p. 45.
[2] A number of the points discussed above are re-analysed in Bach and Horn, op. cit. Chomsky also briefly discusses certain alleged linguistic universals in the domain of phonology, and Chomsky and other theoretical linguists have written at length about phonological universals elsewhere. Phonology is a relatively technical aspect of linguistics which I have avoided discussing in this book; but I believe that non-nativist explanations, often in historical terms but very much less controversial than my Simonian explanation for hierarchical syntax, are available for the phonological characteristics which have plausibly been argued to be universal. See references on p. 185 of my 'Linguistic universals as evidence for empiricism'.

the bulk of my explanations are satisfactory, one might well put such 'loose ends' (if there are such) down to the fact that Chomsky's theory of linguistic universals is under constant revision, so that the inadequacy of the Simonian explanation may reflect shortcomings in the current statement of the universal. (Until recently, for instance, Chomsky believed in the existence of unbounded movement rules, which would appear to be wholly incompatible with Simon's thesis – cf. p. 183 above. Because I read Simon shortly before reading Chomsky's *Reflections on Language*, unbounded movement rules seemed at first to be a worrying anomaly with respect to the evolutionary explanation of linguistic universals; but the worry was scarcely formulated before acquaintance with Chomsky's new 'subjacency' principle dispelled it.) As things stand, it would surely be very much more reasonable to say that there may be one or two cases where we do not yet see quite why some syntactic universal observed by Chomsky is entailed by the fact that languages are products of evolution, than positively to assert that the nature of evolution is not an adequate explanation for certain universals.

What seems clear is that, provided the Simonian account is accepted for the central universals of constituency structure and structure-dependent transformations, any remaining points among the claims made by Chomsky for which my explanations may be felt to be inadequate will be far too meagre to allow us to believe that the central universals might have been produced by biological rather than intellectual evolution. We saw in Chapter VIII that, if syntax were the outcome of intellectual evolution within the individual and/or within the community, we would expect languages to share only those hierarchical properties predicted by Simon (since there will be no mechanism imposing other constraints), while, if it is the outcome of biological evolution, then we expect that various languages will all share some one particular hierarchical structure. (The third logical possibility, that language is the outcome of an un-Darwinian sudden biological saltation, leads to the prediction that all languages should share a common structure which will not, unless by an extraordinary coincidence, be hierarchical at all.) But, obviously, natural languages do not all share one particular syntactic structure; this could not be said even of the European languages, despite their historical relationship, and if it could second-language learning would be a much easier task than it is. Different languages are like different biological species, whose structures contrast in most respects other than hierarchicality, rather than like different individuals of a single species, sharing a particular hierarchical structure. Thus Chomsky's evidence decisively supports the first of the three positions outlined as against the second and third. In other words, Chomsky's evidence favours the creative-mind account of the growth of language over the limited-mind account.

Chomsky is by no means the only scholar working out hypotheses about linguistic universals; as I have said, this is the chief concern of the contemporary discipline of Theoretical Linguistics, whose practitioners are nowadays very numerous. I have concentrated principally on Chomsky's work, because it is mainly he who has argued that these empirical observations have the philosophical consequences which I have challenged. Many theoretical linguists are content to take Chomskyan nativism for granted while evincing little interest in the general philosophical implications of their subject, with the result that they scarcely discuss whether or not non-nativist explanations may be available for their own theories about linguistic universals. If the evidence with which Chomsky supports his nativist argument in fact tends in the opposite direction, it would surely be remarkable for the nativist argument to succeed nevertheless thanks to data not considered by its author.

However, it seems appropriate to round out my case against linguistic nativism with a brief consideration of the chief theories of linguistic universals other than Chomsky's.

To survey all the hypotheses that can be found scattered through the literature would be quite impracticable. Apart from anything else there is no convenient listing of these, nor (equally important) is there a listing of the refutations that have been published. But a far smaller set of theories have turned out robust enough to survive criticism over an appreciable period despite being general enough to have attracted widespread attention with the accompanying serious risk of refutation, and we shall now look at these.

The first of these theories to be considered, that of Joseph Emonds, in fact has a relatively short history but has attained great influence, in part because it enjoys Chomsky's approval.[1] The core of Emonds's theory is that, with certain 'minor' exceptions of which I defer discussion for the moment, all transformational rules in any natural language fall into one of two types: they are either 'structure-preserving' or 'root' transformations. A transformation is 'structure-preserving', essentially, if the constituency structure that results from its application is one that is permitted independently by the base component of the grammar. Thus the Passive rule in English, which transforms e.g. *Russia defeated Germany* into *Germany was defeated by Russia*, is 'structure-preserving' because sentences with the latter structure (namely 'subject + *be* + past-participle + prepositional-phrase') also occur as 'kernel', untransformed sentences – thus e.g. *Jonathan was depressed in Russia* is generated directly by the base rules without the involvement of the Passive transformation. A 'root' transformation, on the other hand, is one that moves some constituent into a position where it is immediately dominated by the 'root' S node, i.e. that turns the constituent into an 'immediate constituent' of the sentence as a whole.

The first point to be made here is that if a transformation is truly 'structure-preserving' in Emonds's sense then it is redundant and cannot justifiably be included in a grammar. The purpose of a grammar is to define the set of all and only the grammatical sentences of a language, so, if a sentence-type can be produced by the base rules alone, there can be no point in adding a transformation to the grammar which generates the same sentence-type by a different route. Emonds does not in fact explain why English grammar needs a rule of Passivization; he merely states that 'Transformational grammarians generally agree' that it does.[2] The reason why Emonds and many other linguists believe in the Passive transformation is that they confuse the syntactic goal of defining the class of sentences of a language with the goal of specifying the semantic relations between those sentences;

[1] J. E. Emonds, *A Transformational Approach to English Syntax*, Academic Press, 1976.
[2] op. cit., p. 65.

because actives and passives are typically paraphrases of one another, it is supposed that a syntactic description must derive them from a common underlying structure. This is a perverse principle; after all, paraphrase is only a special case of the relation of inference between sentences, and no one suggests that the more general relation of inference should be reflected systematically in a syntactic description.

Once we have understood this point, we can revise Emonds's claim so that it reads 'all major transformations are root transformations';[1] Emonds reinterprets all the 'cyclical' transformations proposed by his predecessors so that they are structure-preserving, and hence are not transformations at all. Translated into evolutionary terms, Emonds's claim means that the only syntactic category to have undergone endogenous (as opposed to symbiotic) evolution is the category 'sentence'; endogenous evolution never got going in language until utterances homologous with modern sentences had become established, and then it affected only that largest category.

I shall not pretend that I would have predicted this on evolutionary grounds independently of Emonds. Nevertheless, the finding is fairly easy to understand in evolutionary terms. In earlier discussion I took it for granted that symbiotic evolution in syntax has reached the 'end of the road' in the sentence as we know it – that there is no useful potential construction of a category distinct from contemporary syntactic categories but containing sentences as constituents – because the most inclusive syntactic categories in other languages known to me are broadly equivalent in complexity to our sentences, which would seem an odd coincidence if English sentences were merely the largest syntactic units that had happened to establish themselves so far in a continuing process of evolution. If this is right, then it is plausible to suppose that symbiotic evolution from the one-word-utterance stage to the sentence might have happened quite fast under the pressure of the

---

[1] On pp. 112 and 171 of his book Emonds slightly relaxes his definition of 'structure-preserving transformation' in order to permit non-root transformations to produce certain structures which are not generated directly by the base. I have not investigated what status the very meagre data motivating this modification have with respect to the evolutionary account of syntax.

need for more precise communication, and that sentences would already have existed for the great majority of the period during which language has been evolving; so that endogenous evolution, fuelled by the relatively weak pressure of economy of effort, would have operated only on languages that were already at the sentence stage.

This is, of course, highly speculative. But no more so, surely, that the postulation of unobserved innate mental machinery which imposes subtle constraints on the formal nature of the rules of grammar? Notice how much easier it is for the nativist to explain the various linguistic universals in his terms; whatever universals happen to be discovered, the nativist can always simply say that there exist some corresponding aspects of our unknown innate mental machinery – no one expects him to specify the nature of this machinery, and still less to give independent reasons for thinking that it has the nature which it needs to have in order to explain the linguistic universals. My approach, on the other hand, would be laughed out of court if I were merely to wave my hands and assert that the linguistic universals will ultimately receive some explanation in terms of evolution. I am obliged to specify the relation between evolutionary facts and particular linguistic universals, and to argue that, independently of the evidence of contemporary languages, we would or could have expected linguistic evolution to work as I suggest it did. Since the task facing this approach is considerably more exacting, I see no need to be sheepish about the possibility that this first attempt to apply the evolutionary approach contains some links of argument that are weaker than others.

There remain Emonds's 'minor' or 'local' transformations, which are the one kind of transformation he allows that apply at a lower level than that of the main clause. A local transformation is one which affects in some way (typically, by permuting them) a word and an adjacent phrase or word that are closely linked syntactically, and which does not depend for its applicability on the wider syntactic environment in which the elements are embedded.[1] Thus, a local transformation is responsible for the

---

[1] ibid., pp. 4, 242.

derivation of phrases such as *big enough, single-minded enough* from underlying structures in which the adverb *enough* precedes the adjective or adjectival phrase: *enough big, enough single-minded*. One naturally asks why Emonds posits such un-English underlying structures; the answer is that he postulates a further linguistic universal ('Base Restriction I') according to which categories such as 'Adjective' may only have a single source in the base component of the grammar of any language, so that, since most adverbs of degree (e.g. *too, very*) precede the adjective they modify, all must do so in deep structure in order to avoid the need for a pair of rules

$$\text{Adjectival Phrase} \rightarrow \begin{Bmatrix} very \\ too \\ \vdots \end{Bmatrix} \text{Adjective}$$

$$\text{Adjectival Phrase} \rightarrow \text{Adjective } enough$$

contravening Restriction I.[1]

If one asks, further, why Emonds believes in such Base Restrictions, the answer is that they 'have generally been observed in practice by transformationalists'[2] ('observed' in the sense of 'obeyed' rather than 'noticed', that is). Indeed they have, but why? – it seems perverse to describe phrases containing *enough* by means of rules which first put *enough* in what is always the wrong place for it and then move it elsewhere. Emonds's 'local transformations' and 'base restrictions' hang together, and I believe that a parsimonious theory can dispense with both, leaving Emonds with the single claim that all transformations are root transformations; we have already considered what this means in evolutionary terms.[3]

[1] ibid., p. 14.

[2] ibid.

[3] It may be objected that I am unfair to Emonds's 'local transformations' and 'base restrictions' in that I criticize them through an unusually vulnerable example. I chose the case of *enough* because it is simple to discuss, but I believe that Emonds's definition of 'local transformation' implies that similar arguments could be constructed for his other examples. Another problem with Emonds's work is that he uses a somewhat mystical notion of 'grammaticality' according to which it is permissible to treat a sentence as 'ungrammatical' even though it is commonly used and not perceived by native speakers as odd in any way (op. cit., pp. 24, 35). Cf. Melinda Sinclair, 'The refutability of Emonds's Structure-Preserving Constraint', unpublished M.A. thesis, University of Stellenbosch, 1977.

Emonds's universal hypothesis is a claim about what configurations a syntactic constituent may be moved into: if we ignore 'structure-preserving' and 'local' transformations, a constituent may be moved only into a position where it is directly subordinate to the root. Earlier J. R. Ross had constructed a highly influential (though never formally published) theory about constraints on how constituents may be moved out of syntactic configurations.[1]

For instance, corresponding to any noun-phrase of an English statement it is normally possible to substitute an interrogative noun-phrase which is shifted to the beginning of the sentence, forming a question – thus, corresponding to the statement *John poured the green liquid into the bucket* we can form questions such as *Who poured the green liquid into the bucket?*, *Which liquid did John pour into the bucket?*, *What did John pour the green liquid into?*, questioning the subject, direct object, and head of prepositional phrase respectively – but there are limits to this. Corresponding to the statements *John will arrange a meeting between the foreign candidate and a member of staff*, or *Henry plays the lute and sings madrigals*, it is not possible to form questions such as **Which candidate will John arrange a meeting between and a member of staff?* or **What does Henry play and sings madrigals?* One might suppose that the oddity of these latter questions is a pragmatic matter – that such questions would never in practice be useful, and so we are not accustomed to hearing them. But that is not an adequate explanation. Certain languages (Japanese is a case in point) lack any rule about question-words occurring at the beginning of their sentence, and instead leave them in the same place as non-interrogatives – if the declarative order is *John wants an ice-cream*, then the normal order for a question is *John wants what?* (unlike in English, where the latter word-sequence is not a straightforward question but an invitation to the speaker to repeat a misheard or disbelieved phrase).[2] Speakers of these languages perceive questions such as *John will arrange a meeting between which candidate and a member of staff?* or *Henry plays what and sings madrigals?* as perfectly ordinary, and they mean what

---

[1] J. R. Ross, *Constraints on Variables in Syntax* (M.I.T. Ph.D. thesis, 1967), distributed in mimeo form by the Linguistics Club of Indiana University.

[2] Standard word-order in Japanese declaratives is in fact quite different from that of English, but we need not go into that matter here.

the asterisked English word-sequences 'would mean' if they were grammatical in English. Therefore the oddity of the English sentences cannot be explained in pragmatic terms. Ross argues that the oddity is produced by the violation of a universal constraint on the movement of syntactic constituents, which he calls the 'Co-ordinate Structure Constraint': roughly, no conjunct may be moved out of the co-ordination in which it occurs.[1] This is one of a number of universal syntactic principles proposed by Ross.

Ross's constraint sounds rather arbitrary, and therefore suitable as evidence for the nativist position. Given that our languages contain rules which re-order constituents, why should re-ordering out of co-ordinations in particular be objectionable unless we are born with language-processing machinery that happens not to be able to cope with this phenomenon? However, there is another way of looking at the data. Paul Schachter argues that there is a quite general constraint on co-ordinate constructions which requires that both or all their conjuncts must fulfil the same syntactic and semantic functions – that is why it is ungrammatical to say e.g. *John ate quickly and a cheese sandwich*, since *quickly* is an adverb and *a cheese sandwich* a noun-phrase serving as object.[2] This contraint rules out the asterisked sentences of the previous paragraph, not because they have been derived by moving a constituent in an illegitimate fashion, but because they have ended up with ill-formed co-ordinations: *between and a member of staff* contains no noun-phrase balancing *a member of staff* as object of the preposition *between*, *play and sings madrigals* has a non-finite transitive verb lacking an object before the *and* balancing a finite verb with object after it. Schachter claims that his hypothesis accounts neatly for all the data supporting Ross's Co-ordinate Structure Constraint, together with other data for which Ross has no explanation.

Now Ross's constraint may have been difficult to explain in other than nativist terms, but the same is not true of Schachter's. One consideration which clearly must have played a role in the evolution of complex syntactic systems is that hearers need to understand what is said; a novel syntactic construction which led

---

[1] The precise formulation is given on p. 89 of Ross's thesis.
[2] Paul Schachter, 'Constraints on coördination', *Language*, vol. 53, 1977, pp. 86–103.

to irresolvable ambiguity or unnecessarily acute decoding problems would be unfit for survival. In order to decode a sentence one needs to impose a constituency structure on it and establish the logical relationships between the constituents. When co-ordination first emerged the conjuncts would presumably have fulfilled the condition of sharing syntactic and semantic functions simply because such co-ordinations are most useful in practice. We are more often, perhaps, going to want to say 'John praised Mary; he praised William' than to say 'John praised loudly; he praised William', and (more important) if we do need to say the latter and want to abbreviate it then the contrast in form between the adverb *loudly* and the noun *William* means that there is no difficulty in understanding the logical structure of the sentence 'John praised William loudly'. It is with respect to the former kind of discourse that there will be a motive for the invention of a marker such as *and*, allowing the hearer to grasp the logical role of the various nouns in a sentence such as 'John praised Mary and William'. If the earliest co-ordinations obeyed Schachter's constraint for purely pragmatic reasons, a sensible strategy for hearers to adopt when decoding relatively complex sentences would have been the following: 'If you hear an *and* and you recognize the functions of a constituent on one side of it, look for material on the other side forming a constituent with the same functions'. Once hearers adopted such a strategy, sentences violating Schachter's constraint would systematically have led to misunderstanding, so speakers would have learned to avoid them – and the constraint would thus have been institutionalized as part of the grammar.[1]

---

[1] It might be argued that this account explains too much, in the sense that it predicts that languages should not permit any systematically ambiguous constructions; yet it is notorious that word-sequences such as *old men and women* involve systematic ambiguity. However, although people sometimes say things that are genuinely ambiguous, in my experience there are not usually any real difficulties with phrases such as *old men and women* because in practice it is usually clear from the context and/or the rhythm of pronunciation whether the two former or three latter words should be taken as a constituent. If true, this implies that hearers of the sequence 'Adjective-Noun-*and*-Noun' would not have needed to adopt a strategy (such as 'Assume the adjective goes with just the immediately following noun') which would have led to misunderstanding when the construction was intended by the peaker in the other way. In other cases, where genuine ambiguities would be likely in practice, human languages do seem to institution-

It seems likely that Ross's others universals are to be explained in similar terms. Indeed, Ray Cattell has offered a unified explanation for Ross's three main universal hypotheses which, while perhaps not quite so compelling as Schachter's reinterpretation of the Co-ordinate Structure Constraint, is nevertheless quite attractive; Cattell points out that his account, if valid, robs Ross's data of their force as evidence for linguistic nativism.[1]

Rather earlier than the research just discussed, syntactic universals of another kind, having to do mainly with word-order in simple sentences, were discussed by Joseph Greenberg.[2] Greenberg's universal theories are very different in style from those of Chomsky, Ross, or Emonds. In the first place, Greenberg's proposals are worked out inductively from an examination of a large number of languages drawn from many unrelated and geographically scattered language-families (whereas Chomsky and his followers proposed universal hypotheses based heavily or exclusively on their knowledge of English, and by implication left it to others to examine how 'universal' the properties in question actually are); secondly, whereas Chomsky and his associates are interested exclusively in absolute statements, many of Greenberg's claims are statistical (they often begin 'With far more than chance frequency in the languages of the world . . .'). Linguists of the Chomskyan school in fact held themselves rather aloof from Greenberg's work for a number of years. More recently, since the Platonism of the Chomskyans has come to be tempered by increased acceptance of the desirability of getting to grips with the messy facts of the real world, there has been a measure of *rapprochement*; after examining Greenberg's own ideas, we shall go on to consider a further universal theory which combines some of the virtues of both approaches.

The first of Greenberg's universals, and one on which many of the others depend, is in fact of rather questionable empirical

alize ambiguity-removing constraints on their rules of syntax; cf. J. Hankamer, 'Unacceptable ambiguity', *Linguistic Inquiry*, vol. 4, 1973, pp. 17–68.

[1] R. Cattell, 'Constraints on movement rules', *Language*, vol. 52, 1976, pp. 18–50; see esp. p. 50.

[2] 'Some universals of grammar with particular reference to the order of meaningful elements', in J. H. Greenberg, ed., *Universals of Language*, 2nd edn., M.I.T. Press, 1966.

status. This concerns the order of the elements subject, verb, direct object. In English the usual order (there are exceptions in special circumstances) is 'SVO', as Greenberg symbolizes it, but this is not universal; thus Welsh has the order VSO and Japanese the order SOV. There are six logically-possible orders into which three elements can be permuted, but Greenberg finds that only three of these possibilities occur in practice; there are no languages in which object normally precedes subject (irrespective of the position of the verb, i.e. VOS, OVS, and OSV are all ruled out).

The difficulty about this is that being the first noun-phrase in the sentence may well be part of what we *mean* by calling a given constituent the 'subject', in which case it would be tautologous to say that objects do not normally precede subjects. In the context of English and other European languages we think of the subject as the element with which the verb agrees in person and number, but this is a provincial definition not suitable for discussing 'subject' as a universal notion; there are plenty of languages in which verbs do not inflect at all, and when verbs do inflect it is not always in order to mark 'agreement' with a noun-phrase. (On the other hand, even in English we cannot identify the 'subject' with the 'doer of the action'; there are many cases, e.g. *John was killed, John can see the light*, where the subject is 'done to' rather than 'doer'.) Edward Keenan has attempted to answer this objection by arguing that the notion 'subject' represents a constellation of logically-independent properties, most of which tend in most languages to be shared by a single noun-phrase in each clause, which is thereby identified as the subject.[1] To my mind Keenan does not altogether avert the problem of circularity; some of the other properties in the constellation he describes, e.g. that of being the topic of the discourse, are properties that we might expect *a priori* to characterize the first element of a sentence independently of alleged innate constraints on syntax.

Others of Greenberg's universals, however, are quite clearly empirical. His second universal, for instance, asserts that there is a strong correlation between prepositional and genitive constructions: languages in which prepositions precede the noun-phrases

[1] E. L. Keenan, 'Towards a universal definition of "subject"', in C. N. Li, ed., *Subject and Topic*, Academic Press, 1976.

they govern (as in English *on the shelf*) are almost always languages in which possessed precedes possessor (*the book of John*), while languages in which prepositions follow noun-phrases (properly, languages which have 'postpositions' rather than 'prepositions'), so that they translate 'on the shelf' as, literally, *shelf on* or the like, are almost always languages in which possessor precedes possessed (*John's book*). (English does not offer a good test for this claim because of its alternative genitive constructions.)

I am sure this is a true empirical claim, and it seems very easy to understand in evolutionary terms; it is likely that the two categories of construction were originally the same. That is, it seems very plausible that the earliest way of getting across the information which we nowadays encode in a prepositional phrase such as *on the shelf* might have been to use a genitive construction that would literally translate as something like 'top of shelf'. It would not be very elegant in modern English to say 'Jam top of shelf', but if a foreigner said it no one would fail to understand. The specialization of certain nouns into a separate class of 'prepositions' occurring only or principally in constructions like this would have been a case of endogenous linguistic evolution. Indeed, this evolution has proceeded much less far in some languages than it has in English; in Chinese it is still fairly plain that the postpositions used by that language are related to nouns, although in most cases differences have developed between the postpositions and the cognate words used as independent nouns. If the two constructions originated as one, we expect that they will tend to parallel one another in terms of word-order in the later stages of evolution of any given language, though exceptions are possible if, after the constructions have become distinct, one of them is replaced by a construction involving the opposite order (perhaps by borrowing from another language).

Thus this universal characteristic, though genuine, by no means requires us to postulate innate mental machinery imposing certain word-order properties on our languages; and many of Greenberg's universals can be explained in similar terms. (A large number of them reduce to the notion that languages tend either to put all modifiers before the elements modified or vice versa despite the variety of categories – adjective, subordinate clause, etc. –

which act as 'modifiers'.) Others have even more straightforward explanations. Thus, Greenberg's Universal 44 says that if a language has gender distinctions in the first person it always has gender distinctions in the second and/or third persons, but not necessarily vice versa; thus English has no distinction between masculine and feminine forms of *I*, though we do distinguish *he* v. *she* v. *it*. Naturally so; second and third person pronouns are potentially ambiguous and gender can help disambiguate them, but the word *I* by the nature of things always picks out one individual unambiguously. Greenberg himself is not very friendly towards the nativist approach to language,[1] and §5 of his article sets out to give explanations in terms similar to those sketched here for the various universals in his list. He does not claim to carry out this task exhaustively, but it is hard to believe that the points he fails to discuss would be wholly resistant to such explanations.

The last piece of work we shall consider in detail, Edward Keenan and Bernard Comrie's research on relative clauses, springs out of Greenberg's work but is rather more sympathetic to Chomsky's approach to linguistics – as is suggested by the occurrence of the phrase 'universal grammar' in their title.[2] (Chomsky often describes his linguistic nativism by suggesting that there is an innate 'universal grammar' underlying the diverse surface grammars of various languages.) Keenan and Comrie establish, with copious references to a wide range of languages, a universal 'hierarchy of relativizability' among the various syntactic roles played by noun-phrases. (This is a linear hierarchy, not connected with the branching hierarchy of constituency structure.) English sets no limit on the roles that relative pronouns may play within their relative clauses; a relative pronoun may be subject ('the man *who* played patience'), direct object ('the man *whom* I admire'), indirect object ('the man to *whom* I wrote a letter'), head of a prepositional phrase ('the knife with *which* John whittled the stick'), genitive ('the man *whose* wife wears glasses'), or, at a pinch, object of comparison ('the man than *whom* Mary is taller' – for some speakers it is more natural to say 'the man that Mary is taller

---

[1] cf. Greenberg, op. cit., p. xi.

[2] E. L. Keenan and B. Comrie, 'Noun phrase accessibility and universal grammar', *Linguistic Inquiry*, vol. 8, 1977, pp. 63–99.

than').[1] Other languages are less flexible; thus in French it is quite impossible to use a relative pronoun as object of comparison and say **l'homme que lequel Mary est plus grande*. Some languages are highly restrictive: in Maori and Tagalog, the relative can only be subject of its clause; and, in languages which allow a number of different syntactic roles to be 'relativized', it often happens that some roles are relativized by one relative-clause construction and others by a different one. (Thus, in French there is a special word, *dont*, to express a relative pronoun acting as genitive – though this is not a good example of contrasting 'relativization strategies', since the phrase *de qui* is also used in certain circumstances.) What Keenan and Comrie claim can be stated to a close approximation as follows: of the hierarchy 'subject/direct-object/indirect-object/ head-of-prepositional-phrase/genitive/object-of-comparison', any language will relativize a continuous segment beginning with 'subject' and cutting off at an arbitrary point; and any one relativization strategy, in a language with more than one, will apply to a continuous segment of the hierarchy (the segments handled by alternative strategies may or may not overlap). Thus it is no accident that the one role which French cannot relativize is the object of comparison; if a language fails to relativize just one role, it will always be this one.

Keenan and Comrie in fact say that the position is slightly more complex than this: there are a few cases of 'gaps' where one relative strategy of a language stops at a point on the hierarchy earlier than and not immediately adjacent to the point at which the other strategy of the language begins. However, in the case (Toba Batak, a language of Sumatra) which they discuss in detail (where one strategy applies only to subjects and the other to indirect objects, heads of prepositional phrases, and genitives, leaving direct objects as an unrelativizable gap), if the former strategy *were* extended to direct objects it would lead to systematically ambiguous sentences, and we know that languages avoid this as might be expected *a priori* (cf. the reference to Hankamer's

---

[1] The point of distinguishing 'indirect object' from 'head of prepositional phrase' is that the semantic role 'indirect object' is not necessarily (in some languages, never) marked by a preposition; in English we have 'I wrote *the man* a letter' alongside 'I wrote a letter *to the man*'.

work in the note on p. 197 above). It is not clear from what Keenan and Comrie write whether the second strategy of Toba Batak would in principle be applicable to direct objects, and they point out that the language in any case has a construction which achieves the same effect as relativizing direct objects (it can 'promote' them to subjects and relativize those).[1] So Toba Batak seems to be not so much a language which violates the stated principles as one which is prevented from conforming to it perfectly by the *force majeure* of the need to avoid systematic ambiguity.

The fact that more languages can relativize functions higher in the Keenan/Comrie hierarchy than can relativize lower functions would be explained if there were any reason why it is more useful to be able to relativize higher items, and there is such a reason: as Keenan and Comrie themselves note,[2] to a large extent the hierarchy corresponds to relative frequency with which the respective syntactic roles are instantiated in utterances. For the first three roles this is a necessary truth. Every clause must have a subject while only clauses whose verbs are transitive *can* have an object (noun-phrases appearing with intransitive verbs such as *sleep* are automatically 'subject' irrespective of their semantic relationship to the state of affairs denoted by the verb); likewise indirect objects are possible only with a subset of verbs that also take subject and direct object (it is the presence of the latter which identifies the other object as 'indirect'). The commoner a given syntactic role is in individual clauses, the more occasions there will be when it would be handy to have a way of modifying a noun by means of a relative clause in which the item co-referential with the antecedent plays that role. Given that the differences in frequency between the various syntactic roles are fairly large, it follows naturally that the first relative clauses will have the relative as subject, and whatever construction is used will in time be extended successively through the less-common functions until it reaches one to which it is intrinsically inapplicable.[3]

[1] Keenan and Comrie, op. cit., pp. 68–9.

[2] ibid., §2.2.3.1.

[3] I believe that the related universal claim argued by Bernard Comrie in 'Causatives and universal grammar', *Transactions of the Philological Society, 1974*, pp. 1–32, can be explained in essentially the same way, but I shall not discuss this here.

The one position on the Keenan/Comrie hierarchy which is perhaps not to be explained in terms of frequency is genitive; genitive constructions may well be commoner than the hierarchy suggests. But it is in the nature of the genitive that a relative-clause-forming strategy which works for the functions higher in the Keenan/Comrie hierarchy will often be intrinsically inapplicable to genitives. One very common way of making an ordinary clause into a relative clause is to replace the noun-phrase to be relativized by an invariant pronoun, such as English *that*, appearing at the beginning of the clause: *the meat* [*that John gave . . . to Peter*]. But suppose we tried in this fashion to relativize the genitive *Bill* in *John gave Bill's meat to Peter*; we would get either *the man* [*that John gave . . . 's meat to Peter*], which contains a suffix *'s* not attached to any root (a situation which few languages tolerate even when the result is pronounceable), or, if *'s* is dropped, *the man* [*that John gave . . . meat to Peter*], in which there is no clue about the nature of the connexion between the antecedent *man* and the content of the relative clause. Because the possessor element of a genitive construction is a modifier of another noun which could stand unmodified, deletion of the possessor (unlike, say, deletion of the direct object of a transitive verb) does not leave a gap in logic which calls attention to itself and thus enables the hearer to interpret a relative clause formed by such a strategy. Therefore the genitive will typically be a function which forces a language to come up with a novel relativizing strategy (such as that of moving the whole genitive construction including the possessed noun out of its normal position) rather than merely allowing an existing strategy to be extended to itself; and this may explain the low rank of the genitive on the hierarchy. The object-of-comparison function is lower still, presumably, because *than* constructions are far rarer than any of the other items on the hierarchy.

I could go on to examine further hypotheses about linguistic universals that have been proposed by various scholars. The literature of linguistics contains a wide range of universal proposals, far more than can be discussed exhaustively in this book, from the core hierarchical universals pointed out by Chomsky and disputed, I believe, by no one, to quirky ideas put forward off the cuff in one paper and acknowledged to be refuted by the same writer a publication or two later. Furthermore, not only are the individual properties that have been suggested as possible universals quite diverse, but theoretical linguists differ greatly in how 'wide' or 'narrow' they expect the overall range of natural languages permitted by the ultimate complete theory of linguistic universals to be. Linguists who believe in very 'narrow' limits to linguistic diversity are likely to feel that attempts to explain linguistic universals without recourse to innate mental structure, although perhaps not wrong as far as they go, are sure to be grossly inadequate to the task as a whole.

Certainly my evolutionary account of syntactic universals would be wholly incapable of explaining the picture of human language proposed recently by David Johnson and Paul Postal, to quote one extreme view. According to Johnson and Postal, the correct general theory of language is not so much a set of conditions to which any grammar of an individual human language must conform; it is something more like a specific supergrammar from which any actual grammar must be derived by omitting particular items.[1] That is, suppose we find in English, or in a particular dialect of English, some apparently quirky construction – say the trick, which I think is characteristic of army slang, of interrupting a long word with an expletive (as in *absobloodylutely*); according to Johnson and Postal what has happened is not that a certain group of speakers have learned to perform this particular trick from hearing it used in their community (and have been able to learn it because it is the *sort* of trick that humans can learn, as Chomsky might add), but rather that anyone who speaks a language or dialect *lacking* the construction has learned *not* to use this rule of the innate supergrammar. The German and the Frenchmen begin life 'expecting' (in an unconscious sense) to say things like *unbeverdammtdingt, absosacrélument*, and have to 'unlearn' the construction by exposure to the languages of their particular communities. A linguist who discovers some novel and exotic grammatical construction in a vernacular language of Amazonian

[1] D. E. Johnson and P. M. Postal, *Arc Pair Grammar*, IBM T. J. Watson Research Centre (Yorktown Heights, N.Y.), 1977, §14.3. Johnson and Postal's view is a logical development of an idea proposed by Emmon Bach in 'Questions', *Linguistic Inquiry*, vol. 2, 1971, pp. 153–66.

jungle-dwellers or Central Asian nomads is really discovering a
hitherto unnoticed piece of learned knowledge in the minds of all
of us *except* members of the Amazonian or Central Asian tribe.

Clearly, this approach implies a very 'narrow' range of possible
languages; the theory does not begin to be plausible unless one
assumes, as Johnson and Postal apparently do assume, that the set
of grammatical constructions found in the languages of the world
are fairly few, so that our prima facie impression that every
language and dialect is full of unique or near-unique grammatical
quirks is a mistake. Obviously too, if the supergrammar (which for
Johnson and Postal is itself a highly complex and specific structure) is in our minds from the start, its properties cannot be
attributed to intellectual evolution in the individual. However, as
Johnson and Postal themselves point out, their book of more than
900 pages provides 'little . . . in the way of empirical support for
[their] theory';[1] they are concerned to formalize mathematically
their intuitive notions of what such a supergrammar might be like,
rather than to gather evidence to persuade the sceptic of their case.
(To my mind the idea that we learn what constructions not to use,
rather than what *is* possible in our mother tongue, falls foul of
elementary data about children's acquisition of syntax, a subject
to which I find no reference in Johnson and Postal's book.)

In general there seems to be a rough correlation in Theoretical
Linguistics, whereby those scholars who believe that the range of
possible human languages is very narrow, and narrow in unexpected ways, are relatively uninterested in finding empirical
support for their conjectures, while those who base their claims on
substantial empirical evidence tend to advocate much weaker
linguistic universals which set quite wide limits to the range of
natural languages, and limits which, furthermore, correspond with
well-known, unsurprising characteristics of language such as the
hierarchical constituency structure of sentences. It may be that I
am wrong to ignore the more exotic universal claims. One enthusiastic British proponent of Postal's theories has recently dismissed
the stance of linguists such as myself, who question the empirical
status of much contemporary Theoretical Linguistic analysis

[1] op. cit., p. 5.

without ourselves engaging in such research, as 'self-indulgent methodological agonizing'.[1] Self-indulgently or not, however, I have deemed it worthwhile to discuss here only those universal claims which do appear to be founded on a reasonably substantial basis of evidence.

I have not been able to cover even those exhaustively; and in any case, as already suggested, Theoretical Linguistics is a sufficiently active discipline that seeking to explain its findings is rather like shooting at an unpredictably moving target. Let me content myself by saying that I do not believe I have encountered other well-founded universal hypotheses that are likely to be less easily explained in evolutionary and functional terms than are the universals I have discussed here. Conversely, someone who is unconvinced by my arguments so far will scarcely be swayed by an examination of still more evidence. Either way there seems little point in multiplying instances further. The strategy of seeking to explain various observed linguistic universals in evolutionary terms has proved sufficiently successful up to now to persuade me that it is likely to work also for whatever universals are discovered in the future; I therefore conclude that the common features of human languages reflect not predetermined mental structure but rather the fumbling, step-by-step process whereby the possessors of originally formless minds created and perfected complex patterns of thought and speech by cultural evolution over many generations. The reader must decide whether I have taken him with me.

---

[1] G. K. Pullum, review of Wirth, *Assessing Linguistic Arguments*, *Language*, vol. 54, 1978, p. 399.

X

I have argued that the syntactic characteristics common to the languages of the world are best explained as the consequence of the fact that languages, like other complex cultural possessions, have developed gradually from simple beginnings rather than emerging full-blown overnight; and that this evolution of structure from initial structurelessness cannot have been a genetic process but must, on the evidence, occur afresh in the mind of each human individual. Chomsky's empirical premisses lead to precisely the opposite of Chomsky's conclusions.

It is no accident that Chomsky himself has overlooked the possibility of explaining his linguistic universals in developmental terms. Chomsky often argues that the possibility of explanatory scientific theories of complex phenomena depends on making 'simplifying assumptions' whereby the investigator deliberately ignores many aspects of the phenomena in order to reduce the range of facts he deals with to manageable proportions. This is quite true; thus a physicist working out gravitational attractions between the planets might pretend that each is a perfect sphere – he knows they are not, but it is far beyond him to compensate in his calculations for their actual irregularities. However, in making 'simplifying assumptions' one must be alert to the danger that the considerations one chooses to ignore may be crucial rather than trivial. Chomsky goes on to point out that one of his own simplifying assumptions is that 'learning can be conceptualized as an instantaneous process'.[1] (Indeed, in some of his writings Chomsky seems to treat this not as a counterfactual simplifying assumption but as a datum to be explained; thus he suggests that a nativist account of language acquisition will ultimately need to specify a neural structure which, 'given an input of observed Chinese [e.g.]

---

[1] *Reflections on Language*, pp. 14–15.

sentences', will produce the rules of Chinese grammar 'by an induction of apparently fantastic . . . suddenness'.[1])

In the light of our discussion, this seems to have been a peculiarly unfortunate methodological decision. Chomsky argues that we must inherit fixed mental structure, because he can see no other reason in logic why children should invariably structure the linguistic data available to them in a certain way, given the 'simplifying assumption' that they move from data to finished grammar in one fell swoop. But children structure the data as they do precisely because they do not acquire their grammar in one fell swoop but rather build it up step by step, always using the elements they have mastered so far as basic building blocks when investigating the next level of complexity. Chomsky has put himself in a position comparable to, say, a psychologist who argues for an innate tendency to avoid awareness of things leaving one's home territory on the ground that there is no better explanation for the fact that ships disappear from sight when they get a few miles out to sea, given the simplifying assumption (which in other connexions might be an appropriate one) that the surface of the ocean is perfectly flat.

The considerations we have discussed do not rob the discipline of Theoretical Linguistics of all its general philosophical significance. The notion that the similarities between human languages are not logically necessary, that the hierarchical structure of natural-language sentences (and hence, also, of the formulae of the standard artificial logics) is a consequence of a contingent fact rather than a characteristic which could not conceivably be other than it is – this is a matter of considerable interest for philosophers of logic and others, it is an idea which was wholly novel when first put forward in Chomsky's early writings, and it remains untouched by my argument; only the contingent fact in question has changed from a particular accident of biology to the general fact that languages have evolved gradually.[2] (When I say that the

---

[1] Review of Skinner, *Verbal Behavior*, *Language*, vol. 35., 1959, pp. 26–58, see p. 564 of the reprint in J. A. Fodor and J. J. Katz, eds., *The Structure of Language*, Prentice-Hall, 1964; italics in original removed.

[2] The failure of twentieth-century philosophers of logic to take up the question of the contingency of 'logical forms' may be connected with Gottlob Frege's

notion was 'wholly new' when Chomsky stated it, I must of course qualify this in the sense that no philosophical idea is utterly unconnected with its predecessors – as already said, Chomsky has an obvious intellectual ancestor in Immanuel Kant. But Chomsky has done far more than merely restate Kant's views in language of his own.)

However, while Chomsky may be indirectly responsible for the development of the thesis that the nature of natural languages and artificial logics is a contingent consequence of the nature of evolution (since, if Chomsky had not propounded his nativist account of linguistic universals, it might not have occurred to anyone to work out the evolutionary alternative), nevertheless that thesis is very different from – not to say antagonistic to – the theses for which Chomsky himself argues. Our languages and our logic are not inborn but are learned wholly by experience.[1] We can know as much as we do, not because 'in a sense we already knew it', but because we are creative beings with the ability to formulate fallible but genuinely original concepts and hypotheses in response to genuinely unforeseen experiences. The common features of our languages, and of our other complex intellectual constructs, reflect the uncertain, gradual process by which each of us has built up his structure of belief on a foundation of blank ignorance.

And if this is so, then the foundations of the discipline of 'Theoretical Linguistics' are called into question. Chomsky and other linguists are right, as we have seen, to assert that there are certain contingent limits to the diversity of human languages; but Theoretical Linguistics as understood by its practitioners is much

---

opposition to 'psychologism': cf. *Grundgesetze der Arithmetik*, vol. 1, Hermann Pohle (Jena), 1893, pp. xiv ff., especially p. xvi.

[1] There is also a sense in which logic cannot be learned by experience. It is easy to define logics whose formulae are not hierarchically structured, and therefore it is only the nature of our reactions to experience that causes human logic and language to have this hierarchical character; on the other hand, just as Putnam showed (cf. p. 121 n.1) that decisions about syntactic categories are largely pre-empted once the initial decision to use constituency structure as the basis of grammar is made, so the adoption of the constituency-structure principle for formation rules and the structure-dependence principle for rules of inference undoubtedly fixes the details of a system of logic to a great extent. Cf. §19 of my 'Empirical hypothesis about natural semantics', *Journal of Philosophical Logic*, vol. 5, 1976, pp. 209–36.

more than a mere statement of philosophical principle about the contingency of language. It is seen as a fertile field of substantive research, in which there is room for scores of talented scholars to elaborate increasingly refined structures of hypotheses about limits to the diversity of languages. These general theories of language are of interest partly because they help us to describe features of individual languages in a perspicacious and scientific way, but this is a minor consideration; an adequate formalization of the conceptual structure of English would be an achievement to boast of, but the syntax and phonology of individual languages are thought of as mere 'plumbing', and only pedants (it is insinuated) are interested in these things for their own sake. Most of the glamour of the discipline derives from the idea that the general limits to linguistic diversity reflect built-in features of the machines called minds; that, not yet but some day, linguists will be able to deduce from their general linguistic theory a diagram of the logical circuitry of the apparatus we think with, and all that will be left to the neurophysiologists will be to fill in the engineering details of how the lines and symbols on the diagram translate into the living material of the brain.

Theoretical Linguistics, in this sense, is a mirage. Scientifically-minded linguists can produce descriptions of individual languages, but only of the syntactic and phonological phenomena regarded as 'plumbing' – happily for our species, concepts refuse to be bound over to the good behaviour required by scientific method. For that matter, there are things to be said about linguistic universals in the syntactic and phonological domains, and no doubt the last word has not yet been said about the precise limits to linguistic diversity. But these limits are not clues to inborn machinery as yet unguessed-at by other disciplines; they are merely previously-unappreciated consequences of a process which is in itself perfectly well-known and almost banal. It may still seem worthwhile to some to work out the exact implications for present-day linguistic structure of the fact that languages are evolved systems, but I cannot see that there is much glamour or, indeed, much substance in this task.

It is inevitable that there will be considerable resistance to this message over and above any opposition based on purely intellectual dissent; it disturbs the vested interests of a profession. There are research grants to be gained, lectureships to be filled, reputations to be made by scholars who can claim to be helping to establish the conceptual structure of our language or to discover the machinery of mind encoded in our genes and reflected in linguistic universals. It takes far fewer voices to make the point that these aims are mare's nests. For a don in a Linguistics Department who finds himself responsible for lectures on semantics it is much easier, psychologically, to take his class through the contemporary literature on formal semantic analysis with the attitude that 'there must be something in it' than to spend the term or year insisting that the readings are as valuable as so many patents for perpetual-motion machines.

Some people imagine that scholarly judgements are unaffected by such considerations; they are very naïve. The academic profession is as keen as any other category of labour to avoid large-scale redundancies, and as good at convincing itself of the value of the *status quo*; and, since academics have an unusual measure of control over the circumstances of their own trade, they are relatively successful at surviving 'economic crises' of the intellect. (How many business enterprises would ever need to close if they were financed by government grants awarded on the 'peer review' system?) One cannot expect the points I make to be welcome to the linguistic profession. I hope only that those who disagree will be careful to distinguish intellectual arguments from appeals to the convenience of the academic establishment.

For myself, I am convinced that linguistics must return to its concerns of twenty years ago, namely the scientific description of the varied and fascinating phonological and syntactic structures of different individual languages, and the art of lexicography. If this is pedantry, so be it. At this stage in its history, perhaps our discipline needs fewer Messiahs and more pedants. To quote André Martinet:[1] 'Let us hope that linguistics will soon cease to be fashionable, so that we may again find ourselves among people really interested in language and languages.'

---

[1] Herman Parret, ed., *Discussing Language* (*Janua Linguarum, series major*, 93), Mouton (the Hague), 1974, p. 247; my punctuation.

Index

Items in inverted commas stand for words, concepts, or 'semantic features' indiscriminately.